Second
Edition

Understanding
Executive
Compensation

A Practical Guide for
Decision Makers

Edited by
Irving S. Becker & William M. Gerek
Hay Group

About WorldatWork®

WorldatWork (www.worldatwork.org) is a global human resources association focused on compensation, benefits, work-life and integrated total rewards to attract, motivate and retain a talented workforce. Founded in 1955, WorldatWork provides a network of more than 30,000 members and professionals in 75 countries with training, certification, research, conferences and community. It has offices in Scottsdale, Arizona, and Washington, D.C.

ISBN: Hard back: 978-1-57963-338-7
      Soft cover: 978-1-57963-340-0
      E-book: 978-1-57963-339-4

Editor: Andrea M. Ozias
Design: Hanna Norris, Kris Sotelo
Production Manager: Rebecca Williams

WorldatWork.
The Total Rewards Association
www.worldatwork.org

Table of Contents

Prologue

This second edition of *Understanding Executive Compensation: A Practical Guide for Decision Makers* is a reference guide for compensation committees and other board members, HR professionals, corporate management and other decision makers. Its purpose is to furnish readers with easy access to a wide range of executive compensation topics by providing insight on current best practices, design techniques and trends. *Understanding Executive Compensation* is a hands-on, practical guide that we hope helps in the evaluation and refinement of executive compensation programs.

The main challenge confronting boards and executive compensation professionals today is establishing a consistent and transparent connection between pay and value added. This must be done in a tough economic environment in which regulators, shareholders and even lawmakers carefully scrutinize all aspects of executive compensation, benefits and perquisites — especially the relationship between pay and performance.

We believe companies are well positioned to respond to current challenges. The Dodd-Frank Wall Street Reform and Consumer Protection Act of 2010 and the U.S. Securities and Exchange Commission have raised the bar on governance standards; they and others will continue advancing this process, thus addressing the crucial need to ensure board and senior-executive accountability. The requirements of the say-on-pay provisions under Dodd-Frank and enhanced compensation disclosure have improved transparency of the programs and facilitated competitive analysis, thus providing a clearer idea of how companies think and operate. In addition, accounting rules allow flexibility in designing compensation programs that better reflect pay-for-performance principles. Compensation expense no longer dictates plan preference. This level playing field provides compensation committees with additional vehicles to use in designing executive pay programs that meet business strategy needs. (See "Major Executive Compensation Trends and Challenges Affecting Us Today.")

These issues are only some of the topics we address in this new edition. The following chapters are a compilation of articles by Hay Group consultants from *The Executive Edition* series, supplemented by articles written specifically for this volume. This is not a technical reference per se; in focusing on what works best, we have avoided presenting too much detail on tax, accounting and regulatory issues.

*Understanding Executive Compensatio*n is targeted mainly to a U.S. audience; nonetheless, with its focus on design, we believe it is a useful resource for non-U.S. companies operating in a pay-for-performance environment. In this edition, we have updated and expanded previous chapters with new material and have added new chapters on executive pay disclosure and risk in executive compensation.

The chapters are grouped in three sections:

- "Part I: Executive Pay Design and Strategy" examines issues relating to overall executive compensation strategy and includes design issues relating to the basic components of pay — base salary, annual incentives, equity and nonequity long-term incentives — plus discussions of related topics, such as peer group selection, performance measurement, competitive benchmarking, stock ownership guidelines, executive benefits, equity retention and employment agreements.

- "Part II: Governance, Disclosure and Compensation Committee Initiatives" begins with a discussion of compensation committee governance followed by a chapter on the tools compensation committees use in overseeing executive compensation. We next discuss the basic principles affecting current executive compensation disclosure, followed by a chapter on the recent requirement to address potential risk in executive compensation programs. Next is a chapter on CEO succession planning and the section ends with an analysis of trends in board compensation.

- "Part III: Executive Compensation in Special Settings" addresses the compensation issues that arise in extraordinary situations, such as mergers and acquisitions and initial public offerings.

We also include a chapter on executive and board compensation in tax-exempt organizations, and end with a chapter on international compensation discussing executive compensation issues in seven major countries: Canada, Australia, the United Kingdom, Germany, Italy, China and Brazil.

I would like to thank WorldatWork for publishing this second edition of *Understanding Executive Compensation: A Practical Guide for Decision Makers* and Hay Group for its ongoing support of our executive compensation practice. I also want to thank our clients who furnished insights in working together on executive pay projects.

Special thanks go to Bill Gerek, my co-editor. As editor of Hay Group's *The Executive Edition*, he has created a consistent theme and tone for our executive compensation publications over the years. Most of all, I would like to thank the Hay Group consultants who have contributed their time, effort and intellectual capital to making this book possible.

— Irving (Irv) S. Becker
National Practice Leader,
Executive Compensation Practice

Major Executive Compensation Trends and Challenges Affecting Us Today

Say on Pay

The Dodd-Frank Wall Street Reform and Consumer Protection Act of 2010 requires companies to seek an advisory vote of shareholders on executive pay at least once every three years. This important development gives shareholders a distinct voice in pay matters and imparts to proxy advisers additional clout in influencing the proxy voting process. Having a true pay-for-performance executive compensation program has never been more important.

In addition, a purely legalistic approach to the Compensation Disclosure and Analysis (CD&A) will no longer suffice. Companies and compensation committees need to become effective communicators, providing shareholders and others with clear, user-friendly explanations of the rationale behind their pay decisions. They will increasingly rely on HR and communications professionals to help fulfill their disclosure responsibilities. Nonetheless, under increased scrutiny some may be tempted to play it safe and develop pay programs similar to those of their peers. This may be a mistake. Compensation strategies that work for both executives and shareholders also must consider the unique situation and business strategy of each company.

Institutional Investors

Say on pay has considerably augmented the ability of institutional investors to influence executive compensation. In addition to demanding that compensation committees establish a clear link between what management accomplished and the amount of pay delivered, they can now vote "no" on say on pay and can vote against compensation committee members if appropriate changes are not made.

Institutional investors clearly will continue focusing on performance metrics, thus complicating the work of compensation committees. They no longer simply look at dilution models and vote "yes" or "no"; they now use detailed financial formulas or "black box" approaches to determine pay-for-performance relationships and are active in criticizing companies that do not meet their guidelines. Companies will be tempted to focus exclusively on financial metrics causing them to shy away from nonfinancial measures because they are difficult to disclose and describe. This reliance on only financial metrics may not be in the best long-term interests of shareholders.

Compensation Philosophy

An organization's executive pay programs should be based on a formal, written compensation philosophy closely tied to the primary business strategy. It should be re-examined annually along with other HR programs, such as performance evaluation, communications and management succession.

Long-Term Incentives

Most companies today use some form of portfolio approach to long-term incentives in order to ensure the adaptability and resiliency of their long-term incentive program. The trend of adding performance-based plans — or adding performance features to traditional stock options and restricted stock plans — is expected to continue, thus creating a flexible approach to long-term incentives. Add more disclosure requirements and pressure from institutional shareholders to do a better job of linking pay to performance, and it is not difficult to understand the continued interest in performance-based equity plans. These plans can, however, be complicated to design and monitor, and often increase the workload of compensation committees.

Compensation Committees

Compensation committees will have more responsibility and scrutiny in a post Dodd-Frank environment, similar to that realized by audit committees when the Sarbanes-Oxley Act of 2002 standards were enacted. Committees will be more involved in the details of executive compensation planning and implementation, especially regarding long-term incentives.

In the past, compensation committees mostly focused on annual long-term performance metrics. With the proliferation of long-term performance plans and the need to quantify and justify total pay, compensation committees will have to focus more on long-term performance drivers. They will spend more time ensuring they are choosing the right metrics, monitoring the metrics to assure they are driving the right executive behaviors, and adjusting them as appropriate.

Compensation committees are not as close as management to the operations of the business, often leading to concern about how performance is calibrated and not wanting to establish goals that are too easy or too difficult to meet. The most frequently asked question is, "How do we know we have set the right targets?"

Internal Pay Equity

Because compensation committees continue to be frustrated in relying solely on external market data, expect to see continued interest in internal pay equity analysis. While many companies disclose that they use both internal and external pay factors, their approaches to establishing internal pay equity often suffer from shortcomings in methodology. Internal pay equity too often focuses solely on comparing pay levels without looking closely at what executives actually do in their jobs. By going beyond job titles and pay ratios, companies can better judge what is unique about given executive positions and determine pay levels that are defensible and fair. Once this is accomplished, however, there is still the need to reconcile internal pay equity with external benchmarking.

Alternative View of Pay Levels

With the increased focus on the relationship between executive pay and company performance, many compensation committees are taking a further look at how pay is — or should be — defined. Historically, pay was the total amount shown in the Summary Compensation Table of a company's annual proxy statement. Base salary, annual incentive earned and the grant date fair value of long-term incentives were among the items included. However, when the alignment of pay to performance is examined, equity award grant date fair values (equity opportunity) often differ considerably from what an executive realizes. With these awards, realized gains should align with performance. As companies strive to present alternative views to the proxy adviser models, expect to see more realizable pay analysis.

Volatility of Pay Outcomes

The current benchmarking practice is to look at pay levels and mix of pay against peers — the total compensation value against peers and the value of each element in the mix of compensation. This snapshot approach is useful, but only goes so far. It does not capture a true picture of pay value over time compared to peers. However, consider undertaking a "third dimension" analysis that projects current grant values into the future under a range of outcomes based on the level of incentive awards and performance scenarios. The resulting "volatility score" gives an extended and more accurate picture of the competitive landscape by identifying the effects of potential swings in the pay package. It also is a powerful tool in assessing risk in pay programs.

PART I

Executive Pay Design
and Strategy

1
Compensation Strategy

By Irv Becker and Craig Rowley

Creating an effective executive compensation strategy is a complex process — more so than ever before. On one hand, the strategy must incorporate and reflect important internal issues unique to the company: short- and long-term business objectives, accounting costs for the company, internal pay equity/positioning, industry market competitiveness, administrative processes and perceived value by executives. On the other hand, the strategy must be formulated to withstand external scrutiny from shareholders, regulators, institutional investors, proxy advisers and the press, all of whom increasingly demand information not just on generic guiding principles, but on details of the rationale of specific program design elements as well.

Thus, a compensation strategy must consider many factors and elements if it is to fulfill its purpose of supporting organizational goals, reflecting actual business performance, paying competitively and rewarding executives for value provided. These objectives are valid regardless of the organization's size, industry or developmental stage.

A compensation strategy must be reviewed and revised as the company grows and matures. The need to update the strategy can come from inside the company, such as when a new business strategy is implemented, an acquisition takes effect or new talent must be recruited. The need for revision also can arise from outside the company through changes in tax and accounting rules, the performance of the overall economy and stock market, or increased demand for executive talent in the marketplace. Whatever its specifics, a compensation strategy must have senior executive and outside director buy-in and be accepted and understood by all parties.

This chapter:

- Relates compensation strategy to business strategy and discusses approaches for evaluating the current program, developing performance metrics and maximizing the effectiveness of various long-term incentive vehicles.
- Recommends that organizations look beyond simple pay multiples and consider factors such as job size and complexity in analyzing internal pay equity. The importance of incorporating internal and external pay equity considerations is stressed.
- Explains that, by using work-valuing techniques in addition to traditional market-based approaches, companies can better correlate pay levels with the value executives are expected to provide.

Providing a Strategic Guide for the Compensation Committee

The articulation of a formal executive compensation philosophy has taken on critical importance at public companies in the current executive pay environment of enhanced disclosure and shareholder say-on-pay voting. The need for compensation committees to clearly explain the rationale underlying the design of various pay components of the executive compensation program has grown due to heightened scrutiny by the business press, proxy advisory groups, U.S. Congress, regulators (especially the U.S. Internal Revenue Service [IRS] and the U.S. Securities and Exchange Commission [SEC]), and institutional shareholders, among others.

An organization's executive compensation philosophy must encompass much more than the unhelpful and overused phrases that "we target the market median" or "we pay for performance to attract, retain and motivate talent." The compensation philosophy should offer specific guidance for the compensation committee's numerous decisions concerning executive pay and be used to evaluate the effectiveness of the compensation program by identifying any potential shortcomings in existing plans. The compensation committee should view the philosophy as a tool to influence management's performance and reaffirm the business strategy, not as a perfunctory task to "check the box" on corporate governance compliance.

Surfacing Issues in Compensation Design

In addition to furnishing important information to outside parties, the actual exercise of developing a robust executive compensation philosophy offers the compensation committee an opportunity to learn whether its members are on the same page in the design of appropriate compensation programs. The process needs to consider members' views on target pay levels, mix of pay elements, the comparator peer group or relevant survey data (i.e., the market for talent), performance metrics and targets, and other pay design issues.

The development of a compensation philosophy also can provide needed insight on whether the senior executive team and the compensation committee view the pay program's strengths and areas for improvement in the same manner. Because management has a tremendous personal stake (some may call this "enlightened self-interest") in the compensation program, the compensation committee may discover that its proposed changes actually provoke a long-overdue dialogue with management on various design issues that have been on autopilot for some time. The compensation committee may use this interaction to signal to management the committee's ultimate stewardship of the executive compensation program, along with the importance of needed input from the management team.

Addressing Business Strategy

When compensation committee members and senior management work together as a design team to develop a comprehensive compensation philosophy, it is critical to start with the organization's business strategy. For example, each participant could be asked to explain, in up to three sentences, the annual and long-term strategies for creating shareholder value. These might include initiatives such as acquisition of competitors or complementary businesses, creation or acquisition of new service lines and/or products, an emphasis on international growth, divestitures of underperforming assets, privatization, positioning for a sale and/or rapid organic growth.

Defining the meaning of "high performance" should be explored by the team of compensation committee members and senior management. Each person could outline what superior business and/or operational performance at the company should look like. These descriptions should include financial (e.g., earnings growth) and nonfinancial (e.g., customer satisfaction) metrics. Superior performance also can include qualitative measures, such as the creation of a succession plan or talent management program. The desired outcome is, in a subsequent step, to be able to define clear goals (threshold, target and maximum, where appropriate) for the variable pay plans that promote the agreed-upon business strategy.

Evaluating Current Executive Pay Programs

As noted, the development of a compensation philosophy should involve a candid exchange among the team members concerning the core strengths and possible weaknesses of the current executive compensation program. Ascertaining the program's strengths guards against detrimental changes, while a consensus on opportunities for improvement may surface needed modifications that can promote talent retention and improve financial performance.

To avoid addressing the elements of total direct compensation (i.e., base salary, short- and long-term incentive opportunities) in a haphazard or piecemeal fashion, the team members should agree upon an overall total direct compensation (TDC) competitive market position for executives for planned, budgeted or targeted company financial performance.

In other words, by salary grade or officer title, a competitive market position (e.g., 60th percentile) should be established for a typical competent executive when the organization performs at pre-established annual target levels that are expected (i.e., 50 percent to 60 percent achievable). This competitive position creates an overall framework by which the mix of the three elements of TDC can be "sized."

This approach can be viewed as establishing the size of the TDC "pie," which can then be sliced into three pieces that form TDC. Once this is accomplished for planned performance, the mix of pay elements can be addressed by answering the following questions:

- What is the desired base salary competitive position in the talent market?
- For variable compensation, what percent should be focused on short-term financial results, assuming target financial performance of the organization? What percent should be focused on long-term financial results?
- What percent of long-term incentives, if any, should be in the form of cash? How much equity is available for awards?

Performance Metrics

Once the TDC competitive position and mix of pay elements are established, the process can turn toward the performance metrics of the variable pay program. The dialogue should start with the development of a list of financial and/or operational metrics that drive company success and positively impact share price. Examples to consider could be earnings growth, expense control, revenue growth and profit margin. Next, macro financial performance indicators that outside analysts use to compare the organization to its competitors could be developed. Examples include return on capital, earnings per share and return on assets. Identifying these drivers may help establish both short- and long-term incentive plan performance metrics.

Agreement also should be reached concerning the minimum annual level of return on a shareholder's investment that warrants a financial payout to executives. This threshold return could be expressed as earnings growth or share price appreciation, and should guide the development of performance plan goal setting that results in cash payouts and/or vesting of equity awards.

Finally, the method of evaluating financial and operational performance metrics should be established, which could include absolute internal financial targets, performance relative to industry peers, performance relative to analysts' expectations or performance relative to an index (e.g., S&P 500). Measuring performance relative to peers can motivate best-in-class performance during weak economic seasons; measuring performance relative to realistic internal goals promotes participants' engagement by focusing their attention on specific outcomes that they believe they can influence.

Long-Term Incentives

The compensation philosophy also should address the use of long-term incentive (LTI) vehicles (e.g., stock options, performance shares, time-vested restricted stock). Therefore, a conversation around the proper role(s) of LTIs in executive compensation programs can help with the compensation committee's selection of the appropriate instruments. Examples of the role of LTIs and potential vehicles are shown in Table 1-1.

Numerous other questions and procedures could be addressed by compensation committee members and management that may affect the executive compensation philosophy and its effectiveness:

- What multiple of base salary should executives hold in stock?
- How can the philosophy be communicated so that all parties understand it and have buy-in toward the compensation program?
- To what degree should individual behavior/performance factor into base salary increases and the size of incentive awards each fiscal year?
- To what degree should public disclosure affect the design of the executive compensation program and levels of compensation?
- To what degree should the company be involved in the planning and funding of executive retirement?

TABLE 1-1

Examples of the Role of Long-Term Incentives and Potential Vehicles

Desired Role of LTI	Potential LTI Vehicle
Retain executive talent	Time-vested restricted stock
Encourage capital accumulation in rising market	Stock options
Encourage capital accumulation in flat or depressed market	Time-vested restricted stock
Drive company performance	Performance shares/units
Promote stock price appreciation	Stock options
Provide tax efficiency for the executive	Restricted stock units
Promote actual ownership	Time-vested restricted stock

- How should decisions concerning which benefits/perquisites to offer be made (e.g., employee feedback, best practices, peer-group prevalence, general industry prevalence)?
- How might the compensation philosophy affect shareholders' say-on-pay voting?

Each compensation committee needs to take seriously its vital role in establishing a comprehensive philosophy that guides all aspects of executive compensation. The more that senior management can be engaged in this process, the more likely the total compensation program will increase perceived value to those executives, thereby increasing the likelihood of retaining talented executives and motivating them to performance that increases the organization's value.

Additionally, the compensation philosophy should be reviewed regularly to ascertain that it responds to changing organizational and economic conditions, and continues to effectively aid executive pay decisions.

Building Internal Equity

Compensation committees increasingly are asking questions about what internal equity is and how to implement it as part of a well-designed executive compensation process and program. Major organizations have discussed internal equity in their proxy statements.

The concept of internal equity isn't new. However, the discussion of internal equity — which focuses on pay relationships between executives — has become carelessly oversimplified in many cases. Focusing only on pay relationships between executive roles without understanding how those roles differ can yield information that is not only meaningless, but potentially debilitating to the health of an executive compensation program.

A Useful But Often Misunderstood Concept

We all know how quickly the landscape for executive compensation has changed — and is changing. Shareholders and compensation committees have become proactive in challenging the externally focused, peer-group driven approach to benchmarking executive pay. Many have complained that an over-reliance on external market data from a peer group or survey has led to a "ratcheting" effect, where the same group of comparator organizations benchmarks against each other's pay levels, to find that what was a 75th percentile market positioning one year is a 50th percentile positioning just two years later.

Market comparisons encourage the lower-paying companies to accelerate their pay increases to meet the market. The result has been an ever-escalating executive pay structure that compensates on a mindset that an organization's executives need to be paid at least at the market median rather than on the actual demands of the role or its performance.

As a result, the need for a true internal equity-based approach — one that helps compensation committees understand the market but be driven by internal fairness — has never been more apparent.

What Is Internal Equity?

Debates and discussions on internal equity typically define the term narrowly as the pay relationships between different positions at different levels in a single organization. This approach looks to understand whether executives in that organization are paid appropriately relative to each other rather than relative to the external market. However, the concept of internal equity also should examine pay differences as a function of organization structure, job size and incumbent performance. While some may consider internal equity to mean the relationship of the CEO's pay to the next level of executive reporting to the CEO, that focus may be overly simplistic.

In managing the concept of internal equity, companies have been encouraged by some commentators to use "pay multiples," or one position that is targeted at roughly "x" times another position. For example, this concept is promoted by the suggestion that the CEO should be paid at a level that is no more than two times that of key executives reporting to the CEO. In building on this questionable approach, some companies use pay multiples to manage the internal equity among executives. This ensures that an employer's pay relationships are linked to each other rather than to the external market (which may lead to a greater, or in some cases smaller, multiple). While the internal fairness of executive pay is very important, a simplistic approach that does not consider other relevant factors is misguided.

The Problem with Multiples

The problem with a multiples approach is that top organization structures are not the same across a peer group and, as a result, not all executive roles at a given organizational level are equal in value. Some organizations have a narrow span of control, and possibly a chief operating officer is the top position reporting to the CEO. Another organization may operate as a holding company, with group heads reporting to the CEO. Still others may have a more integrated structure, with either vertical or horizontal integration of businesses.

In short, not all organizations — and, therefore, not all executive roles — are structured similarly. As such, a pay multiple that is appropriate for one employer may be entirely meaningless for another due to differences in structure.

In addition, an individual executive's pay is a function of the background of how the incumbent secured the job, as well as his/her sustained performance and potential. A CEO recruited from the outside by a company in a turnaround situation likely will be paid more than a newly appointed CEO in a more stable organization who is promoted from within.

For example, consider two separate companies with "group head" positions accountable for $2 billion in revenue in a parent company with $5 billion in total revenue. In most surveys, both the CEO and the group head positions would be valued as the "same sized" job. Look at the facts in Table 1-2 more closely.

Using traditional market data, the CEOs of both companies would be priced as each heading a $5 billion international company. Both group heads would be priced the same as well, relative to group heads managing $2 billion in revenue. Using an approach based on job content, the first company's CEO position likely would have a higher market value than the second but, using traditional

TABLE 1-2

Company Example Assumptions

Dimensions/Company	A	B
Parent Company:		
Revenue	$5 billion	$5 billion
Countries (with assets)	40	5
Employees	12,000	5,000
Value added	High	Low
Complexity	High	Low
Group Head		
Revenue	$2 billion	$2 billion
Countries (with assets)	30	3
Employees	5,000	1,500
Value added	High	Low
Complexity	High	Low

Company A

The chairman of the board is the former CEO. The CEO was "homegrown" and came out of the group-head position a year ago. Currently, the incumbent is paid low relative to market references. The company has 12,000 employees in 40 countries, and key staff functions are decentralized. The relatively new group head (one of three) reports to the CEO, was a candidate for the CEO position and was managing a smaller group prior to the decision to fill the CEO position with the current incumbent. The group head is paid slightly above market for this position. The group head is accountable for five separate high value-added, high gross-margin industrial product businesses that are characterized by proprietary technologies and consultative relationships with customers. The group has 5,000 employees in 30 countries around the world. North America represents 40 percent, Europe 40 percent and Asia-Pacific 20 percent of assets, employees and revenue generation.

Company B

The CEO recently was recruited from the outside and given the chairman of the board responsibility, as well. Pay to recruit the best candidate is above market references. The company has experienced performance issues and the new CEO has a mandate to turn performance around. The company sells into 10 countries, with assets in five of these. All business operations are based in the Americas, and there are 5,000 employees. Key staff functions are highly centralized. The group head reports to the CEO. The incumbent was promoted up from the head of manufacturing position, and the former incumbent was given an early retirement package. The new incumbent is paid below market references. The group-head position (one of three) has responsibility for two commodity products manufactured in a single plant location. Raw material accounts for 75 percent of product value, and gross margins are relatively low. The group employs 1,500 employees in the United States, Canada and Mexico. It manufactures in the United States and exports 15 percent of its production to Canada and Mexico, where distribution centers and sales offices are located.

market pricing, both would have the same market value. The same is true for the group head position — the market value of the job in Company A would be higher than in Company B using a job content-based approach that recognizes complexity as well as size. As discussed here and amplified in Table 1-3, a job-content approach to defining job size would result in a difference in both job size as well as market value for these positions.

Incumbent pay would be driven by the situation and by incumbent background as well. In Company A, the ratio of the CEO's pay to that of the group head would be expected to be much smaller than in Company B. It would not make sense to say that the multiple should be two times in both companies. Further, the multiple would narrow in both companies if a chief operating officer position was established.

A More Balanced Approach

The answer is to look not only at job titles and the size of the organization, but also at the jobs themselves: How big and complex are they? What do they actually do? They key is to understand the size of each role. In addition, incumbent experience, performance and prior compensation history should be considered.

Job sizing allows a more informed snapshot into the internal equity of pay practices. Simply put, it focuses on the design of each job and essentially looks to rank (or score) jobs based on their content and complexity.

TABLE 1-3

Job-Content Approach to Defining Job Size

Survey Level/Company	A	B
1	CEO	
2		CEO/COB
3		
4	Group head	
5		
6		Group head

Job Sizing

There are various ways to size jobs. One approach is grounded in the common sense view that most compensation committees should understand their executive roles well enough to know which are materially bigger or smaller, and thus be able to group them into different levels. Another well-established job-sizing method takes a more precise approach by applying a job evaluation methodology, which evaluates each role while examining three dimensions:

- **Know-how.** The total of every kind of knowledge and skill required for acceptable job performance.
- **Problem solving.** The intensity of the mental process that employs know-how to identify, define and resolve problems.
- **Accountability.** The job's autonomy, the impact of the job and the nature of the impact on end results.

In the case of senior executives, accountability is the most highly weighted factor, while a different weighting is likely appropriate in the case of lower management positions. Using the aforementioned methodology, the weighting for the CEO position has approximately half of the value in accountability, with know-how and problem solving splitting the remaining half.

However job sizing is done, what results is a ranking or score that represents the size of each role relative to other executive jobs; this allows an examination of the relationship between their size and their pay. With this information, it is clear whether the organization's bigger jobs are paid more than the smaller jobs — a critical test for the internal equity of pay practices.

For example, look at the pay practices for the sample company in Figure 1-1. In this example, each point represents an executive's pay and the relative size of the job. Note how the points all hover closely around the central trend line for the organization, indicating that this organization does a good job of paying executives in line with the relative complexity and size of their roles. Now look at the organization in Figure 1-2. In this company, there is far more dispersion in the pay practices, with many smaller jobs being more highly paid than some of the organization's bigger jobs.

As an example, take Dave and Bill, the two circled executives in Figure 1-2. While Bill's role actually is bigger than Dave's role, Dave is paid more — nearly 50 percent more. There may be good reasons for paying these two individuals differently. For example, Dave may have been in his current job for a number of

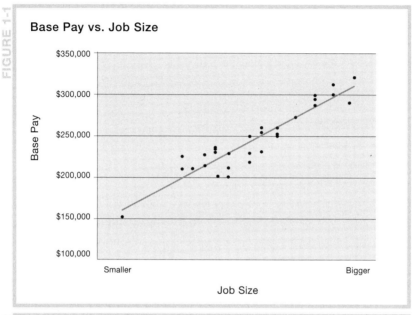

FIGURE 1-1

Base Pay vs. Job Size

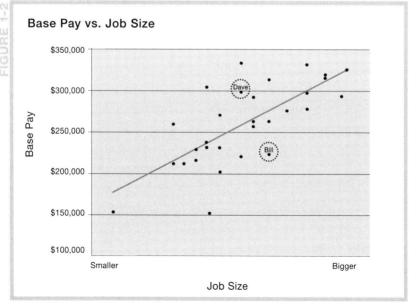

FIGURE 1-2

Base Pay vs. Job Size

years and his performance may be outstanding, and he may have high potential to move up several organization levels. Bill, on the other hand, may be new in the job and promoted several grades internally, but has yet to prove himself in his current job. If both incumbents reported to a common executive position, the ratio of each would be far different to the boss.

While these differences in pay may be rational and explainable, the relationships of salary relative to job size and responsibility indicate this organization may have an issue relative to internal equity as compared to the company represented in Figure 1-1.

External Benchmarking Still Matters

Taking an internal equity approach absolutely does not mean that a company should avoid incorporating external benchmarking into the process. However, the market should be viewed as a point of reference, not a mandate on precisely how a position should be paid. Before making a decision on pay, external market data should be balanced against the internal perspective.

Balancing internal equity with external benchmarking can be done in myriad ways. In its simplest form, compensation committees can consider internal equity alongside external market competitiveness, balancing the need to pay executives at a certain level of competitiveness with the need to pay executives appropriately relative to other roles and incumbent factors. Pay levels for executives should be a function of:

- Organization structure
- Size and complexity of the job
- Incumbent experience and demonstrated performance
- Potential (will current pay keep other interested employers at bay?)
- Succession (can pay for increased responsibility be managed effectively?)
- Internal equity (will pay be viewed as fair, all factors considered?).

Managing All Factors

However it is done, integrating internal equity into the compensation benchmarking process will move compensation governance going forward, as it adds another important dimension to looking at executive pay.

That said, there is a danger in examining internal equity in a vacuum. Using only a blind application of a pay-multiple approach can lead to recruitment and retention issues for some executives, and overpayment for others. Neither of these outcomes should be acceptable to shareholders.

For these reasons, it is clear that both the relative size of an organization's executive jobs and the "going rate" matter. Using internal equity in pay decisions forces a company to account for how its executive roles are unique. Compensation committees that consider internal equity alongside external competitiveness are able to create an executive compensation program that balances fairness and competitiveness with what jobs actually do, and that helps ensure that compensation decisions are not at the mercy of the market, but make sense — all factors considered.

Connecting Pay with Value

Research from Hay Group suggests that taking into account the complexity of the job in addition to traditional benchmark measures (e.g., revenue) provides the best solution and enhances faith in compensation determinations. Executive-level positions from Hay Group's U.S. Executive Compensation Database were studied to better understand the relative importance of the variables that commonly are considered when designing executive compensation packages. The relationship among the variables was measured by the correlation coefficient, which represents their statistical validity as predictors of base salary.

Base salary was more strongly correlated with the size and complexity of the job, as measured by Hay Group's proprietary job-sizing method, than with the size of the organization (as measured by revenue). However, accounting for both factors is a better predictor of base salaries than using only one variable.

Implications

On the surface, defining a competitive pay level seems easy. Companies have embraced a free-market approach by paying their executives similar to other executives in a representative group of peer organizations. The size of the company — typically defined by revenue — is the most common approach to recognize company and job differences when determining a competitive compensation level.

However, relying solely on a market-based approach could provide a false sense of security. Although size is an important consideration, it does not adequately address the value that the job is adding to an organization. For example, even in organizations of similar size, not all chief financial officer positions are created equally. Factors such as importance of international markets, type of ownership and capital structure greatly influence job complexity, hence the value that these jobs add to the organization. Some CFOs have accountability for other factors, such as information technology, administration and strategic planning; others do not. These additional variables should be considered when determining an appropriate pay level, much the same as companies use a host of financial measures to evaluate investment alternatives.

Although work-valuing techniques have been used for decades, many companies abandoned them because they felt the burden of maintaining these systems did not outweigh the benefits of having a highly disciplined compensation administration process. However, these methods instill a level of rigor and objectivity to the executive compensation process that greatly increases the confidence of decisions that cannot be found through market pricing. And they better connect the value that a job adds to the organization with the commensurate level of pay, which enables boards to rationalize their determinations with stakeholders.

2
Peer Groups

By Cory Morrow

Increased disclosure requirements, shareholder activism and media attention have reinforced a market-based approach for executive compensation analysis and design. Given the high level of scrutiny associated with executive compensation, devising an appropriate peer group is an important activity for the compensation committee. Directors are faced with publicly disclosing peer-group companies, explaining the selection criteria used in developing the peer group, and defending the peer group's appropriateness for benchmarking compensation, performance analysis and program design.

In this environment, the development and use of a compensation peer group is a critical tool for assessing the competitiveness and appropriateness of the various elements of a company's compensation programs. Utilizing a properly constructed peer group can provide a valuable perspective on issues such as compensation levels, performance benchmarks, pay elements, and short- and long-term incentive plan design. Each company needs an objective and systematic approach to constructing a peer group that best fits its unique organizational characteristics, one that goes beyond simply targeting executive pay levels and allows the committee to assess compensation in relation to the value delivered to the company and shareholders.

This chapter:

- Introduces the sources from which companies can benchmark executive pay and describes the factors used in the peer selection process. It also outlines an approach that results in a more comprehensive picture of competitor practices by supplementing proxy peer analysis with functional job information from a larger database of employers.

- Discusses the need for a dual analysis that not only targets compensation at a percentile of market, but also uses business performance analysis to rank executives' annual and total direct compensation against the company's performance relative to competitors.
- Discusses the use of external performance comparisons in setting and validating performance measures across various time periods and, ultimately, how peer group analysis and market data can be used in setting executive compensation.

Proxy and Survey Comparison Groups

Companies generally have two alternatives for benchmarking executive pay: broad comparative groups using survey data and company-selected peer groups.

Survey databases are an excellent source for broad, robust data for almost any type of executive position. General market or all-industry databases provide the broadest scope of data for compensation comparisons. These databases are particularly appropriate for corporate and staff roles in which industry expertise is not necessarily required and executives can move fairly easily between industries. General market data may also be appropriate for organizations in niche industries or with few direct competitors of similar size. Alternatively, many surveys are available for specific industries. This allows benchmarking to markets that are more similar to the subject organization but still provide deeper levels of data.

In terms of matching executives to a database, the most precise approach is to use job size/grading or possibly a multivariate analysis that also allows for considerations such as employee numbers and internationality. This methodology can be the best way of capturing the scale and complexity of a business while still using a wide set of comparators; however, the downside is a loss of transparency. Whether this level of sophistication is necessary depends on the organization's circumstances. In our experience, such an approach is the most appropriate for:

- Organizations that are the top or bottom of a comparator group
- Injecting some rigor in the process of assessing the appropriate effect of an organization change to pay levels

- Comparing roles below the C-suite level where job title matching alone can be extremely imprecise, particularly in today's complex matrix structures in which roles with the same title often have very different responsibilities.

Best Practices in Proxy Peer Group Selection

U.S. Securities and Exchange Commission (SEC) disclosure requirements (see Chapter 14) as well as increased activism by shareholder groups are leading compensation committees to take a closer look at the process for determining executive pay. One area receiving significant attention is the selection of an appropriate peer group for executive pay comparisons.

For benchmarking of named executive officers, developing a custom peer group of other publicly traded companies can be the best source of competitive data. Not only is this a source for compensation values, but it also can provide details on incentive program design, benefit and perquisite offerings and other executive policies, such as severance and change-in-control agreements.

Comparator peer groups are used by compensation committees to inform executive compensation decisions, including the establishment of target levels for executive pay and the design of short- and long-term incentive compensation programs. A peer group used for compensation benchmarking should be constructed:

- **Specifically for the individual company.** Because each organization has unique characteristics, the comparator group must be custom-built for that particular entity.
- **Based on a set of sound design principles and criteria.** Beginning the peer group design with a set of principles helps ensure that the process is sustainable and objective. It also avoids a course that many shareholder activists suspect is too often followed — starting with the answer and working backward.

The most effective peer groups typically include 12 to 20 companies that represent the company's market for talent (where it looks to recruit executives and which organizations poach its talent). Fewer than 12 companies may not provide statistically significant results and can be skewed by outliers; more than 20 companies introduces the likelihood that the group has gone beyond true "peers."

In developing a compensation peer group, the focus should be on design principles that drive the success of the individual company and reflect its market for executive talent. Selection criteria for developing a peer group commonly include:

- **Organizational size.** Size is measured by revenue for most industries, but asset-based for some industries (particularly financial institutions). A general rule suggests peer companies should be between 0.5 times and 2 times the size of the subject organization. Although some companies look at market capitalization, caution is needed when considering this measure. Market cap typically is not the preferred measure of scale because market capitalization:
    - Can be volatile, which should not have an effect on pay
    - Is aligned to (expected) profitability rather than scale. Therefore, it can understate comparisons for companies in low-margin sectors and arguably inflate salary and annual incentive benchmarks for speculative enterprises.
- **Industry.** Use of industry classifications, such as Global Industry Classification Standard (GICS) codes, can help identify companies either narrowly in common sub-industries or more broadly in industry groups or sectors. The broader classifications may be more appropriate for companies that operate multiple lines of business, or simply when there is an insufficient number of companies in the narrower classifications.
- **Business model/complexity.** Organizations may choose to screen companies or refine the groups by only selecting companies with similar business models. For example, a company that develops, produces and markets its product may choose to exclude companies in the same industry that only provide a related service, but do not actually develop and produce a product.
- **Global versus domestic operations.** Companies that operate on a global basis with executives that have accountability for global results may exclude (or limit the number of) domestic-only companies and vice versa.

- **Regulatory environment.** For many companies (e.g., utilities), regulatory complexities play a significant role in executive responsibilities; in those situations, constructing a peer group with companies that have similar complexities would be appropriate.
- **Founders of family-run businesses.** These types of executives tend to have different compensation arrangements than typical market practices and, therefore, it may be inappropriate to include these companies in a peer group (unless the subject company is a founder/family-run business, in which case it may actively seek to include these types of organizations).

Peer groups should be reviewed annually to ensure they remain relevant and continue to meet the aforementioned criteria. Companies often need to be removed due to mergers, acquisitions, going private, bankruptcy, regulatory changes and other developments.

Of course, these standards need to be adapted to the particular organization. For example, in some industries, the number of companies that truly could be considered peers is quite small. An independent U.S. corporation's most direct competitors may be relatively small divisions of much larger U.S. employers (or foreign-owned companies) that do not file proxy statements, or privately owned companies for which data is difficult to obtain. In this case, a design principle that requires selecting the corporation's closest business competitors would be inappropriate. In other instances, a company may compete for talent with much larger organizations, and it may be appropriate to include such companies in its peer group. (See "Suggested Attributes of a Peer Group.") By following these practices, a compensation committee will be able to develop a peer group of companies that provides valuable and representative data on market compensation practices.

Using Comparator Peer Groups in Shareholders' Best Interests

A compensation committee should use the peer group to compare compensation levels (how much) and design (forms of pay delivery). The "how much" analysis should be informed by title-match benchmarking (e.g., CEO, CFO) and compensation rank where sufficient title matching is not possible (e.g., second highest-paid officer).

Suggested Attributes of a Peer Group

The development of an appropriate peer group involves a consideration of various factors, but should include at least the following four attributes:

Be Current

Markets are dynamic. As a result, a corporation that was an appropriate peer last year may have changed its focus, modified its line(s) of business, been acquired, experienced a dramatic change in performance or even gone out of business. For these and other reasons, a company may no longer truly be a peer. Similarly, the company itself may have changed, either by organically growing faster than its peers or through acquisition, divestiture or by entering/leaving various markets. Accordingly, effort is required to evaluate the companies included in the comparator group on an annual basis. In addition, it is essential to understand the peer companies being utilized by institutional shareholders to assess a company's pay-performance relationship. Where this data is available, it is worth taking the effort to compare these peer groups to the one approved by the compensation committee.

Be Composed of a Representative Number of Companies

A base number of organizations are key for the validity of the summary statistical compensation data. Companies with a few direct competitors often focus on too narrow a group of potential organizations and may face difficulties establishing a valid peer group. Consequently, for purposes of compensation benchmarking, it is important to loosen the rigidity of the selection process to create a sample size that is sufficiently robust to provide meaningful data from a statistical viewpoint.

Be Reasonable in Relationship to Peer Companies

More specifically, an appropriate peer should be reasonably related to the companies used in the performance graphic in the corporation's annual report, particularly to the industry line-of-business index. Because a large portion of executive pay is variable and often linked to corporate performance, best practices suggest that there should be commonality among the companies used to determine whether compensation is appropriate and those used to illustrate corporate performance.

For example, there may be a disconnect if the company's compensation peer group consists of companies in the Dow Jones Industrial Average Index — all household-name, large-capitalization corporations — while the company's performance graph contains relatively unknown, small capitalization companies. Also, shareholder interest groups compare key aspects of a company's program to business peers, especially when looking at share allocations.

Be Performance Based

Frequently, comparisons are made on the basis of organizational size, not performance. The most useful size metric generally is company revenue. While there is a strong correlation (especially with base salary) between revenue size and pay (within the same industry), other variables may need to be considered.

The levels should be viewed not only by total dollar amount, but also by the mix of pay at the peer companies ("mix of pay" refers to the relationship among fixed salary, short-term variable cash and long-term equity or cash).

Given that a large percentage of executive pay is at risk and not in the form of guaranteed compensation, it is useful to examine a company's compensation structure in comparison to that of its peers. This may include a review of target incentive award opportunities, types of equity used and performance metrics selected.

The decision about the type of awards can be informed by current peer group and market practices, but primarily should be driven by assessing which award vehicles most closely align executive pay with the organization's strategic goals.

Comparing Performance of Peer Group Companies

If a compensation committee only uses a peer group to assist with the establishment of top executive pay levels, its task is incomplete. To understand the overall benefit that executives provide to shareholders, the compensation committee should compare the company's performance with that of its peer group. This comparison allows the compensation committee to determine the degree of alignment of executive pay with actual business performance relative to the comparator peer group, and functions in the best interests of the company's shareholders. Results of this pay-for-performance analysis provide insight into the relationship between executive pay levels and company performance as well as whether pay is commensurate with the performance level achieved (i.e., where a company provides executive pay above median, does it consistently exceed peer group median performance?).

In exploring this question, compensation committees should look for a directional, as opposed to precise, relationship between pay and performance. It is unrealistic to expect a company that performs at the peer group's 40th percentile to have its executive compensation pegged precisely at the 40th percentile. However, if this company properly aligns its pay programs with performance considerations, shareholders should reasonably expect executives' compensation to be directionally equivalent to that of company performance and fall between the 25th and 50th percentiles of the peer group.

As shown in Figure 2-1, area B displays a pay-for-performance directional relationship; areas A and C do not. Concerns with the shaded areas include:

- In area A, executive compensation may be viewed as an excessive expenditure of the shareholders' assets because compensation rank is significantly higher than performance rank. In this case, the compensation committee may consider one of the following:
  - Freezing or slowing the growth of base salaries
  - Modifying the relationship between performance and payout
  - Lowering the payout opportunities
  - Raising the performance metric targets
  - Changing the performance metrics
  - Modifying relative performance metrics that compare the company's performance against a peer group.
- In area C, there may be a risk of losing talented executives because performance rank significantly exceeds compensation rank. In this situation, retention concerns may cause the compensation committee to raise salaries, increase payout opportunities and/ or review the performance metric targets.

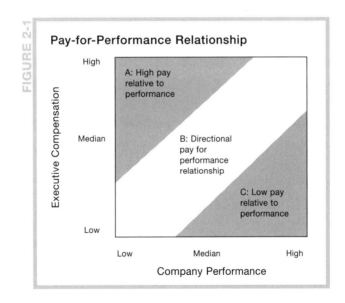

FIGURE 2-1

Pay-for-Performance Relationship

Executive Compensation (vertical axis): High, Median, Low

A: High pay relative to performance

B: Directional pay for performance relationship

C: Low pay relative to performance

Company Performance (horizontal axis): Low, Median, High

External Performance Comparison

A robust pay-for-performance analysis does not involve merely a comparison of a company's absolute business performance to its internal, committee-approved performance targets (absolute performance goals). It is possible for a company to repeatedly achieve or exceed its internal financial and nonfinancial goals, resulting in incentive awards paying out at or above target levels, but still fall behind the performance of its peer companies. A pay-for-performance analysis should analyze a company's performance relative to its peer group's performance (relative performance goals).

Another benefit to a comparison of company performance relative to peer group, a compensation committee is able to validate the performance goals it establishes for its executive variable pay programs. The analysis can reveal whether the internal performance goals warrant the corresponding payouts when compared to the peer group's aggregate historical performance.

For example, an examination might reveal that the one-year earnings growth goal established by the compensation committee for target performance corresponds to the historical 25th percentile earnings growth of a comparator peer group. Such a discovery might prompt the compensation committee to increase the annual incentive plan's earnings growth target and/or significantly lower the payout opportunities.

Performance Measure Selection

Once a comparator peer group has been approved by the compensation committee based on the agreed-upon criteria and principles, performance measures are selected and then weighted. Determining the proper number of performance measures requires a consideration of the company's circumstances. While multiple measures may enable a compensation committee to address various factors relevant to performance and limit any potential "gaming," or the measures that can occur when only one measure is used, too many measures may lose desired focus and prevent the program from being meaningful. Only in atypical situations have we seen well-crafted programs using more than four measures.

Performance Measurement Periods

Performance for the selected metrics might be evaluated for both one- and three-year (possibly up to five-year) performance periods for each company. Then, for example, each company's CEO cash compensation and total direct compensation can be ranked and plotted against its corresponding composite performance ranking.

Figure 2-2 shows an example of CEO cash compensation versus one-year company performance, with a ranking of one representing the best performance/highest compensation. As shown, Company Alpha has the best composite one-year performance ranking, as well as the highest CEO cash compensation. However, Company Charlie, with the third-highest performance ranking, is next to last (or in 11th place out of 12 companies) in cash compensation. Absent other retention factors, Company Charlie may be at risk of losing its CEO to another company unless changes are made to the CEO's cash compensation program, and/or above-market long-term incentive awards are granted.

Although no analysis of executive pay relative to company performance will be all encompassing, the approach suggested can show whether a directional relationship exists between pay and performance. Given the increased corporate governance requirements and outside scrutiny of executive compensation, it is crucial that compensation commit-tees make efforts to assure investors that they truly are overseeing an executive compensation program that aligns pay and performance.

Use of Peer Groups in Setting Compensation

Once a peer group is established and data are collected, the work is not done. Compensation committees have a responsibility to apply their judgment in evaluating peer-group data. For example, after selecting the suitable peer companies based on the afore-mentioned criteria, we may find that an organization's revenue is at the 30th percentile of the group. If this organization has a philosophy of paying at the median of its market, is it proper to target the median of its peer group? Perhaps the company should lower its target positioning to better match the size of its desired peer group. Similarly, if a company has been under-performing, it may be inappropriate to select only high-performing peer companies

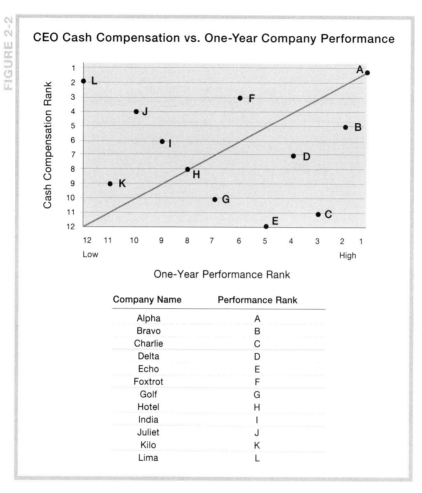

FIGURE 2-2

CEO Cash Compensation vs. One-Year Company Performance

Company Name	Performance Rank
Alpha	A
Bravo	B
Charlie	C
Delta	D
Echo	E
Foxtrot	F
Golf	G
Hotel	H
India	I
Juliet	J
Kilo	K
Lima	L

and target at the median of that group. Some consideration needs to be given to these factors so that the compensation philosophy works in alignment with the peer group.

Market data will always have a role to play in setting executive pay. How else can the compensation committee be assured that pay is not excessive, but sufficient to attract and retain its key talent? In any case, the approach chosen for benchmarking needs to be appropriate. This means selecting the right comparators, taking the context into account and looking at competitiveness in various performance scenarios. Ultimately, a compensation committee needs to rely on its business judgment while using benchmark data as one input, but not as an absolute answer.

3
Base Salary

By James Bowers

As its name implies, base salary is the foundation for the other components of an executive compensation program. It reflects the more qualitative aspects of an executive's performance and is used by executives to meet financial needs.

In most organizations, a salary range is used with a spread of about 50 percent to 70 percent — typically plus or minus 20 percent to 30 percent of midpoint or market reference point, reflecting the organization's desired competitive position. While many employers state a desired market position of median or average, the range is there for a reason. Where an executive fits in the range usually is a function of a number of other factors, with the best being sustained performance over time. However, position in the salary range also may be heavily influenced by other factors, such as the incumbent's salary in a former job or geographic considerations where a higher cost of living requires paying more to attract and retain executives. Also, employers often establish salary ranges based on a combination of internal equity and external competitiveness, but market data and internal equity considerations do not always perfectly align.

While the mantra in many organizations is to "pay the market," especially when it comes to base salary, the fact is that many variables go into determining base salary — some tangible, some intangible. Base salary is important to the executive because it is, relative to other forms of compensation, more of a constant and it also should reflect the value of the jobholder's role and the incumbent's performance to the organization.

Base salary grows with job responsibilities, but ironically becomes a smaller part of total compensation as job size progresses. For CEOs of large capitalization companies, base salary is typically below 20 percent of target total direct compensation. Base salary's percentage of compensation for top executives has been decreasing in recent years as performance-based incentives (both short- and long-term) have been growing in potential value at a faster rate than base salary that, for executives, now keeps pace (percentage-wise) with what is awarded to all other employees.

This chapter:

- Discusses the importance of the base salary component in the total compensation equation. It defines the purpose of salary and its use as the starting point in determining the value of annual and long-term incentive awards as well as benefits programs, such as pension, long-term disability and paid time off.

- Explains how executive pay can be affected by many factors (e.g., geography, industry mix, desirability, supply/demand, executive negotiations). While geographic pay distinctions often are based on cost-of-living considerations for nonexecutive positions, the effect of other factors, such as supply and demand, location desirability, quality of lifestyle, quality of education and job availability for family members likely are stronger influences over executive pay.

Base Salary: The Foundation of Total Compensation

Base salary is the least complex form of compensation, yet some would argue it is the most important when viewing pay in the workforce. For top executives, base salary typically is not the most meaningful form of compensation in terms of value, but it can have a significant bearing on the actual value of other pay components that often are expressed as a percentage of base salary.

Overview of Salary

The term salary dates back to the Roman Empire when Roman soldiers were paid in a valuable commodity — salt — that could be bartered for other goods and services. "Salary" actually means "salt money." Despite the importance of salary in history, its significance often is misunderstood and confused in the press with other forms of compensation.

Salary typically is the foundation of other forms of compensation. Annual and long-term incentives commonly are derived from salary (e.g., a percentage or multiple), while the value of benefits often is based on salary.

With the current focus in the press on executive pay, salary may be viewed negatively by shareholders and other interest groups if it appears too high from some perspectives. One consideration in setting salary for a public company's CEO, as well as any of its other highest-paid executives subject to Internal Revenue Code (IRC) section 162(m), is that the tax law does not consider salary to be performance-based compensation exempt from the $1 million deduction limitation.

In addition to driving the value of other forms of compensation, salary is an important part of the attract-and-retain equation. It is not considered as strong in its ability to provide motivation to an executive; arguably, compensation is only motivational when it is at risk. Under this view, fixed compensation is not motivational. Psychologists generally have maintained that salary is a hygienic factor rather than a motivational one. That is, salary either satisfies or dissatisfies, but does not motivate or change behavior. For lower level jobs, salary is important to meet basic needs (e.g., security, ability to provide food and shelter for self and family). While these needs may be lessened for executives due to higher pay levels, security cannot be ignored as a psychological factor for executives, especially in today's market.

Relation to Market

Determining an executive's base salary typically is a function of the market and the value of the position and person in it to the organization. Most organizations measure the market for executives on the basis of position function and either organization size (revenue) or job size (job evaluation). It is important to balance the two, as many executive jobs are structured uniquely to fit the organization's strategy and incumbent capacity. Job information in surveys tends to be much more generic and functional-hierarchy based. Matrix management positions are consequently difficult to market price.

Employers often claim that they establish the market reference or midpoint of a salary range on the basis of market median. "Market" is based on organizations of comparable size and complexity.

Approximately 80 percent of organizations believe their pay is at market median yet, as measured in compensation surveys, actual pay around median varies significantly — especially at executive levels. The typical salary range (+/-20 percent to 30 percent) around market reference produces a pay spectrum from about the 10th percentile to the 90th percentile of market for most executive positions. Actual pay around market reference is based on incumbent experience, performance and tenure in a given job.

Many companies maintain that salary is largely paid for incumbent factors, including how one performs the job, and not just on achieved results. As such, competencies and behaviors are significant factors in determining the appropriate salary increase and resulting new salary.

In recent years, budgets for salary increases at most organizations have been in the range of 3 percent to 4 percent. Increasingly, salary budgets are a function of company economics as well as market salary projections. Internal organization guidelines for individual increases typically can call for increases from 0 percent to two times salary increase budget, while still complying with the overall budget. The amount of an increase should be based on performance and salary level relative to the reference. In reality, most executive increases are tightly clustered around the overall merit budget. Thus, salary increases do not provide much incentive to perform better, considering the narrow range of increases for performance.

Managing Salary

Given the amount that salary represents as a percentage of total compensation, it would seem that salary should be managed more effectively and with greater differentiation than it typically is. Some employers let the market drive executive salaries and do not manage salaries to reflect the performance and value of the person and position to the organization. A more effective approach involves managing the market as a reference rather than as a mandate for how much an executive should be paid. In addition, the salary range should reflect demonstrated performance over time as opposed to pay for tenure.

Managing salary is important because it is the foundation for other compensation programs and represents one of the largest fixed costs in managing an enterprise. (See Table 3-1.) At a market reference of $100,000, the typical range is +/-$20,000 to $30,000. However, an incumbent paid at the maximum versus the minimum would find a total direct compensation difference of $80,000, assuming target short- and long-term incentives as a consistent percentage of base salary. This does not include the value difference in benefits (e.g., income replacement and retirement).

Having a competitive compensation policy and paying competitively can be two different things. It is important to manage salary so it drives the appropriate total compensation. Salary matters.

Other Considerations

When organizations search for talent from the outside, potential recruits often focus on increasing their salary. But employers should exercise care not to distort internal pay relationships. Instead of paying more salary and affecting internal equity, signing bonuses

TABLE 3-1

Impact of Salary on Total Direct Compensation

Salary	STI %	STI $	TCC*	LTI %	LTI $	TDC**
$80,000	50%	$40,000	$120,000	50%	$40,000	$160,000
$100,000	50%	$50,000	$150,000	50%	$50,000	$200,000
$120,000	50%	$60,000	$180,000	50%	$60,000	$240,000

TCC* = total cash compensation (salary plus annual incentive pay)
TDC** = total direct compensation (TCC plus long-term incentive pay)

and restricted stock can be helpful in both attracting and retaining top talent. It can be argued that salary is "forever." Two execu- tives — one paid $80,000 and the other paid $120,000 for the same position — will generate quite different compensation costs over time. The difference over 10 years is roughly $1 million in total direct compensation, assuming a 4-percent annual increase. Not small change.

Geographic and Other Pay Differentials

Geographic differentials receive a fair amount of attention, even at executive levels. Traditionally, an employer could determine a pay differential based on a combination of the compensation practices in a given geography and a cost-of-living differential; the resulting factor would be applied to whatever market data the organization used to benchmark. There is a legitimate question as to whether geographic pay differentials should apply to highly compensated executives.

Rather than geography, the more appropriate consideration is an economic one: market supply/demand and market pay rates. Often there is a correlation with cost of living, but not always. Sometimes desirability or new entrants into a market are strong considerations. Executives tend to be shrewd negotiators and often will reference costs of living as a negotiation point, especially as it relates to base salary (which pays living costs). Consider the company that moved from high-cost New York City to a Southern city with a much lower cost of living. Executives offered a transfer of work location demanded more money, as they did not want to disrupt family and, in some cases, working spouses with a move. One could be certain the reverse would result in increased pay, too, with the cost of living reinforcing the argument of moving from a Southern city to New York City.

Do Geographic Premiums Exist for Executives?

Geographic pay differentials do exist at executive levels, but be careful in defining the reason; pay differentials between different locations undoubtedly exist, as the cost of labor is discernibly higher in some areas than in others. This may be cost-of-living influenced, but desirability and nature of competition for talent is a big factor. For example, a large metropolitan area (e.g., New York City) certainly is influenced by living costs, but perhaps more heavily influenced by the fact that it is an international corporate location and a concentration for the relatively highly compensated financial services sector.

Most organizations look locally before venturing outside of the core geographic area. While these organizations may find executives who move across the country for their jobs, typically they look first at the local markets. Employers are more likely to recruit locally and implement pay practices that are comparable to their locales.

Various resources are available for determining geographic pay premiums. Special geographic "cuts" of general market data frequently are used to compare pay levels at certain job levels to the rest of Hay Group's relevant database. Many surveys already include views of data that reflect different geographic pay practices. And, time and again, geographic pay differences have been found in the data — even at the senior-most levels of organizations.

One of the most popular resources is the Economic Research Institute (ERI), which offers a premier database that uses a combination of publicly available published survey data and its own survey data to represent the geographic pay differences at different salary levels.

Over the years, Hay Group's research has found higher pay on the East and West coasts of the United States than in most non-coastal cities. The differential relative to national averages can be as high as 20 percent for selected metropolitan areas on the East and West coasts.

Problems with Using Geographic Differences

Accounting for geographic differences can over-inflate pay structures if not thoughtfully addressed and implemented. Consider the financial services industry. New York City remains a significant hub of financial activity in the United States, where financial services organizations still abound.

Assume a bank based in New York City uses a financial services salary survey to develop a salary structure with midpoints that are targeted at the market median. Also assume that the organization uses a data source that says New York City pay levels for a given salary are 15 percent higher than national market pay levels. The organization then benchmarks its positions, applies the 15 percent differential to the benchmarking results and uses this information to create the midpoint of its salary band.

However, a closer look at the salary survey reveals that, of the 100 survey participants, 30 already are in New York City. Therefore, applying the 15-percent premium would result in some double counting — and a salary range that would overpay people relative to the intended market benchmark.

Best Practices in Using Geographic and Other Differentials

Understanding the "right" pay differential has significant implications for how organizations benchmark and set pay. Finding the pay differential for a given locale is easy enough; determining the appropriate pay differential for an organization is more challenging. There are five core precepts in considering geography to benchmark and set pay:

- **Understand your competitive market for executive talent.** From where does the organization recruit? Which organizations might poach its executive talent? Where might executives go if they were to leave?
- **Understand your benchmarking resources.** Do the resources being used to benchmark pay practices already account for differentials in pay practices in some way? If using a survey, examine the participant list or contact the firm that provided the survey to request more information on participants in a certain geographic area. The degree to which a geographic area already is represented in the summary data should inform the degree to which a premium should be applied. If using a customized peer group, the competitive market for executive talent is theoretically already represented, and likely would not call for a geographic adjustment.
- **Consider whether different positions call for different premiums.** In some industries and locations, certain positions are affected more by geography than others. For example, the preponderance

of pharmaceutical companies in New Jersey has created a somewhat specific pay market for New Jersey-based "pharma" roles. However, when hiring for finance roles in these organizations, the presence of the high-paying New York City-dominated finance market may come into play. In such cases, organizations may need to account for a geographic premium differently for the pure pharma roles than for their finance roles.

- **Reflect any geographic premium in the organization's pay philosophy.** Simply put, an organization should define and document the degree to which the competitive market for executive talent is geographic in nature. The employer then should provide guidelines on how it accounts for this in benchmarking and making pay decisions.

- **Take your temperature.** Finally, it should be apparent whether the current pay program and pay levels are working for this executive population. Understanding which parts of an organization's total value proposition (e.g., pay levels) are most important to executives, along with how the executives view the various components, should help determine whether the organization should reflect a geographic pay differential. Looking at turnover and executive morale should provide important context here.

4
Annual Incentive Pay

By Garry Teesdale and Martin Somelofske

Annual incentives can best be defined as compensation tied to performance, measured relative to a performance standard and earned during a 12-month period. People often use "annual incentive" and "bonus" interchangeably when, in fact, they are two different things. An incentive focuses on motivating and rewarding desired behaviors and results based on planned metrics and defined results, while a bonus tends to be after the fact and discretionary.

Annual incentives, which originated at Bethlehem Steel in 1911, were for many years essentially profit-sharing vehicles to reward non-owner managers. By the 1960s and 1970s, these plans had evolved into a tool reinforcing the importance of a company's budget (i.e., target bonuses tied to budgeted earnings). In the late 1980s and early 1990s, organizations began to consider tying bonus awards to performance using a measure of value. Today, annual incentives in many forms are ubiquitous in U.S. and foreign companies.

It is important to remember that annual incentives are just that: annual. Companies often let their plans continue unchanged year after year without considering changes in company goals or operations. Most often, companies revisit their annual incentive plans when a major corporate change occurs, such as a transaction or restructuring, a new strategy or a new CEO. At this point, the old incentive model may no longer be appropriate, or a symbolic change may be required.

In other situations, companies may feel the current plan is not working — that there is a disconnect between the actual or perceived level of performance and payments received by employees. This was the case during recent periods of economic turmoil when many companies struggled to determine annual incentive goals and payment levels. Another reason for change is when an organization realizes it is not in line with the market or has heard about an interesting new annual incentive approach and wishes to determine its feasibility.

In any of these situations, it is critical to have an annual incentive design that forges a strong link between performance and payout level. Without an effective design, the annual incentive plan simply becomes a bonus.

This chapter:

- Reviews how annual incentives can affect individual and team performance and discusses design considerations such as plan purpose and objectives, eligibility, funding, calculating awards and payout alternatives.

- Addresses the difficulties in administering and budgeting for an annual incentive plan and discusses the issues that arise in an economic downturn, including steps companies can take to maintain the efficacy of the plan while company performance remains below par.

The Design of Annual Incentives

Short-term variable compensation has become a critical component of most employers' total rewards programs. Diverse perceptions exist regarding the use of variable pay. (See "Advantages and Disadvantages of Variable Pay Programs.") As the use of annual incentive plans continues growing, companies question whether they influence behavior and/or improve performance beyond what could be attained in their absence.

Design is the foundation of an effective annual incentive plan. To be effective, an annual incentive plan must increase performance focus by encouraging the delivery of specific goals and desired behaviors. Implementation also is critical — the programs communicate and reinforce messages around corporate aims and personal performance.

An effective plan also should link the cost of such compensation to affordability, align the amount and mix of pay with market

Advantages and Disadvantages of Variable Pay Programs

Advantages

- Reinforce desired employee performance and behaviors.
- Align individual goals and objectives with organizational goals and objectives.
- Create a strong alignment between productivity, costs, revenue and performance.
- Support a performance culture by differentiating the rewards paid to top performers versus average or below-average performers.
- Maintain competitiveness in the labor market.

Disadvantages

- May be difficult to administer given the difficulties in tracking and measuring performance.
- Require a variable cost structure, which is more difficult to budget than straight salary costs.
- Employees can develop an entitlement mentality if measures are not understood.
- Short-term incentives may encourage short-term vision.
- May discourage the right behaviors if improperly designed.

norms, provide defensive support against accusations of paying too much, and achieve favorable tax treatment.

Six critical questions should be considered in designing annual incentive plans:

- What is the plan's purpose?
- Who will participate?
- What should the objectives, measures and standards be?
- What should the level of opportunity be?
- How is the plan funded?
- What are the payout alternatives?

Plan Purpose

Understanding why a company may need to alter or develop a new annual incentive plan is the first step. As design is a critical success factor, it is important for a company to understand the real issues behind its reasons. (See Table 4-1.)

TABLE 4-1

Incentive Plan Design Issues

What a Company Says ...	What the Real Issue May Be ...
"Our annual incentive plan may not be aligned with typical market practice."	"We need comfort that our plan is 'normal.' Is there anything new we should know about?"
"I read an article about EVA-based (or RONA, sales, etc.) incentive plans — that's what we need."	"Our current performance measure(s) may not be the most effective."
"Our incentive plan is broken."	"The plan didn't pay out. The problem could be a design, target-setting or calibration problem — perhaps performance was poor."

Plan Participation

Eligibility in a variable pay plan depends on both the organizational compensation philosophy/strategy and several key decision factors:

- At what organizational level does the employee reside? How does that position affect organizational performance?
- Should employees who have poor performance ratings be eligible for participation?
- Does it matter if an employee is eligible for other variable pay plans?
- Is the employee full or part time? How does that affect the employee's contribution?
- When does eligibility begin?

Most companies with broad-based annual incentive plans provide awards to about 70 percent to 80 percent of the employee population. Companies use various criteria to establish annual incentive plan eligibility — typically one or two factors are used to determine eligibility. Position title/ reporting relationship are the most common criteria used, followed by salary grade/band.

FIGURE 4-1

Performance: Objectives, Measures and Targets

Performance Objectives

What are the organization's performance goals?

1. Increase profit?
2. Grow sales?
3. Reduce costs?
4. Improve quality?

Plan Objectives, Measures and Standards

Performance measures play a key role in the design of variable compensation plans. Before a company determines performance measures, it first is essential to determine the intended goals/ outcomes of accomplishments (objectives) and how the results will be measured (standards), as outlined in Figure 4-1.

When selecting the performance measures to use, a company first should examine the business strategy and determine how it wants to achieve the business results. The next step is to determine how individual and/or team contributors can affect those results and what performances are needed to achieve organizational goals.

There is no shortage of performance measures; finding the appropriate balance among corporate, business unit and individual metrics is an ongoing challenge for most organizations. Financial measures can be placed into three categories: accounting, value-based and company value, as in Figure 4-2.

A majority of companies rely on two or more performance measures, often combining financial measures with some assessment of individual performance. The most common measures applied are revenue, operating income, business unit performance and individual performance.

An assessment of individual performance in determining participants' awards typically is based on formal assessment. Individual

Performance Measures	Performance Targets
What measures and indicators do we use to measure progress against these goals?	How do we set the necessary standard of achievement to get a bonus payment?
1. EBITDA?	1. Budget?
2. Market share?	2. Relative to peers?
3. Cost per unit?	3. Versus last year?
4. Returns per unit?	4. Absolute target?

FIGURE 4-2

Three Categories of Financial Measures

	Accounting	Value-Based	Company Value
Measures	• Earnings • EPS • ROE • ROA	• EVA • Economic profit	• Discounted cash flow • Net present value
Measurement Period	• Distinct (results-based)	• Distinct (results-based)	• Forward-looking
Underlying Rules	• GAAP • Lower of cost • Double entry • Industry rules • Revenue realization	• Capital charge • Economic logic	• Cash flows • Cost of capital

reviews and qualitative measures are used more frequently for individuals lower in the organization.

Opportunity Level

The level(s) at which an incentive plan measures and rewards performance can have a significant effect on its overall effectiveness. A company must determine at what level performance should be measured, as well as how it will differ by employee/group. For example, should support staff be held accountable for overall corporate performance? Or should the CEO's performance be measured against individual goals?

Once the proper levels of opportunity are defined, the next step is identifying the appropriate weighting. A company must determine how measures at each level should be combined to determine a final award and the degree of influence that discrete measures should have on the overall payout.

The measurement focus of incentive plans should be tailored to meet the organization's operating structure. To determine the appropriate balance, an organization should consider:

• Business unit profiles and growth prospects
• Amount of interaction and interdependency between business units and corporate

- Degree to which an executive can control key performance measures at various levels
- Management and corporate culture.

Award Calculation

After identifying the annual incentive plan measures, associated performance objectives and individual award opportunity, it is time to examine how to combine them. Specifically, it is time to think about issues associated with performance measure weightings. While there are numerous possibilities, companies typically employ one of three approaches:

- **Additive.** Awards are calculated separately for each performance metric and added together to determine the incentive payout. Metrics are independent of each other; metrics with greater importance (i.e., organizational impact) are weighted more than less critical performance targets.
- **Multiplicative.** Award for performance on one metric is adjusted based on performance of another metric. Metrics are mathematically linked to reward for a balanced performance against both metrics simultaneously (high performance on one metric is at the expense of another).
- **Matrix.** Levels of performance on two measures from axes of the matrix. The annual incentive is determined by the intersection of performance level of each measure. Like the multiplicative approach, measures are mathematically linked to reward for balanced performance against both measures simultaneously.

Payout Range

A payout range — the award amounts provided to participants based on performance outcomes — can have a significant influence on behavior and compensation. The two critical components of any payout range are:

- **Threshold.** The level of performance below which no incentive award is provided.
- **Maximum.** The level of performance above which no additional incremental awards are earned.

It is common practice to set the range of performance targets relative to the company's business plan for the current year (e.g., target achievement equals 100 percent of plan). Thresholds and maximums are then developed around this target.

The payout range can be symmetrical or asymmetrical. A symmetrical range allows the threshold for payment at the same percentage below the target as the maximum is above it, whereas an asymmetrical payout range typically provides more upside potential to plan participants. (See Figure 4-3.)

Whether a payout range is asymmetrical usually is associated with a company's philosophy to reward proportionately more for performance that is above target and less for performance that falls below objectives. A critical consideration in determining appropriate leverage is the relative positioning of performance targets to industry norms. If the performance targets are industry-leading, the plan could reflect higher-than-average opportunity, with modest downside leverage and high upside leverage.

Conversely, if the performance targets are within industry norms, high leverage may be appropriate on both sides of target.

The odds of attaining goal levels are an important consideration when setting incentive plan goals. Participants must believe that at the onset of the performance period the goals have a reasonable likelihood of being achieved. If the goals are too stringent, the participants will discount them and virtually ignore the targets. If the goals are too easy, the plan will not drive stretch performance. From an employee motivation and incentive design perspective, Table 4-2 lays out a rule for the odds of attainment when setting performance goals.

Many companies establish a minimum or threshold level of performance that must be achieved to receive any payout under the incentive plan. "Circuit breakers" commonly are built into the funding of the incentive pool or serve as the threshold of performance for one of the plan measures. Some companies still allow incentives below the threshold under certain circumstances, at least partly negating the purpose of the threshold.

Not all threshold levels operate as circuit breakers. A company may set a threshold for measures that are mutually exclusive, thus

FIGURE 4-3

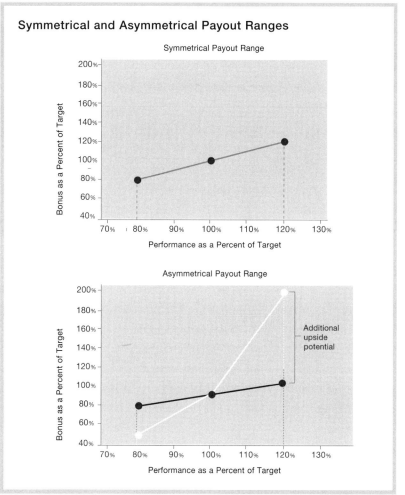

Symmetrical and Asymmetrical Payout Ranges

TABLE 4-2

Attainment of Performance Levels

Performance Level	Odds of Attainment
Threshold	8 out of 10
Target	5 out of 10
Maximum (Stretch)	2 out of 10

allowing some portion of the bonus to be paid if performance exceeds threshold on one measure while falling short on the other(s).

Dealing with Economic Turmoil

Determining annual incentive plan goals and appropriate payout levels can be especially challenging during periods of economic turmoil. Management and compensation committees struggle with ways to maintain effective incentive plans while business plans and goals fall below normal or desired levels of performance. In many cases, normal objectives for maximizing short-term profit give way to improving cash flow and better positioning for future profitable growth. This often leaves employees feeling that they are working harder than ever with little hope of achieving established performance thresholds. On the other hand, management and compensation committees need to maintain fiscal responsibility and control compensation costs in line with reduced performance.

One way to deal with the situation is to widen normal performance ranges. For example, if threshold performance goals are normally set at 80 percent of planned performance, the threshold may be reduced to 50 percent of plan, often coupled with a corresponding reduction in the amount of threshold-level incentive payment (e.g., 25 percent of target payment rather than 50 percent of target payment). Some organizations go a step farther and provide enhanced incentive opportunities to drive performance past target and toward established maximum performance levels.

Another approach is to fund some level of an incentive payment pool for high-performing employees for improving the business or achieving specified strategic goals under a difficult set of circumstances even though current financial goals are not achieved. In the end, it is important to achieve a balance among annual profit, growth and performance, and setting goals with reasonable odds of attainment that drive employees to achieve desired results. At some companies, payments for achievement of short-term milestones or strategic goals are deferred in the form of restricted shares. In that way, the level or value of payment is linked to continued employment and the effect that short-term achievements have on future share value. However, once economic conditions start settling down, it is important for a company to return to a more normalized performance and goal-setting approach with an appropriate balance between short- and long-term compensation design.

Plan Funding
The way an organization funds incentives plays an important role in achieving a fair balance between the interests of shareholders and plan participants. Funding for cash-based incentive plans focuses on pools of money, whereas funding for equity-based plans focuses on pools of shares. There are two common approaches used to determine overall annual incentive plan funding:

- **Sum of targets.** The aggregate amount of awards to be paid under the plan is determined by adding the target awards of all participants. Companies usually then modify the pool resulting from the aggregate targets based on a formal schedule relating to performance.
- **Financial results-based formula.** A fund is established using a percentage of a financial measure (e.g., 3 percent of net income) or a percentage of a financial measure that exceeds a hurdle rate (e.g., 5 percent of net income in excess of an 8-percent return on equity).

The challenge with the sum of targets approach is, depending on the measures and the company's ability to correlate the different payout levels with performance, it does not necessarily link to the employer's ability to pay these incentives. Conversely, the financial results-based formula is relatively rigid on whether bonuses will be paid at the level earned. To address these challenges, the solution for many companies is a combination of both approaches.

For companies establishing a maximum pool, the most common method to express the maximum pool is as a multiple or percentage of the target pool. It is not uncommon for a company to set an overall limit on the amount it will pay out in any one year. This limit sometimes is called a "stakeholder protection clause" because it protects stakeholders against possible windfall payments under the plan due to unforeseen events.

Payout Alternatives

In some cases, a company may want to provide senior managers with flexibility in choosing how they receive their incentive payout. There are two general types of incentive payout alternatives that employers most commonly offer to employees:

- **Deferral opportunities.** In addition to base salary, many companies allow participants to elect to defer receipt of all or a portion of their incentive awards/payments.

- **Cash-bonus exchange.** Companies also may allow employees to exchange a portion of their target or actual annual cash bonus for stock options and/or time-vested restricted stock.

Why would a company offer these opportunities, and why would an employee take advantage of them? (See Table 4-3.)

Annual incentives are an important part of total compensation. Employees may not always see the link between base pay and organizational objectives, whereas variable pay provides visibility about how their actions affect the company and its achievement of goals. The plan design is critical for any annual incentive pay plan to be both effective and to align employee performance to organizational objectives.

TABLE 4-3

Employee and Company Benefits

Employee Benefits	Company Benefits
Tax effectiveness: Delays tax on the exchanged incentive value (until employee realizes value from equity award).	**Stock ownership:** Provides an additional opportunity for employees to increase their ownership levels.
Additional upside/wealth accumulation potential: While the exchange for equity-based compensation entails more risk than cash, it also provides significantly more upside potential.	**Tax/income statement effectiveness:** Improves cash flow for company in the short-term (though long-term EPS effects may be less beneficial).
Flexibility: Furnishes ability to customize pay, a growing market trend.	

5
Public Company Long-Term Incentive Compensation: An Equity-Based Focus

By David Wise and Tony Wu

For senior executives in public companies, equity-based long-term incentives (LTIs) usually are the largest component of the pay package, often exceeding base salary and annual incentives by several multiples. Owing to the multi-year vesting periods and the potential for significant rewards, LTIs are a powerful and highly visible tool in retaining top executive talent. In addition, equity-based compensation is the principal agent in aligning company leadership with shareholders.

In the 1980s, 1990s and early 2000s, stock options dominated LTI plans. More recently, changes in accounting, governance reforms, market downturns, shareholder scrutiny and concerns about high dilution levels have combined to alter both the design and use of LTIs. More than any other factor, however, the required expensing of stock options under accounting rules adopted in 2004 prompted significant strategic changes in LTI practices.

In addition to accounting rule changes, updated proxy requirements for compensation disclosure began drawing attention to practices and plans that previously might have been known only to a handful of company insiders and board members. Further, disclosure requirements demanded that companies explain why certain plan elements were used in addition to what existed. Thus, it became incumbent upon executives and compensation committees to rethink and re-evaluate their equity plans based on their specific business needs and strategies, all while taking into consideration how their shareholders were likely to view their plans.

In recent years, companies have broadened their approaches to LTIs and now often use a portfolio approach to making LTI grants by spreading more value over a combination of vehicles. The biggest gains have been seen in performance-share plans and performance-vested restricted stock plans that combine both share price increase and other key company-wide performance to determine incentive value.

Many issues have to be addressed in designing LTI programs: the potential value of company shares, management's perception of share value, the optimum number of shares authorized for use, the effect of run rates and stock overhang, to name only a few. In this environment, setting performance goals has taken on a heightened importance in LTI design. Many companies are challenged just setting annual goals, let alone having to project multiple-year targets. Determining accurate performance measures that trigger appropriate plan payouts is, of course, crucial to the success of these plans. Our objective is to provide practical insights on how companies can transition to a more balanced, strategic approach to LTIs.

This chapter:

- Examines how LTIs fit into an overall pay strategy and what compensation committees and senior management must do to address the share dilution and pay-for-performance issues relating to LTIs.
- Discusses the design flexibility available to companies seeking to include performance conditions in full-value stock awards. Considerations such as leverage, performance measures, goal setting, performance periods and eligibility for performance-vested plans also are addressed.
- Reviews the key accounting issues relating to LTIs, focusing on performance shares and performance-vested restricted stock.
- Recommends that companies examine their stock option program for efficiency and perceived value from both shareholder and executive perspectives.

Strategic Considerations for Long-Term Incentive Plans

Direct compensation in its many forms — base salary, annual bonuses and LTIs — is the single greatest expense for most companies in the United States. Accordingly, employee rewards represent a significant component of the financial strategy and decision process for any successful business.

Because the compensation system is such a significant component of an organization's overall financial structure, it is strategic almost by definition. Nowhere is the strategic nature of the compensation program more evident than in the design of executive LTI programs. Specifically, an LTI program is:

• Likely the key element in a company's ability to attract and retain top executive talent — those individuals who develop and implement strategic business plans

• Costly and creates significant multi-year liabilities, creating long-term commitments for the company

• Highly visible; no board of directors or compensation committee wants to be in the position of defending compensation practices similar to excessive arrangements that have been reported at some well-known and respected organizations.

With the increases in proxy-related disclosure requirements, shareholders of public companies gained more and better information with which to evaluate a company's LTI program. As these shareholders began paying more attention to these disclosures, and as they were given more power with which to affect a company's compensation decision-making, LTI practices began changing. Gone are the days in which companies would simply disclose that their program designs were a function of market practices and competitiveness; the U.S. Securities and Exchange Commission (SEC) and shareholders began demanding that companies demonstrate the link between their programs and their strategy.

Understanding Constraints in Granting Long-Term Incentives

LTI issues go beyond pure compensation design. They introduce issues relating to accounting, tax and use of a company's share pool — each of which provides some constraints. There is real expense and potential dilution of shareholder value in employee grants of LTIs to be considered, which add levels of complexity when compared to other elements of the executive pay package.

These constraints are critical for all companies to understand as they look to balance their HR objectives with the cold, hard facts of their LTIs' effect on financials and share availability.

Key questions in this process include:

- How many shares are available for the company to grant?
- When will the available pool of shares expire?
- What is the company's current stock overhang relative to peer and shareholder benchmarks?
- What will be the expense impact of each type of share granted? How well does that expense correlate to perceived value on the part of recipients?
- What are the tax implications — to the recipient as well as the company — of the different LTI vehicles being considered?

Knowing the 'Hot Buttons'

The landscape for LTI compensation changes annually, and every company needs to know what market trends suggest and what shareholders watch. As the largest part of an executive's compensation package, LTIs tend to attract significant shareholder attention on issues that relate to dilution of their share value and the pay-for-performance orientation of the company's program.

Some of the key questions companies need to ask regularly go right to the heart of these "hot buttons":

- What is the right level of shares for the company to use annually (i.e., run rate)?
- Do additional equity grants provide additional motivation or retention value to an executive who already has a significant stake in the business?
- Do executives own enough shares to demonstrate adequate alignment with shareholders? Are the company's share ownership and retention guidelines/requirements set at the right levels?
- How long is "long term"? Should changes be considered that better align the vesting of these incentives with the time horizon for the company's business challenges?
- How much (if any) of the company's LTI mix should be performance-vested vs. service-vested?

- What should happen to unvested shares upon termination? Should they vest immediately, continue to vest, or not vest at all?
- What should happen to unvested shares upon a change in control? Should they vest immediately or continue to vest?

While none of these questions necessarily has a single right answer for every company, many shareholders will have strong opinions on them. No compensation committee should ever be surprised by their shareholders' reaction to their LTI program, which puts pressure on the compensation team to ensure that each and every one of these issues is given adequate attention and planning.

Performance Shares and Performance-Vested Restricted Stock

Regulatory and corporate governance developments, combined with the refinement of a key design feature, have breathed new life into the use of performance shares and performance-vested restricted stock in LTI programs. Full-value stock award plans like restricted stock — long-favored by recipients but often loathed by skeptical investors — have shown an increase in use since the stock option expensing rules changes. Today, however, the inclusion of performance criteria has become an essential feature in these plans to meet shareholder demands for good governance and paying for performance.

Service-Based, Full-Value Plans (Restricted Stock)

Executives who receive traditional restricted stock awards are granted the right to shares of company stock, usually without cost, once prescribed terms and conditions are satisfied. In conventional practice, terms and conditions were limited to time-based vesting. Stay on the job for, say, four years, and the stock becomes yours, either ratably over time (graded vesting) or all at once (cliff vesting) at the end of the restriction period. In the interim, you may be a beneficial owner, meaning you receive dividends and can vote your shares.

All in all, this tends to be a good deal for the executive. The downside is limited (restricted stock does not go underwater), and the cost cannot be beat (by contrast, an executive must pay the exercise price for a stock option). Once restrictions lapse, the executive may sell shares or use cash (often from bonuses) to pay the resulting tax. However, from the viewpoint of wary investors, this often is deemed too good of a deal; they tend to want to see more executive skin in the game and performance hurdles that are more robust than merely staying employed.

Adding Performance Conditions to Full-Value Awards

In recent years, the use of performance shares and performance-vested restricted stock has surged for a combination of reasons. First, changes in the accounting rules eliminated a compelling advantage in favor of stock options by requiring companies to recognize a charge to earnings on fixed option grants issued at fair market value. This heavily debated action evened the playing field for other compensatory equity-based programs with stock options from an accounting perspective.

Additionally, with shareholders becoming more involved in all matters relating to executive pay, companies became more focused on the levels of dilution that resulted when the majority of LTIs were granted through stock options. Using performance shares or restricted stock helps conserve shares because companies obtain more mileage from the full value of a restricted share than from the fair value of a stock option, which always will be worth less than the underlying price of the stock.

Most notably, performance shares are designed in part to respond to the perceived lack of pay-for-performance orientation from which service-vested vehicles suffer. Performance share plans (PSPs) provide a more direct link to performance than stock options or other service-based LTI vehicles by using two different levers to align pay and performance: the accomplishment of key goals (typically financial, operational or shareholder driven) that determine how many shares are earned, combined with the value of those shares earned at the end of the cycle.

PSPs are now viewed favorably by external constituencies, particularly when used as the dominant vehicle in an LTI program.

Designing Performance Share Plans

One key benefit of a PSP is the considerable design flexibility offered. However, before a PSP can be rolled out, numerous design features have to be thought through (including details), as each decision contains financial, cultural and operational implications.

Leverage

PSPs usually have a degree of leverage, which refers to the relationship between performance and payout levels. Typically, these plans operate similarly to annual incentive programs in that there are scaled payouts available for performance that is both below and above target goals. A common leverage curve provides something on the order of 50 percent of target shares for achievement of threshold performance, and 150 percent or 200 percent of target shares for achievement of stretch performance. (See Figure 5-1.)

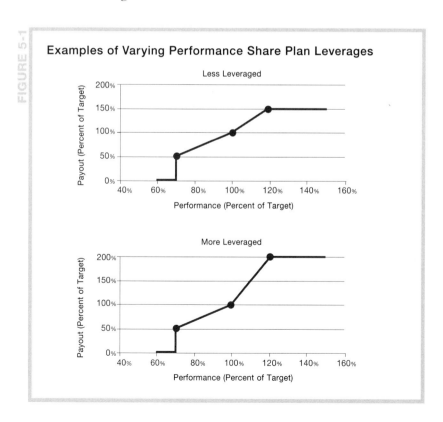

FIGURE 5-1

Examples of Varying Performance Share Plan Leverages

In both examples, shares are earned at a faster pace for incremental performance above target levels than they are below target levels. Achieving the right leverage relationship should be a function of a company's overall pay philosophy, business strategy and performance orientation. For example, a more leveraged curve may be appropriate for entrepreneurial organizations where executives are expected to take on more risk in an effort to drive the success of the business. In these situations, executives would be more generously rewarded for outstanding performance, but held more accountable for below-target performance. A flatter leverage curve, on the other hand, might be appropriate for a company with a less leveraged business strategy.

Performance Measures

A primary challenge with using performance shares is the difficulty in setting challenging yet achievable goals for an extended time. To set goals, companies often rely on the forecasting abilities of their finance and strategic planning teams to develop realistic projections. However, while many companies use objectives that are absolute in nature, goals also can be relative.

Absolute goals typically are financial in nature but, increasingly, companies are adopting other, more strategic measurements that capture needed longer term business transformations (e.g., sales or market share growth in a key product category). Relative goals almost always are financial in nature and look to compare the company's performance against a peer group or broader index (e.g., the company's total shareholder return or top-line growth versus its peer group). Balancing the benefits and drawbacks of each approach, many companies may use both types of measures in their plans, allowing them to balance absolute performance with outperformance.

While there is an ongoing debate about the use of objectives and subjective measures in annual incentive plans, most long-term plans make use of only objective measures that are easily measurable. There are several practical reasons for this. First and foremost, in the United States, section 162(m) of the Internal Revenue Code (IRC) stipulates that for compensation to be considered "performance-based" and, therefore, eligible for tax deductibility, associated performance goals for a few top-paid executives (i.e., CEO and next three highest paid executives other than the CFO) must be objective so that a third party can clearly determine whether goals have been attained. These goals cannot be subject to discretionary assessments that could increase the amounts. Second, the accounting rules penalize equity-based awards that are not based on the objective performance criteria, requiring such grants to be treated with liability accounting instead of the preferred equity accounting treatment.

Goal Setting

Many companies struggle with how to set the bar on multiple-year performance plans. There are various strategies for addressing this issue, including looking at historical performance against targets or budgets. However, best-practice goal setting suggests that the objectives should balance both realistic probabilities to achievement, as well as fairness to shareholders. Both of these elements should be a function in part of the company's strategic plan, internal and external performance expectations, odds of attainment of different performance outcomes, and participant perception, to name a few.

Common chances of attaining the key performance levels are shown in Table 4-2. If goals are too difficult, participants will have low perceived value of the plan and ignore performance. If goals are too soft, the plan will not drive the performance that shareholders are seeking.

Eligibility

Performance plans typically have been limited to senior executives as they represent the key players in driving the success of the business. Current practice limits performance shares to the executive level, as lower-level employees may not always grasp the performance share design concept as it relates to their own positions. The less a participant understands about the award and the less ability to influence the outcomes, the less value that he/she ascribes to the award.

Performance Period

Most plans tend to include a three-year performance period, which is a function of the maximum length of time in which many companies are comfortable forecasting performance, as well as what is considered to be a market-standard vesting period. However, there are plans in the marketplace that are designed from one to five years. Such plans should maintain some alignment with the time horizon of the company's strategic challenges.

Accounting Considerations

The effect on a company's financial statements often affects the types of incentive compensation provided to executives. Accordingly, key accounting considerations may influence awards of performance shares and performance-vested restricted stock.

Financial Accounting Standards Board (FASB) Accounting Standards Codification (ASC) Topic 718, formerly FASB 123R, requires that all equity-based compensation granted to employees be accounted for at fair value, measured at grant date. Stock-based awards, including stock options and full-value share plans — whether time- or performance-vested — are classified as equity awards (as opposed to liability awards), assuming payments are settled solely in company stock. Dividends or dividend equivalents (if any) paid during the vesting or performance period are not recognized as additional compensation cost unless the underlying awards are subsequently forfeited and the dividends are not repaid. However, accounting implications vary depending on the type of measures selected.

Performance Conditions

For awards that may vary on the basis of performance conditions (as opposed to market conditions), accruals are recognized over the amortization period and are intended to reflect the probable payout outcome. At the end of each reporting period, the company has to assess the likely performance outcome. Expense recognition then tracks payout amounts based on this estimated performance outcome until the next period when this process is repeated.

If the probable performance outcome changes during the subsequent reporting period, expense accruals need to be adjusted to track new estimated corresponding payouts. Because the number of shares that can be earned likely will differ from target levels, the tracking of awards can cause volatility in compensation expense, as predictions for the likely outcome of shares earned will vary by reporting period. Expense accruals will fluctuate over the course of the performance period depending on whether probable performance outcomes go up or down. (See Figure 5-2.) One advantage of linking performance shares to a performance condition is the reversal of the expenses if the performance condition is not met. Examples of performance conditions include revenue, earnings, cash flow or return-based efficiency measures (e.g., return on equity).

Market Conditions

For performance awards that may vary on the basis of market conditions (in which the stock price is a factor in triggering the award's vesting), the grant-date fair value is determined based on a Monte Carlo valuation model, stimulating all possible outcomes over the term of the award. The resulting output is a single value incorporating the economic effect of the market condition over time. Expense is fixed at grant date and amortized over the performance period. (See Figure 5-3.) The expense is irreversible if the market condition is not met. Examples of market conditions include stock price and total shareholder return.

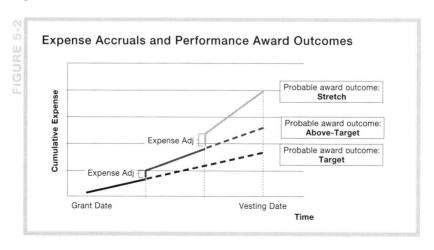

FIGURE 5-2

Expense Accruals and Performance Award Outcomes

Cumulative Expense

Probable award outcome:
Stretch

Probable award outcome:
Above-Target

Expense Adj

Probable award outcome:
Target

Expense Adj

Grant Date

Vesting Date

Time

FIGURE 5-3

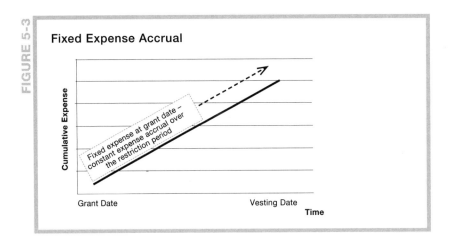

Fixed Expense Accrual

Cumulative Expense

Fixed expense at grant date – constant expense accrual over the restriction period

Grant Date   Vesting Date

Time

Income Tax Deductibility

To obtain income tax deductibility under IRC section 162(m), a PSP must be approved by shareholders and contain one or more performance metrics, thereby qualifying as performance-based compensation. Goals must be set either prior to the beginning of the performance period or within 90 days of the beginning of the performance period with the outcome substantially uncertain and no more than 25 percent of the performance period having passed. Unearned shares typically do not carry voting rights and participants may or may not be paid dividend equivalents throughout the performance period.

Other Considerations

Other design implications for a PSP are:

- **Share usage.** Performance shares are full-value awards and often are counted as more than one share toward the equity pool (i.e., shares available for award issuance) for the share usage and Institutional Shareholder Services (ISS) burn-rate calculations. Depending on the plan's leverage curve, companies typically reserve their shares at stretch payout levels up front to ensure that the number of shares required is available at the time of payout. If the actual number of shares paid out is less than reserved, the excess number of shares reserved is available for future grants. To avoid an "against" vote recommendation from a shareholder proxy advisory group, burn-rate levels typically need to be kept within a range of market-standard levels.

- **Number of tranches.** The number of award tranches also has an effect on the ultimate design. Assuming a three-year performance period, a company may issue one award tranche at grant that spans over the entire performance period, or three award tranches, one tranche at the beginning of each year of the performance cycle. One award tranche simplifies the accounting requirements, as this award is considered to only have one grant-date fair value. The latter, multi-award tranche design requires the company to determine a grant-date fair value for each award tranche. This not only adds to the accounting complexity, but the administrative complexity as well (e.g., tracking of performance for each award tranche).

- **Grant process.** LTI awards typically are granted annually. With such an approach, multiple awards overlap, therefore creating "glue" in the position. Executives are less willing to leave three award cycles on the table if another opportunity presents itself. However, with three award cycles come three sets of overlapping performance measures; a commitment generally must be made to the nature of metrics selected, as vastly different overlapping metrics may dilute the performance message and confusion as to which goals to focus on may arise. Therefore, rather than measuring goals annually, three-year cumulative goals are measured to determine award payout.

Growing Use of Performance Shares

Performance shares are playing a more prominent role in an executive's total compensation package as pay for performance, corporate accountability and shareholder value creation have become increasing focal points in today's executive compensation environment. Performance shares clearly have an advantage over time-vested equity vehicles. Design flexibility, a direct link to performance, favorable accounting treatment, and the perceptions of shareholders have made performance shares a favored long-term incentive compensation delivery vehicle in the boardroom. However, a properly designed plan requires careful thought, rigorous modeling and refinement, as even the slighted design decisions may have lasting program implications. While the complexities may seem overwhelming, PSPs are increasingly viewed as the best answer in balancing executive pay, shareholder interests and financial performance.

Stock Option Efficiency and Perceived Value

While the accounting changes that require the expensing of stock options have spurred companies to look at different plan designs, stock option efficiency (from both a shareholder and an employee perspective) also has become an issue for consideration.

Stock options have low share-usage efficiency relative to other equity vehicles. To deliver the same expected equity value to employees, a company has to grant significantly more stock options than full-value restricted shares, which have built-in value at grant.

Since the introduction of stock option expensing, companies must consider the expense efficiency of stock options. In this process, two critical questions are being asked about their LTI plans:

- **What is the stock option value actually realized by employee per dollar of expense?** While stock options have the potential to deliver significant value to option holders, they may have zero realizable value unless they are in the money when exercisable. In companies where share price performance is poor, companies will incur expense for a vehicle that delivers no value to employees.

- **What is the gap between the perceived value of stock options and the expense taken by the company?** The binomial and Black-Scholes stock option valuation models provide an expected value of stock options. In theory, stock option recipients should value these options at the same levels produced by the valuation models. In reality, however, an employee's perception of the stock option value is typically much less than the expense value, creating a potentially significant inefficiency.

Perceived Value

For certain employees at some companies, the perceived value of stock options can be less than 50 percent of the option valuation. This means that, for every dollar of stock option value granted, the recipient credits the company with delivering less than 50 cents of value. Simply put, the employee would believe that a cash payment of 50 cents or less would be a fair exchange for a stock option grant.

The degree to which this discount exists involves a number of factors, including:

- **The company's recent share price history.** For companies with strong share price history where stock options have vested in the money, the perceived value of stock options is likely to be much higher than in companies with stagnant price history.
- **Salary level and personal wealth situation.** Higher-paid employees such as executives tend to value stock options higher than lower-paid employees. In large part, this perception may be due to the fact that lower-paid employees generally have nearer-term cash needs and are more inclined to focus on the potential that a grant may yield little or no gain.
- **Personal risk profile.** Employees who are risk averse will place less value on vehicles that have the potential to finish underwater.

As companies begin looking at alternatives to stock options, it is imperative that they consider perceived value at different levels of their own organizations. Understanding how employees value these vehicles can provide significant opportunity to create LTI packages that increase perceived value, reduce share usage, limit expense and/or provide greater expense efficiency. (See "Examples of Perceived Value.")

Share Conversion Ratios

As in the Company A example, many employers have long used a standard 3:1 stock option to time-vested restricted share conversion ratio based on the approximate expense relationship. For companies where the perceived value of stock options is relatively high, this ratio can re-create the perceived value.

However, in companies where the perceived value is significantly lower than the expense relationship — like Companies A and B — there is an opportunity to either increase perceived value or reduce expense. As illustrated, Company A was able to increase the perceived value of the grants with a 3:1 conversion, while Company B was able to reduce the expense of the grants with a 4:1 conversion.

Examples of Perceived Value

Company A: Changing the LTI Mix to Increase Perceived Value

Company A is considering a move from stock options to time-vested restricted stock and wants to increase the perceived value of the LTI grant while maintaining the same current expense. The company grants an employee $90,000 worth of LTI value through 30,000 stock options, with a $9 current share price and a $3 option valuation.

However, the company's recent share price performance has been modest. Some previous grants are currently underwater, and an internal survey finds that most employees value the stock options significantly less than the expense value would suggest, discounting the expense value by approximately 33 percent (for a value of $2 per stock option). As a result, the employee values the $90,000 grant at approximately $60,000.

In switching to time-vested restricted stock, the expense value of each restricted share will be $9, or three times each stock option, using 10,000 shares to create an LTI grant with the same $90,000 expense.[1] A survey by the company determines that employees tend to give roughly a 12-percent "haircut" to restricted shares (or $8 per option), for a perceived value of $80,000.

For Company A, this switch from options to restricted shares results in an increase in the perceived value of the grant by $20,000, while maintaining the same expense.

[1] In current plan design, restricted shares increasingly also have performance hurdles. Although performance will have some impact on perceived value, the discussion and examples have used "plain vanilla" time-vested full-value shares to illustrate the point.

Company A	Value Granted	Share Price	Expense Valuation per Share	Perceived Value	Number of Shares Needed	Expense Taken	Perceived Value
Stock Options	$90,000	$9	$3	$2	30,000	$90,000	$60,000
Restricted Stock	$90,000	$9	$9	$8	10,000	$90,000	$80,000

Company B: Changing the LTI Mix to Reduce Expense

Company B is similar in all ways to Company A, but rather than looking to create the same expense, the company wants to re-create the same perceived value.

At Company A, time-vested restricted shares were substituted for stock options based on the expense relationship of $9 to $3, or a 3-1 ratio.

However, when we look at the perceived value of the two vehicles — $8 for restricted shares and $2 for stock options — we see that these actually relate in a 4-1 ratio. Using the 4-1 ratio translates into a conversion of only 7,500 time-vested restricted shares, down from 10,000 at Company A.

Here, Company B has created the same perceived value, while reducing the expense of the LTI program by $22,500.

Company B	Number of Shares Granted	Share Price	Expense Valuation per Share	Perceived Value	Expense Taken	Perceived Value
Stock Options	30,000	$9	$3	$2	$90,000	$60,000
Restricted Stock	7,500	$9	$9	$8	$67,500	$60,000

Other Considerations

Clearly, the implementation of a comprehensive LTI program should not be driven by expense, perceived value and share usage concerns in isolation. In particular, maintaining adequate performance criteria in LTI packages has become more critical than ever. As mentioned, it is common for restricted share plans to have performance features.

While these performance-based programs typically have a perceived value lower than that of time-vested restricted shares — as the number of shares or units to be delivered is not guaranteed — they also can be useful because fewer shares are needed and the awards may maintain a higher perceived value than stock options.

Each company has different needs, business objectives, employee mixes and shareholders. Compensation committees need to look at various considerations involving expense, share usage, retention concerns, perceived value, company performance and performance leverage to determine the right course. The one-size-fits-all approach is rarely a viable one. A portfolio approach, through which multiple vehicles are used to consider these issues at different levels in the organization, is recommended.

As a starting point, however, companies need to research and understand how employees value the different LTI vehicles being presented to them and use this information to develop their portfolio.

6
Long-Term Incentive Compensation in Private Companies and Business Units

By Daniel Moynihan

Long-term incentive (LTI) pay is a critical component of most executive compensation packages. LTIs help recruit and retain high-performing executives, encourage specific executive behaviors and align executive financial interests with those of shareholders. In addition, LTIs can focus executives on what is best for the organization well into the future and, when well-designed, promote superior corporate performance that directly benefits shareholders. Employers are seeking methods of compensating executives that are based on sustained, long-term performance.

The basic objectives for LTI programs hold true for both public and private companies. Public companies have considerable flexibility in designing LTI programs through stock options, restricted stock, performance shares, phantom plans and other forms of equity compensation, as well as cash programs. Ongoing equity grants, however, are not usually effective in private companies. In these businesses, equity generally is illiquid and subject to numerous restrictions that cause executives to substantially discount the value they place on any such awards. Also, founder-owners (or their families) are seldom willing to dilute their ownership stakes.

The following pages focus on approaches to non-equity LTIs specifically designed for private companies and the business units within public companies where compensation strategy dictates an LTI focus on business unit rather than corporate performance.

This chapter:

- Explains why a performance unit plan is a viable LTI for a private company and what financial and nonfinancial performance measures may be used in the plan design. We illustrate how performance unit plans actually work through two examples — a single performance factor example and a matrix example.

- Describes a value creation plan, an easy-to-administer and easy-to-understand LTI vehicle in which participants share in an incentive pool that varies up or down based on company or business unit "economic profit." Using an example, an explanation is provided about how a measure of profit is defined and how the incentive pool is determined and awarded.

- Includes an overview of how phantom equity is being used in private companies, as well as within units of larger publicly traded businesses.

The Performance Unit Plan Alternative

Performance unit plans (PUPs) often make good sense for private companies. They are one of the available performance plans that link cash payments to the operating performance of the company during a multi-year performance period. Unlike annual bonuses, PUPs tie financial rewards to the company's long-term performance while avoiding prolonged financial obligations.

Under a typical PUP, participants receive a fixed number of performance units, each with a target value. Each grant of performance units relates to a performance period that usually stretches over a three- to five-year horizon. The final value of the units at the end of the cycle depends on the achievement of pre-established performance objectives. Depending on the company's objectives, performance periods may run sequentially or they may overlap.

Performance Measurement

A PUP relies upon carefully selected performance measures to evaluate executives' contributions. Performance measures must be well understood and performance expectations must be well communicated if a program is to be effective. A properly designed PUP focuses executives on achieving desired results and promoting actions consistent with the business strategy.

Financial and Nonfinancial Performance Measures

Nonfinancial measures can be quantitative (e.g., market share, product mix, productivity, cost position) or qualitative (e.g., customer satisfaction, quality, service level, process excellence).

Financial measures are more traditional and typically found on company accounting statements. They typically are income-based (e.g., net income, operating income, earnings per share, revenue) or return-based (e.g., return on equity, return on assets, return on capital).

The overriding role of financial performance is to link behavior with value creation. As this link becomes more straightforward and transparent, the measures generally become more effective. The selection of financial measures requires a balance between accuracy and complexity. The financial measures that most accurately reflect the value of the company tend to be the ones that are the most complex.

What and How to Measure

The performance measurement involves two decisions: what to measure and how to measure. Performance measures identify what to measure, and performance goals establish target levels of performance against those measures. Goals can be established using internal or external benchmarks. While internal benchmarks or an absolute goal-setting method have been the most common approach, external standards or a relative goal-setting method are becoming more popular.

At the end of the performance period, actual performance against objectives is evaluated. Based on this evaluation, the performance unit value is determined. Each unit has a target value if the plan's target performance is achieved for the period. The actual performance unit value varies depending upon the long-term performance during the period. It is common in most plans to have a threshold performance level so that the performance unit has no value if the threshold level is not achieved. The unit value for threshold performance typically is 50 percent of target value. Likewise, a maximum performance level is established correlating to a maximum unit value, which commonly is set at 150 percent or 200 percent of target value.

Single Performance Factor Example

In the single performance factor approach, only one measure is used to determine the incentive payout. While perhaps the simplest structure (because it uses only one measure), it does not diversify an executive's incentive opportunity. (See Figure 6-1)

In this example, the awards are generated in a range of zero to 150 percent times the target award based upon sales growth performance versus goal. Under other designs, multiple factors may be considered without the payout opportunity representing the sum of performance on all measures.

Matrix Example

A second method of determining incentive plan payouts uses a matrix. In this approach, two measures are used to determine the incentive payout. This method is more complex than the single factor, and an advantage is that the combination of the two measures can be weighted differently at varying performance levels to reflect strategic priorities. (See Figure 6-2.)

Looking at a matrix of performance measures, if a company was below target in sales but above target in earnings before interest and taxes (EBIT) margin, the plan still can pay out at 100 percent of target. (See "Advantages and Disadvantages of PUPs.")

Overall, a PUP can be easy to administer and explain, and it provides executives with an alternative to a stock-based program in which such an equity award is not practical or desirable.

The Value Creation Plan Approach

In many cases, a viable alternative to stock-based LTI awards can be found through the use of a value creation plan (VCP) that shares a portion of earnings above a pre-established threshold with executives. A VCP can be understandable for participants and relatively simple to administer based on measurable returns at the business-unit level or consolidated level (for private companies).

In essence, each VCP participant has an ownership interest in an LTI pool that grows or shrinks based upon the private company or business unit's performance relative to the annual expected return

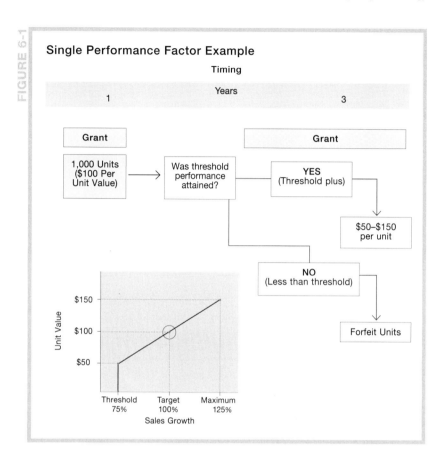

FIGURE 6-1

Single Performance Factor Example

Timing

Years

1   3

| Grant | Grant |

1,000 Units ($100 Per Unit Value) → Was threshold performance attained?

YES (Threshold plus)

$50–$150 per unit

NO (Less than threshold)

Forfeit Units

$150

$100

$50

Unit Value

Threshold 75%   Target 100%   Maximum 125%

Sales Growth

on investment in the entity. A VCP eliminates the need to settle upon a method to value company stock (for private companies), set multi-year performance goals or establish peer group or index benchmarks.

Designing the Program

To establish a VCP, a measure of profit must be defined and understood by all participants. Examples include EBIT, net operating profit after taxes (NOPAT) and bottom-line net income. Also, a return measure must be defined, such as return on equity or return on invested capital (debt and equity). The threshold return must be periodically adjusted as the cost of investment funds and/or debt-to-equity ratio change. Further, as the private company's or business unit's capital base grows, so too would the required profit to meet the expected threshold return to investors.

FIGURE 6-2

Matrix Using Sales and EBIT Margin

EBIT Margin Performance				
110% 11%		$104.5 MM 100%	$107.25 MM 125%	$110 MM 150%
105% 10.5%		$99.75 MM 75%	102.38 MM 100%	$105 MM 125%
100% 10%	0% Payout	$95 MM 50%	$97.5 MM 75%	$100 MM 100%
95% 9.5%		$90.25 MM 37.5%	$92.63 MM 50%	$95 MM 75%
90% 9%		$85.5 MM 25%	$87.75 MM 37.5%	$90 MM 50%

0% Payout

95% $0.950 billion	97.5% $0.975 billion	100% $1 billion

Sales Performance

Advantages and Disadvantages of PUPs

Advantages:

- Risk/reward balance can be precisely engineered.

- No shares are required.

- Design can result in low or zero payments during sub-par performance cycles.

- Charge to earnings is capped because there is a maximum payout.

- Can be used to reinforce mid-term performance objectives.

- Relatively easy to communicate.

Disadvantages:

- Difficult to set long-term performance goals.

- Subject to liability accounting treatment.

Sharing Ratio

When a VCP is created, a sharing ratio needs to be established whereby a portion of the private company or business unit's annual economic profit is contributed to an LTI pool. The sharing ratio is based upon market target awards and determined at the start of the plan and held constant for a defined period. If an economic loss occurs (i.e., earnings below the expected threshold return), then

$112.75 MM	$115.5 MM	EBIT $
175%	200%	Payout as a percent of target
$107.63 MM	$110.25 MM	EBIT $
150%	175%	Payout as a percent of target
$102.5 MM	$105 MM	EBIT $
125%	150%	Payout as a percent of target
$97.38 MM	$99.75 MM	EBIT $
100%	125%	Payout as a percent of target
$92.25 MM	$94.5 MM	EBIT $
75%	100%	Payout as a percent of target

102.5%	105%
$1.025 billion	$1.050 billion

the sharing ratio's proportion is deducted from the incentive pool. The annual contribution (or deduction) is then allocated among the plan participants' account balances using a predetermined formula.

This two-step exercise occurs annually over the life of the plan. To mitigate risk for the participants, a floor could be placed upon deductions from the incentive pool; a corresponding limit could be placed on annual contributions to the pool to limit the company's liability. Special provisions would be crafted regarding a potential sale of the company/business unit or if the private company completes an initial public offering.

Example

For an example of how a VCP could work, consider the co-founders of a debt-free private company who want to establish an LTI plan for their senior executive team but are unwilling to dilute their ownership in the company. The co-founders decide to set up a VCP that rewards executives for NOPAT above a threshold return on the co-founders' equity in the company.

In this example, the sharing percentage of NOPAT that exceeds the company's cost of capital would be added to the incentive plan pool annually and allocated to the individual participants' accounts according to formula. To the extent that NOPAT is lower than the cost of capital, the incentive pool would be reduced using the sharing percentage. (See Figure 6-3.)

Vesting for each year's contribution to the LTI pool typically would be over at least three years, and distribution of a portion (e.g., one half) of the vested amount could be provided for at that time. The remaining portion of the vested balance could be required to remain in the pool until a fixed date in the event of a below-threshold performance year (which would cause the pool to shrink). Distribution could even be in the form of parent-company stock for participants who are employees of a business unit of a publicly traded company.

The design would need to take into account the potential application of the tax rules governing nonqualified deferred compensation plans under Internal Revenue Code (IRC) section 409A. If section 409A applies to the specific design, its deferral requirements would

FIGURE 6-3

Illustration of a Value Creation Plan

A	Calculate NOPAT at end of year	$5,000,000
B	Calculate owners' equity	$40,000,000
C	Factor in cost of capital …	X 10%
D	… to get to threshold return	$4,000,000
E	Subtract threshold return from NOPAT to get economic value creation	$1,000,000
F	Apply the sharing ratio …	X 15%
G	… to get contribution to incentive pool	$150,000
H	Allocate contribution among plan participants (as shown below)	

$$\frac{\text{Individual's target}}{\text{Sum of participants' target}} \quad x \quad \text{Contribution to pool}$$

need to be satisfied to avoid taxation and penalties when there is no longer a substantial risk of forfeiture (e.g., on vesting).

A VCP rewards investors before rewarding executives by motivating the executive team to focus on attaining an earnings level above the cost of the investors' capital. For executives in business units, a VCP provides a performance metric directly connected to their business unit's financial performance, which they can influence more directly than the parent company's overall stock price. A VCP can be easy to administer and explain, and it provides executives an alternative to company stock where such an award is not always practical or desirable.

Phantom Stock

A tool that has languished in obscurity at public companies, phantom stock recently has shown signs of emerging. While the reasons for public companies to turn to phantom stock are varied (i.e., uncertainties in the financial markets, insufficient authorized shares for actual stock awards), it is a compensation device that deserves more consideration. Phantom stock can provide valuable attributes of equity and help with motivation, focus and retention.

The basic concept of a phantom stock program involves a company's agreement or promise to pay the recipient of an award an amount equal to the value of a certain number (or percentage) of shares of the company's stock. Commonly structured through the award of units, a phantom stock program enables a company to make an award that tracks the economic benefits of stock ownership without using actual shares. Because phantom stock is a contractual right and not an interest in property, the tax event for the executive and the employer occurs at the payment in settlement of a properly designed phantom stock arrangement.

Phantom stock plans are shadows that mimic their real equity counterparts; phantom stock and shadow stock are terms that often are used interchangeably. Although shares of real stock can be traded at will, phantom shares or units take on value only when key contingencies or vesting conditions are met. A phantom stock plan typically does not require investment or confer ownership, so its recipient does not have voting rights. It is essentially an upside opportunity, as participants' investments typically are limited to their services; they stand to gain from any upside growth of the company.

Valuation

In making awards under a phantom stock plan, there is a determination of the value of a phantom share or unit in connection with awards to one or more participants. Valuations also will be needed for periodic reporting to participants (and to actual shareholders and the SEC if used by a public company) as well as for determinations of amounts payable at the time of settlement.

Phantom stock programs can be simply designed. However, they should be created to meet the company's specific needs and objectives in protecting the unique knowledge and skill base that is represented by those key employees selected for awards. The two types that are most prevalent are:

- The appreciation-only plan (much like a stock appreciation right)
- The full-value plan, where the award includes the underlying value of the unit (like a restricted stock unit).

Generally, a phantom stock plan or agreement spells out how the program operates and how payments are determined, along with other various details, often including:

- Eligibility criteria
- Vesting schedule
- Valuation method or formula
- Settlement and payout events
- Handling of various termination events, including:
  - Retirement
  - Death
  - Disability
  - Dismissal
  - Resignation
- Restrictive covenants
- Form of payment
- Provisions for the sales of the company
- Any funding vehicle

Design and Accounting

Accounting is a key challenge of phantom stock. Historically, phantom plans have been viewed as undesirable from an accounting perspective because of the resulting liability accounting treatment. This creates volatility on the company's income statement, which is something that concerns most CFOs. Generally, for accounting purposes, phantom shares must be treated as an expense over the required service period, and the company does not receive its income tax deduction until the benefits are paid out. This timing is similar to other equity awards, but can prove to be not as advantageous in periods when the value of the award increases. With liability accounting, the accounting expense and corresponding tax deduction are the same. When real equity is used, the company may get a tax advantage, as the expense can be locked in at grant while the tax deduction can grow as the value of the equity grows.

In addition, coming up with cash to cover phantom payouts can be tricky. Phantom stock plan gains (in appreciation-only programs) or current fair value (in full-value programs) must be paid by the company versus the public markets which is the case when using publicly traded equity. Finally, phantom stock programs typically are subject to the often complex rules applicable to nonqualified deferred compensation under IRC section 409A, so care must be taken in their design.

Why Use Phantom Stock for LTI Awards?

Phantom stock can help in getting an executive team to think and act like equity partners. It creates a sense of ownership in the success of the business because having phantom stock means the participants have skin in the game. The concept of being an equity partner by having phantom stock can create the same feeling of connection as the more traditional equity tools (e.g., stock options, restricted stock).

In addition to its incentive components, a phantom stock program involves deferred compensation and can act like golden handcuffs in retaining key executives. Phantom stock most often is used by privately held companies, but some publicly traded organizations are using phantom stock or similar cash-based LTIs as well.

Phantom stock plans can be especially useful in providing the economic benefits of equity without diluting shareholders. Because recipients of phantom units lack voting rights, a company can issue these units without altering the governance of the company or worrying about dilution issues. Phantom stock does not directly dilute the value of real outstanding shares. Phantom stock awards do, however, have a significant effect on cash flow at payout. This is why some plans have a conversion feature and may pay out in actual stock.

Another advantage to a company is the ability to design an award so that an executive receives no benefit unless vesting conditions are met and, under the appreciation-only model, the company's value has increased. The fair market value of the stock is commonly used by public companies, while private companies have various approaches. For example, a professional valuation may be preferred but viewed as too costly; many companies then turn to book value. Other approaches include a formula using revenue, EBITDA, net income, or a combination of relevant measures; a formula also can help with consistency of the valuation over time.

There are many reasons a company would consider a phantom stock arrangement:

- A public company may find that it has insufficient authorized shares to award the desired amount of awards that require actual stock.
- A company's leadership may have considered other plans but found their rules too restrictive or implementation costs too high.
- The owner(s) may desire to maintain actual and effectual control, while still sharing the economic value of the company.
- There may be ownership restrictions for certain types of entities (i.e., sole proprietorship, partnership, limited liability company), such as the S-corporation 100-shareholder rule.
- The objective is to provide equity-type incentives to a restricted group of individuals.
- A corporate division that can measure its enterprise value and wants its employees to have a share in that value even though there is no real stock available.

• A desire to focus on an event or contingency (e.g., sale, merger, IPO).

Typically, a phantom plan can provide a more flexible alternative that is not subject to the same restrictions as most equity ownership plans. For many, the simple desire to use an equity-like vehicle without giving up true ownership may be reason enough to implement. In considering a phantom stock program, the advantages and disadvantages in Table 6-1 should be evaluated.

Who Is Using Phantom Stock?

Phantom stock is not only a private-company phenomenon. According to Hay Group research of proxy filings, some well-known, publicly traded companies are using this tool to attract, retain and motivate select groups of employees.

Phantom stock is a traditional LTI vehicle rather than a fad. While trends come and go, cash-based LTI plans do have a place in the executive compensation portfolio. While these plans generally are simple and provide flexibility to the company, they also can raise various issues that must be considered carefully. In the appropriate situation, a phantom stock plan can keep the company spirit alive in the executive suite.

TABLE 6-1

Pros and Cons of Phantom Stock

Advantages:

- Allows employees to share in the growth of the company's value without being shareholders
- No equity dilution, as no actual shares are awarded
- Powerful retention tool when combined with vesting
- Board/compensation committee has flexibility to design plans based on their own discretion
- Can be tied to overall company or business unit results
- No employee investment required
- Can provide for dividend equivalents
- Design can permit phantom stock to be converted into actual equity
- No income tax until proceeds are converted to cash or real stock
- Potential tax deferral of employee compensation
- Retirement benefit opportunity.

Disadvantages:

- If paid in cash, can be a financial drain on the company's cash flow
- At a private company, may require outside valuation on an annual basis
- Company needs to communicate financial results to participants
- Payments to employee are taxed as ordinary income
- May affect the overall value of the business in a transaction
- IRC section 409A rules add complexity and difficulty in achieving objectives.

7
Performance Measurement
for Incentive Pay Plans

By Michael Ippolito and Matthew Kleger

The importance of pay for performance as a principle of executive compensation philosophy can hardly be understated. Entire books and hundreds of articles and conference presentations have been devoted to showing the techniques and strategies needed to align executive pay with company performance. Recently, the focus on pay — especially the dollar amounts reported in the press — has distracted attention from performance, which should be the focal point of any pay-for-performance discussion.

Currently, there is no unified, standard way to address the performance side of the equation and multiple metrics are in use. Total shareholder return (TSR) can be helpful in measuring management performance if it is used with a balanced management methodology that combines a TSR approach with other operating metrics that more accurately reflect the current status and expectations of long-term growth. The challenge is in determining the most effective measures given the company's unique circumstances. Once a metrically sound framework is in place, setting performance goals at realistic levels from both the company and executive perspectives can be a relatively unambiguous process.

This chapter:

- Addresses the conditions under which effective goal setting takes place and the threshold, target and maximum performance levels used for short-term incentives, as well as the pros and cons of using absolute versus relative performance goals in setting incentives.

- Discusses how performance should be defined and measured and introduces a "cash value added" approach that connects corporate performance metrics with shareholder return.
- Explains in more detail the techniques used in incorporating TSR in plan design. Taking a "high definition" approach in choosing and implementing a TSR comparator group is recommended — one that entails testing, weighting and ranking the comparator-group companies. Examples of when to not use TSR also are reviewed.

Setting Goals for Incentive Plans

With the increased scrutiny on executive compensation and greater transparency due to enhanced disclosure requirements, having a pay-for-performance compensation philosophy is practically a must for companies. Companies not only need to show a relationship between executive pay and company performance, but also must demonstrate they pay the appropriate level for performance. The pay-for-performance relationship should create and reinforce shareholder alignment.

A main challenge in designing an incentive plan is being able to forecast company performance and set goals at the right level, especially for periods longer than a year. Executives are motivated and the likelihood of desired performance increases under incentive plans when the following conditions are met:

- Executives have a line of sight in which they understand the performance goals and view them as achievable.
- There is a clear link between performance and pay.
- Executives view the pay associated with the incentive plan as meaningful (i.e., large enough to justify the effort required to achieve the performance goals).

If performance goals are not appropriately set, there can be negative consequences. If performance goals are set too high, executives will not be motivated, knowing there is little likelihood of achieving the targets. At the other extreme, if executives consistently and easily achieve performance targets, they are being sent the wrong message that superior performance is not required to receive an incentive payout.

As noted in discussions of incentive programs in this book, short-term incentive plans typically have pre-established performance levels:

- **Threshold.** A floor that represents the minimum level of performance that must be achieved before an incentive can be earned. The most prevalent threshold payout level is 50 percent of target.
- **Target.** The expected and/or planned (budgeted) level of achievement or a realistic goal that is achievable and meaningful.
- **Maximum.** The total incentive opportunity that may be earned for superior performance, sometimes referred to as a "cap." The most common maximum payout levels are 150 percent and 200 percent of target.

The level of performance relative to target that should correlate with threshold and maximum payout levels can be difficult to calibrate. A simplified approach would be to set the threshold performance level at 80 percent or 90 percent of target performance and set the maximum performance level at 100 percent or 120 percent of target performance. For example, if revenue is the performance metric and the target is $1 billion in revenue, a maximum performance level based on 120 percent of target, or $1.2 billion, may be reasonable. However, if TSR is the metric and 10-percent TSR is the target, 120 percent of target (or 12-percent TSR) likely would set the maximum goal too low.

Calibrating threshold and maximum goals appropriately can depend greatly on the performance metric. One way to test the reasonableness of the goal-setting process is to estimate the probabilities of achieving the performance levels and compare them to standard achievement frequencies (as discussed in Chapter 5 in the section titled "Performance Shares and Performance-Vested Restricted Stock").

Goal-Setting Approaches

There are two basic approaches companies can use in setting the right goals:

- **Absolute or internal approach.** Goals are set based on the company's year-over-year performance, and budgets are developed assuming the projected growth of the company. An internal approach requires a strong planning process and is difficult in industries in which external events can have a dramatic effect on results. Performance goals usually are effective when there is rigor around the goal-setting process and goals are based on the company's strategic and operating objectives. This technique can be enhanced if shareholder expectations are incorporated in the process.

- **Relative or external approach.** Goals are focused on how the company performs relative to its competitors or peers. A relative or external approach measures the company against direct competitors that are affected by similar macroeconomic factors and compete in the same market or with the same products. This method eliminates the need to set internal company performance goals because it focuses on how the company performs against its peers. It also mitigates the risk of setting the goals too high or too low.

A potential drawback to a relative approach is that selecting a peer group may be difficult for some companies. It may be particularly challenging for companies with a unique business model or in a consolidating industry. Also, the relative approach sometimes can result in unintended payouts. Even if a company outperformed the majority of its peers, it is possible that its absolute performance was poor and it created negative value for shareholders. This situation can be addressed in the following ways:

- The compensation committee may apply negative discretion in determining the incentive payouts. Therefore, the compensation committee would have the ability to pay no incentives if the company did not create any shareholder value.
- In addition to the relative goals based on performance compared to the peer group, an absolute threshold (or "circuit breaker") can be established under which no incentives are paid if the threshold performance level is not achieved (i.e., if the company does not reach an $X level of EBITDA, no incentives are paid). In cases in which the circuit breaker is tripped, all incentive payments become discretionary.

Considerations

In selecting a goal-setting approach, companies should consider several factors:

- **Management process.** How much rigor and structure is in the process? How much information is available to management regarding shareholder and analyst expectations and peer company metrics?
- **Strategic priorities.** What are the company's business objectives and ability to forecast performance based on the company's life cycle and maturity?
- **Company performance.** How volatile is the company's performance on an absolute basis and relative to peers historically?

Setting goals for incentive plans is a subjective process that requires much discussion and consideration. The board of directors and management should be able to provide sound rationale for the goals and approach selected.

'Say on Pay'? What About Performance?

For nearly two decades, a pay-for-performance debate has dominated the corporate governance agenda. While great progress has been made in enhancing transparency and aligning the interests of management and shareholders, there has been surprisingly little consensus on what constitutes best practices in performance management. Boards and investors must hold management accountable for achieving performance objectives that are comprehensive, actionable and value creating.

For compensation professionals, aligning executive pay with performance is the great work in progress of our time. The plot is well understood: Align management with investor objectives by rewarding executives for their enterprise's performance and voilà ... all stakeholders are satisfied.

So why does the drama continue to escalate? Because the mainstream focus to date has been on the pay side of the equation.

While significant and important progress has been achieved, the critical problem of effectively assessing performance remains largely unaddressed. Unless and until this changes, the plot will continue, intensifying during worsening economic times.

Defining Performance

Pay for performance depends entirely on the definition of performance. While executive pay is an easy target, it is a distracting sideshow to the management imperative of assessing and improving corporate performance. So why has progress been so elusive? The two primary reasons — comparability and complexity — are well-known:

- First, establishing standards for industries or enterprises that have different economic dynamics can be contentious at best. The question "Who had a better year, the World Series champion or the Super Bowl winner?" illustrates the point.

- Second, "corporate performance" math is difficult to measure and not necessarily supported by historical accounting measures. Much like a horse race, corporate performance is best thought of as a firm's position at any given point in time relative to its long-term objectives. While the past is certainly prologue, current expectations define performance, not vice versa. It is a world in which "What have you done for me lately?" is trumped by "What can I expect from you tomorrow?"

Measuring Performance

Because the capital markets trade on these expectations daily, the U.S. Securities and Exchange Commission (SEC) established TSR as the de facto definition of corporate performance. To further this point, the Dodd-Frank Wall Street Reform and Consumer Protection Act of 2010 provided for the SEC to promulgate rules requiring a proxy disclosure showing "the relationship between executive compensation actually paid and the financial performance" of the company, taking into account shareholder return. For some companies, there are very good reasons to use relative TSR as a performance measure for incentive plans. For example, in mature businesses that are cyclical and/or significantly affected by external factors, relative TSR can be an excellent way to assess the achievements of management in the prevailing market, economic and regulatory context.

As previously stated, relative TSR is most relevant for mature, cyclical businesses. Conversely, relative TSR is of limited validity for certain types of companies:

- Companies targeting substantial growth
- Companies in a turnaround situation
- Companies that are not competing with other companies for customers to any meaningful extent
- "Grow or die" companies (e.g., startups, turnarounds).

Absolute performance is what matters most in these companies. If relative performance is to be used at all, it might be used as a multiplier to the incentive award rather than as a primary measure.

While TSR is as good as any other measure, it is imperfect and there are some concerns with using this singular metric as the standard bearer for measuring performance:

- **TSR depends on two random, arbitrary points in time.** The same company can simultaneously be the best among its peers for one timeframe and the worse for another.
- **TSR is not actionable.** The CEO has no more control over the share price than does the factory-floor worker. The case of Enron demonstrated the ill and unintended effects of CEOs who attempt to make TSR actionable.
- **TSR is a short-term performance measure.** Irrespective of the timeframe selected, TSR fluctuates with the daily vagaries of the capital markets. It is possible, for example, for an enterprise to have achieved a five-year TSR of 20 percent one day and 0 percent the very next. Can CEO performance actually go from top quartile to bottom quartile in a single day?

Ultimately, corporate performance must be assessed based on a broad framework of interrelated metrics that influence current expectations. To succeed, the framework must, first and foremost, be economically sound. The "performance mathematics" must ensure that as levers are pressed, expected values are achieved and perceptions are influenced accordingly. Performance measurement also must be comprehensive and balanced. History is replete with pay-for-performance issues stemming from improvement in measured revenue growth offset by nonmeasured asset expansion. Finally, the assessment approach must be easy to implement. If it cannot be readily understood and tracked by all stakeholders, it will not work.

Figure 7-1 is an example of a performance management framework that connects capital market expectations with actionable enterprise operating metrics. The framework begins with establishing a corporate performance metric that is highly correlated to TSR. Metrics like cash-value added (CVA), summarized in Figure 7-2 (using the "residual value" definition), have become attractive choices in recent years because of their efficacy and simplicity. Forecasted CVA has a strong correlation to TSR because it is tied directly to the discounted cash-flow valuation of the enterprise.

While CVA is important because it is the sum of the moving parts of performance, the actionable levers of growth, profitability and asset management are the important focal points. By establishing plans and targets in each of these areas in accordance with forecasted CVA, performance improvement can be measured and effectively managed for the long term. From a board and investor point of view, the framework provides the rest of the story to the TSR metric and enables effective assessment of performance in the context of executive pay.

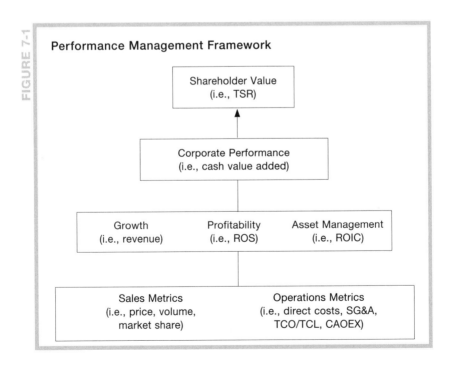

FIGURE 7-1

FIGURE 7-2

Cash-Value Added (CVA) Defined

Cash-Value Added:	Operating cash flow - capital charge
Operating Cash Flow:	Net income + depreciation +/- changes in net working capital
Capital Charge:	Total invested capital x weighted average cost of capital

---

Although this approach is not immune to the aforementioned issues of comparability and complexity, it is a useful paradigm for establishing a standardized approach to corporate performance management. As investors become increasingly frustrated by subpar returns, they will shift their attention from pay to performance. Boards and management that take action now will be well-served by staying ahead of this inevitable plot twist.

Incorporating Relative TSR in Incentive Plan Design: A High-Definition Approach

When incorporating a relative TSR measure into an incentive plan, not all companies take a high-definition view in selecting and implementing a TSR comparator group, despite the fact that the choice of comparator group can have a big effect on incentive plan outcomes. Similarly, high-definition thinking may allow an organization to reduce the level of random noise in the comparator group, which may in turn make the use of relative TSR more appealing to executives who often are suspicious of its use as a performance measure.

Historically, the common approach with relative TSR plans was to base the comparator group on the most obvious alternative investments for a shareholder. This reflected the origins of relative TSR in the relative performance-driven bonus plans operated for mutual fund managers themselves. In the early days, this often meant simply using the S&P 500 or some other very broad comparator group. However, hindsight and experience have exposed this as low-definition thinking. Such broad comparator groups include a high degree of randomness due to the very different degrees of volatility and cyclical exposure faced by different sectors and businesses. In addition, when looking at the stock market in high definition, we see that the U.S. shareholder base has become more diverse in the past 10 to 15 years and the alternative investments are not always obvious.

With this richness and diversity in both the shareholder base and the nature of potential alternative investments, it becomes necessary to think about relative TSR in a different way. In essence, this means considering which businesses face broadly similar economic, market, regulatory and operational challenges. This generally includes direct business competitors and/or businesses with a similar profile in terms of products, sectors and locations. Size also can be a factor, but wider size variations can be accepted for TSR than would be appropriate when selecting a peer group for compensation benchmarking purposes.

Of course not all businesses have competitors that look like them or face the same challenges. For example, in some highly consolidated sectors there may only be a handful of competing firms, and some of these may not be listed on a stock market. In these circumstances, assuming that TSR remains a valid metric, it becomes necessary to choose on the basis of factors such as:

- **Correlation.** How well does the historical TSR of different sectors correlate to our company/sector?
- **Volatility (beta).** How does the historical share price volatility for different sectors compare to our company/sector?

Having developed a potential comparator group, it is important to model and test this group. This means tracking TSR for the potential comparators over several overlapping historical performance periods and computing what the plan would have paid in these scenarios. This modeling allows the following key questions to be addressed:

- Do the performance outcomes fit with what we believe about the historical performance of our business?
- In a small group, are any comparators miscorrelated? Why? Does the miscorrelation invalidate the outcomes? Is this likely to recur?

- In a larger group, are many sectors miscorrelated to us and our main competitors?
- In a global group, are any countries miscorrelated?

Ideally, this exercise answers whether the proposed group is suitable and/or highlights any necessary modifications. It is possible that the modeling will produce a set of notional historical payments that seem to be driven by random factors rather than the performance of the business. In this event, either the proposed comparator group needs to be significantly revised or the use of relative TSR as a measure needs to be re-thought.

Some companies may have a small number of highly relevant comparators and a larger number of companies with whom they have some similarity. In this case, the aim is to make sure the comparator group is large enough to be robust without it being dominated by the less relevant comparators. The answer here could be to weight the companies in the comparator group such that the most relevant companies have a larger effect on the result.

When assessing performance against a comparator group, there typically are three approaches:

- **Sample ranking.** This is the simplest and most common approach, and would be the low-definition default choice. However, under this approach incentive payments are sensitive to the level of clustering of comparator companies. Therefore, incremental improvements to TSR may have a very large or very small effect on plan vesting/payouts.
- **Percentage outperformance.** An example of this approach provides for full vesting/payout where TSR is at median plus 10 percent per annum, with linear interpolation used between median and this level. This approach avoids material differences in incentive awards arising from small differences in performance. However this approach does require a percentage outperformance target to be set for full vesting/payout.
- **Smoothed ranking.** This is a compromise option between the two approaches described above. For example, TSR at median- and upper-quartile companies is calculated with vesting/payout between these points calculated by linear interpolation. Again, this avoids

material differences for incentive awards arising from small differences in performance.

In the authors' opinions, simple ranking works best for very large comparator groups. Otherwise, the other methods are preferable. If the comparator group is very small, the percentage outperformance approach generally works best.

Although not addressed in detail in this chapter, any high-definition approach requires active consideration of the following issues:

- **Start and end dates.** Generally, the authors believe TSR should be measured from grant date to payout/vesting date, although some companies measure performance over the financial year.
- **Share price averaging period.** Generally, the authors recommend an averaging period of at least one month.
- **Treatment of companies leaving the comparator group.** This typically depends upon the comparator group being used to measure relative performance.

8
Executive Retirement Benefits/Deferred Compensation

By Melissa Rasman and Adam Meyers

Deferred compensation arrangements can help employers attract and retain key executives by furnishing benefits beyond the basic executive compensation package. These executive retirement programs have become increasingly prevalent in recent years. They are found in various forms in two-thirds of all organizations, and in an even higher percentage of larger publicly traded companies.

Broadly defined, a deferred compensation arrangement consists of an individual agreement or a plan whereby an organization pays compensation to one or more of its employees at a future date for services rendered in a prior year. The term "deferred compensation" encompasses both tax-qualified and nonqualified arrangements. Due to the limits on contributions and benefits under qualified plans, nonqualified programs usually are used for executive deferred compensation arrangements.

Employers typically use two basic categories of nonqualified deferred compensation plans: nonelective plans (commonly referred to as supplemental executive retirement plans [SERP]) and elective deferral plans. The key difference is that employers fund nonelective plans, whereas employees contribute their own earnings to elective plans. Some employers offer plans that provide both nonelective and elective deferred compensation.

This chapter:

- Discusses the strategic objectives of a SERP program and the technical considerations that affect SERP design. Examples are furnished of three customized design alternatives depending on the status of the SERP participant.

- Explains why the costs of a SERP are a crucial consideration and the five basic principles that underlie executive pensions. There also is a discussion of the rationale behind SERPs, including the role that executives themselves play in a SERP design.
- Reviews the purpose and objectives of an elective deferred compensation program and the applicable tax and accounting rules that govern these plans. Key features and disadvantages of these plans also are discussed.
- Addresses the use of performance-based SERPs that reward criteria other than, or in addition to, the passage of time to motivate and reward executive performance. Plan features that an employer may wish to consider are described.

SERP Design and Organization Strategy

Supplemental executive retirement plans (SERPs), as the name suggests, are designed to supplement a company's existing qualified retirement plans. Although executives generally are covered by the same qualified retirement plans as the rest of the employee population, tax-qualified retirement benefits are subject to limits on:

- Salary taken into account for plan purposes
- Benefit levels that can be provided (in the case of defined benefit plans)
- The amounts that can be contributed to a participant's account for a given year (in the case of defined contribution plans).

Due to these restrictions, the overall benefit levels provided under qualified plans are lower for the executive population relative to their compensation level than for the general employee population. To make executives whole for the effects of these limits, employers commonly establish SERPs. Further, organizations often design a SERP to provide a higher level of retirement income (relative to an executive's compensation) than is provided under their tax-qualified plans. These richer SERPs usually are designed to attract and retain executives. According to a Hay Group survey of executive benefits, the most popular income replacement ratio is 60 percent, which for many highly-paid employees would be impossible to achieve through tax-qualified retirement plans.

A SERP must be unfunded, and coverage must be limited to a select group of management and other highly compensated employees; otherwise, legal mandates under the Employee Retirement Income Security Act of 1974 (ERISA) generally would make a SERP unworkable. Generally, SERP benefits are taxable to the executive (and deductible by the employer) when paid, subject to two key exceptions:

- Employees of tax-exempt employers subject to Internal Revenue Code (IRC) section 457(f) are taxed when their benefits are no longer subject to a substantial forfeiture risk (i.e., are vested).
- Executives of any type of employer may be taxed as vested benefits accrue if provided under a plan or arrangement that fails to meet the legal constraints on timing of benefits elections, distributions and funding under IRC section 409A (which are discussed in the third section of this chapter).

Design flexibility has been critical to the popularity of SERPs. A SERP can be used to:

- **Attract mid-career hires.** Help supplement benefits to executives who are hired later in their careers; this can be an important recruitment tool for high-performing executives.
- **Assist in succession planning.** Offer an executive early retirement to allow for necessary succession planning.
- **Attach golden handcuffs.** Retain an executive who may consider leaving for either retirement or a competitor.
- **Provide competitive benefits.** Close the gap between the existing qualified plans and what the market offers.
- **Reward executive performance.** Better align the interests of executives and shareholders.

A SERP's value to an executive and its strategic impact can be affected by certain critical factors, as discussed in "Key Value Parameters."

Examples of Customized Design Alternatives

Different situations may call for different designs. In examining three familiar scenarios, common design considerations are noted.

First, consider the mid-career hire. Assume that a struggling company is dramatically changing its market strategy and the current executive team has little such experience. The company

Key Value Parameters

Replacement Ratio

The target percentage of an executive's pay that the SERP is designed to pay annually during retirement. It is designed to help an executive maintain his/her accustomed standard of living in retirement. The most popular replacement ratio is 60 percent of an executive's total cash, with nearly 80 percent of organizations with SERPs providing ratios in the 50 percent to 70 percent range.

Definition of Pay

The pay definition is critical to understanding SERP value. A 60-percent replacement ratio can look very different depending on whether it is pegged to salary versus total cash (salary plus annual incentive) or total direct compensation (total cash plus long-term incentive).

Most organizations use total cash in their definition of compensation for SERP purposes. About one-quarter of organizations define compensation as base salary only, while a small (and declining) number include both long- and short-term incentives. Arguably, using LTIs in defining pay is inappropriate. An LTI is intended as capital accumulation for the long-term, and it should not be replaced in a program that is designed to re-create a comparable post-retirement standard of living.

Average Pay Period

SERP values can be substantially affected by the final-pay averaging period. In companies where pay leverage and the resulting year-to-year differences are low, choosing a highest period will have little effect. But in companies with highly leveraged pay packages, such a plan could result in a significant windfall for executives. The most common choices are the highest consecutive three- and five-year periods.

Definition of Service

In this context, service refers to the minimum amount of time an executive must work with the company to earn a full retirement benefit. Retiring with less than the plan's service minimum usually requires pro-rating the targeted replacement ratio.

For companies that have a tradition of long-tenured executives, the service period may make little difference to executives. But for the increasing number of companies that recruit top executives from competitors later in their careers, the service period may be a critical determinant in the recruiting package. The typical minimum service period is 15 or 20 years. However, special provisions are sometimes crafted to recruit key executives closer to retirement.

Vesting

The vesting schedule also can have a significant effect on a SERP's value. The most prevalent practices are based on an executive's tenure with the company, with roughly one-half of the SERPs using a cliff-vesting schedule that provides 100 percent vesting after a specified period of years of service (e.g., three, five, 10 years), and the remaining organizations using either graded vesting, 100 percent immediate vesting or vesting at a particular age.

Retirement Age

Allowing executives to receive full benefits at an earlier age is becoming more popular. Consistently, the prevalent retirement age has been 65, but there continues to be notable prevalence for unreduced early retirement at ages 60 or 62.

Careful consideration should be given to any lowering of an unreduced retirement age. While there may be strategic reasons to facilitate an executive's early retirement, such changes can substantially increase the SERP's cost. In addition, company stakeholders may not benefit if the early retirees are vital to the company and no adequate succession plan is in place.

Actuarial Assumptions

The actuarial assumptions used to convert an annual target benefit to a lump sum can be significant. In practice, the selection of these assumptions — which include the assumed interest and mortality rates — can be both subjective and negotiable.

Balancing Design Considerations

Each component of a SERP can be used more effectively to achieve desired results when companies do a better job of ensuring that their SERP design is driven by organizational strategy.

Organizations must ask critical questions regarding both strategy and the current makeup of the executive team. For example:

• How important is retention of the current executives in helping the organization meet its strategic objectives?
• Has the succession plan provided a strong enough executive pool with the right skills and competencies to lead the company where it needs to go?
• Does the organization need to recruit a new executive from a competitor to better enable that strategy?
• Is the current retirement package competitive enough to prevent executives from being poached by a competitor?

Generally, it is beneficial to have one program design that can serve most of the executive population. However, in many cases, the need to retain or attract particular top executives may necessitate a customized plan design.

hopes to attract an executive from a competitor that has had success with a similar strategy. The design considerations here will be around making the SERP's upside attractive while also building in performance leverage.

Second, consider the golden handcuffs situation in which a company wants to retain its successful CEO by motivating the executive to retire later rather than earlier. Here, design considerations are around giving the executive more opportunity to obtain a larger SERP payout by staying past age 65.

Then there is the typical rising executive who is being promoted from a senior manager to a top executive. While the company's strong preference would be not to lose such an executive's talents, the board may believe that, given the company's strong succession plan, a replacement can be found if needed. Design considerations focus on increasing leverage to influence performance, with the understanding that consistently poorer performance could result in low payouts.

Each of these situations may call for a different approach to SERP design. (See Table 8-1.) In each case, the mix should be tailored to the organization's particular needs and objectives.

Executive Pensions/SERPs: An Approach Based on Core Principles

With enhanced disclosure of executive pensions in recent years, particularly large (and arguably abusive) arrangements for top

TABLE 8-1

Alternative Approaches to SERP Design

	Replacement Ratio	Pay Definition	Pay Period
Mid-Career Hire	40%	Total direct (total cash + LTI)	3-year period average
Golden Handcuffs	60%	Total cash (base + bonus)	Highest 3-year period average
Rising Executive	50%	Total cash (base + bonus)	3-year period average
Typical Case	60%	Total cash (base + bonus)	3-year period average

executives have attracted the attention of shareholders, proxy advisers and the press. Relevant questions to consider are:

- Are the programs reasonable and appropriate?
- Is the true potential cost reasonably determinable?
- How were they designed and approved in the first place?

Why the Cost of Executive Pensions Is Important

Executive pensions can be quite expensive, often constituting a significant portion of the value of an executive's total compensation. Historically, many executive pension arrangements were not fully and clearly disclosed to shareholders, although this was significantly improved by the enhanced disclosure rules issued by the SEC starting in 2006. However, even now the costs may not be well understood.

The most highly leveraged executive pension is the defined benefit SERP. Defined benefits (DB) plans are backloaded, with the funding cost increasing substantially as pay increases, particularly as the executive gets closer to retirement age.

For example, assume a long-serving executive covered by a 60-percent-of-final-salary defined-benefit SERP is appointed CEO two years before retirement. Further assume that this resulted in his base salary increasing from $1 million to $1.5 million. While his projected annual pension benefit increased from $600,000 to $900,000, the single lump-sum cost increased approximately $3 million. Even spread over his two remaining years, this would cost roughly $1.5 million per year, or 100 percent of his annual salary per year. This is before any bonus is even included in the pension formula. It would not be surprising to find that no board or compensation committee member was aware of this leverage

Minimum Service	Vesting Requirements	Retirement Age
10 years	5-year graded	60
15 years	10-year cliff	70
20 years	15-year graded	65
15 – 20 years	15-year graded	65

and that the salary decision was made without even considering the consequential pension cost.

Although a fairly extreme example (but based on a real case), this hypothetical situation illustrates just how important pension issues can be. One-year value transfers of 50 percent to 150 percent of base salary to executives through final pay executive pensions are common. The closer to retirement age this occurs, the more this "hidden" cost is leveraged. If incentive plans appear unlikely to pay out, final salary pension plans can provide a strong motivation for an executive to negotiate a salary increase.

Core Principles

Employers should reflect on certain core principles as guidelines for appropriate practice in developing executive pension programs:

- **Core Principle 1.** The provision for an executive pension is part of the rewards package the executive receives for work carried out for the organization and, as such, should be treated as part of the total compensation package, not as a separate entitlement.
- **Core Principle 2.** Realistic cost estimates of any pension proposals should be disclosed to compensation committees or other decision makers. In the case of DB plans, the cost estimates should reflect the value being transferred to the executive as well as the leveraging and phasing of that transfer — not simply the current cost charge or contribution. Salary comparisons — internal or external — and salary adjustments should consider the added effect due to significant differences in pension costs.
- **Core Principle 3.** Aside from any pension provision required by law or under a tax-qualified retirement plan available to all employees, the executive should determine the extent, if any, of the total compensation package that is apportioned to a pension.
- **Core Principle 4.** The provision of executive pensions generally should be made on a defined contribution (DC) basis (rather than on a DB basis). This DC (e.g., a percentage of base salary) then should be a component of the total compensation package each year. The particular amount of that component each year can be actuarially determined to produce target benefits each year of

retirement, just like a DB SERP. Under a DC approach, deferred compensation is shown as an account balance that recognized the cost attributable to each year of employment.

- **Core Principle 5.** In accordance with enhanced executive compensation disclosure rules, the cost of executive pensions must be more fully described. In particular, DB plans often contain potentially costly ancillary benefits and special features in addition to the basic target replacement ratio. Examples are subsidized (unreduced) early retirement provisions, the inclusion of LTI awards in the definition of compensation, granting additional years of service for short-term executives, providing unrestricted joint and survivor benefits, and numerous other features.

Rationale

Providing a sound overall compensation package for a top executive was the focus in developing these core principles.

- Senior executives are, relative to most employees, highly paid. They have more opportunity during their working lifetimes to acquire significant assets or wealth to support that lifestyle in retirement.

- In addition, senior executives have more flexibility to determine and apportion the income level to spend currently versus save for retirement. Because this apportionment can vary substantially from person to person, it is more appropriate to allow the executive to make this decision than the employer. It is less appropriate for the employer to take on the financial risks associated with providing a high level of guaranteed benefits or to determine the extent to which executives should defer consumption.

- Executives should have the opportunity (and responsibility) for choosing the level of retirement income or target replacement ratio that they need and re-apportioning their total pay accordingly. In this process, executives can use an equivalent DC schedule that will produce this target. In other words, executive pensions should be considered more of an elective deferred compensation plan, although structured as employer-funded SERPs.

- Most executives are intelligent, responsible individuals who are relied upon by their employers to make sound decisions on complex issues in their work. They often have responsibilities regarding asset values far in excess of their own pension assets. It is therefore appropriate that they take responsibility for determining the portion of their compensation packages allocated to retirement benefits.

Which Pay Components Should Be Used in Determining Pensions?

Variable pay has become a standard portion of executive compensation packages, and the level of retirement income generally is considered relative to pay. However, retirement income is not expected to be as volatile as pay can be from year to year. Accordingly, some judgment should be applied in targeting an executive's fixed retirement income to a variable rate of compensation while in active employment.

It can be appropriate to include annual bonuses in the definition of pay for purposes of determining pension contributions or benefits. Annual bonuses can be considered as part of the standard of living developed for an executive over the years. However, LTIs represent special awards that are intended to be capital accumulation devices in and of themselves (as is a SERP). Therefore, the inclusion of LTI in the definition of annual pay for pension purposes is redundant and inappropriate.

In some circumstances, the inclusion of annual bonuses in the pension formula is purely cosmetic. For example, an annual pension of 60 percent of base salary at retirement is the same as a pension of 50 percent of total cash compensation for an employee with a 20-percent bonus. A company may believe that one approach appears less controversial than the other even though they both produce the same benefit.

Removing Executive Distractions

A common argument is that DB plans enable an executive to ignore his/her personal financial security concerns and focus on the company's business, as opposed to the distractions attendant with the variations in a DC structure.

If the employer wants to take such a paternalistic approach, this can be addressed by providing a basic level of DB protection. Beyond such a minimum, the second core principle would be applied.

Elective Deferred Compensation Arrangements

Nonqualified deferred compensation (NQDC) plans that are funded by executives through elective deferral arrangements also can help employers attract and retain key executives by furnishing benefits beyond the basic executive compensation package.

A nonqualified plan is not required to meet the coverage, vesting, funding or fiduciary responsibility rules of ERISA. Most of ERISA's reporting and disclosure requirements and the tax-qualification requirements under the IRC also are inapplicable. However, a nonqualified arrangement does not receive the favorable tax treatment accorded a qualified retirement plan.

Because nonqualified plans are exempt from the most restrictive provisions of ERISA and the IRC, they can be designed to cover selected executives. In fact, these plans generally cannot be made available to rank-and-file employees.

Elective deferred compensation plans enable an executive to defer payment of a portion of his/her compensation to a future date. Under a properly designed plan, executives of for-profit businesses can defer tax on compensation until they receive it without risking forfeiture if they voluntarily terminate employment; executives of tax-exempt organizations do not have this option due to special tax rules applicable to tax-exempt employers. Therefore, elective plans are a more valuable benefit in the for-profit sector.

Purpose

Elective NQDC plans are similar to section 401(k) plans in that a covered employee may elect to set aside a portion of his/her compensation for payment in the future. Such plans have several advantages:

- **Deferrals of compensation in excess of the statutory limitations on qualified plans.** Nonqualified plans can make up for regulatory limits on pre-tax contributions to tax-qualified plans, such as section 401(k) plans, and can recognize pay that may not be taken into account under a qualified plan. Because nonqualified plans allow executives to defer compensation above the statutory limitations, they can be used to supplement retirement benefits under a company's qualified retirement plans and provide for other future financial commitments.

- **Reduction of executive's current income taxes.** Current taxable income is reduced by the amount of compensation that is deferred. However, compensation will be taxed at ordinary income tax rates that are in effect when distributions are received. If the executive is in a lower income-tax bracket when distributions are made (compared to the applicable rate when compensation is deferred), there may be additional income tax savings. On the other hand, if the applicable tax rate is higher, the executive could pay more in taxes than if the compensation had not been deferred.

- **Tax-deferred accumulation.** Income tax is not paid on earnings credited to a deferred compensation account until distributions are received, allowing the deferrals and earnings to compound on a pre-tax basis.

- **Recruitment and retention of key employees.** An employer can use these plans as a recruitment incentive and retention tool. Many executives seek arrangements to supplement the company's retirement plans. In addition, these executives may be more likely to continue employment to avoid triggering a taxable distribution upon termination or, if vesting is deferred, forfeiting all or a portion of the benefit accrued.

- **Coverage and design flexibility.** Because there are no coverage, eligibility or nondiscrimination requirements applicable to nonqualified plans, an employer can provide these benefits to a select group of executives or highly compensated employees; coverage of other employees could subject the plan to the reach of ERISA. Because there are fewer formal requirements applicable to NQDC plans than to qualified plans, nonqualified programs are simpler to establish and maintain. In particular, nonqualified plans have no funding requirements.

Taxation and Accounting

General rules on how NQDC is taxed and how it is treated under the accounting rules are summarized in Table 8-2.

Under a taxable employer's deferred compensation arrangement that satisfies applicable tax law standards, neither the compensation nor the earnings on the deferrals is taxable to the individual

TABLE 8-2

How NQDC Is Taxed and Treated Under Accounting Rules

	Company Accounting	Company Taxation	Individual Taxation
Compensation Earned	Charge to earnings	No tax deduction	FICA tax
Compensation Received	No charge to earnings	Tax deduction	Ordinary income tax

until received. When the employee recognizes taxable income and incurs tax liability, the company receives a tax deduction in the same amount. In most cases, the company will have recorded an expense on its books at the time the compensation was earned, even though the tax deduction might not apply for many years.

Applicable Tax Laws

Although NQDC plans have fewer restrictions than qualified plans, specific rules must be followed to accomplish the deferral of an employee's taxable compensation

- **Constructive receipt.** If an executive can obtain funds at any time upon request or has control over them, the amounts are currently taxable under the long-standing doctrine of constructive receipt, regardless of whether the executive actually obtains the money. To avoid constructive receipt, a deferred compensation agreement must be entered into before the deferred income is earned or available; the arrangement also must substantially restrict the executive's ability to access the funds until a predetermined time or event (at which time it will become taxable). These requirements were formalized as part of IRC section 409A.
- **Section 409A.** Section 409A imposes a series of requirements on NQDC arrangements; its rules govern when deferral elections may be made and when they may be modified, when deferred amounts may be distributed, and how they may be funded. Unless an exception applies, a nonqualified arrangement must meet these requirements in form and operation. Section 409A accelerates income taxation and imposes a 20-percent tax penalty, as well as

interest payments, on a covered executive if a plan is noncompliant. See "Section 409A and Elective Deferred Compensation Plans" for more information about specific rules that apply.

To avoid current taxation of deferred amounts under the economic benefit and constructive receipt doctrines, nonqualified plan benefits must be unfunded and subject to the claims of general creditors. In the case of the company's insolvency or bankruptcy, the executive's right to receive payments may be no greater than that of any other general unsecured creditor. Although nonqualified plan benefits must be unfunded, they typically are informally funded, with funds set aside in trust accounts to cover the plans' liabilities while maintaining exemption from most ERISA requirements. These funds remain assets of the company and are within the reach of creditors in the event of insolvency or bankruptcy.

Section 409A and Elective Deferred Compensation Plans

Initial Deferral Elections

In general, elective participant deferrals are irrevocable and must be made before the start of the calendar year in which the related services commence. The election must identify the amount to be deferred, the length of period of deferral and the form of payment. For performance-based compensation relating to services performed during a period of at least 12 months, a participant's initial deferral election may be made at any time before the six-month period prior to the end of the performance period — if it meets certain criteria. For example, participants in a bonus plan that has a calendar-year performance period could make deferral elections regarding such bonuses anytime on or before June 30 of the calendar year in which the amounts are earned.

Changes to Deferral Elections

A subsequent participant election to delay a payment or change the form of payment must not take effect for at least 12 months and must further defer the payments for at least five years. If the payment is scheduled to be made on a fixed date, the subsequent deferral election may not be made sooner than 12 months prior to the date the amount is scheduled to be paid. In general, these restrictions also apply to changes to distribution provisions initiated by the employer.

Distributions

Payments of deferred compensation may only be made at a specified time or under a fixed schedule that is objectively determinable, or upon certain specified events — separation from service, death, disability, change in the ownership or effective control of the company or unforeseeable emergency, in each case as defined by the IRC and tax regulations

Informal funding can increase participant security but falls short of true funding. Two common informal funding devices are:

- **Rabbi trust.** An employer-established grantor trust into which the employer determines how much money or other assets are placed for the provision of benefits. These assets must remain subject to the company's creditors.

- **Corporate-owned life insurance (COLI).** Death proceeds or loans are used to recover benefits payments provided by the plan. COLI involves an employer's investment in cash-value life insurance policies that insure the lives of selected executives. The company pays the premiums, retains ownership and receives tax-free proceeds when the participant dies.

If assets are transferred outside of the United States or restrictions are triggered by an employer's poor financial health, section

Acceleration of Payments

Deferred compensation payments generally may not be made before the permissible payment date or event specified in the plan. This anti-acceleration rule effectively bars distribution of benefits upon plan termination, except under very limited circumstances.

Six-Month Delay to Specified Employees

Payments to a specified employee of a public company triggered by a separation from service must be delayed at least six months following the separation, except in the event of disability or death of the specified employee. For purposes of this provision, "specified employee" generally includes "key employees" of public companies as defined in the "top-heavy" rules governing benefits provided under tax-qualified retirement plans.

Restrictions on Setting Aside Funds

Section 409A limits the ability of an employer to informally set aside assets to pay deferred compensation benefits.

Economic Benefit

Under the economic benefit doctrine, income realized in any form by an executive is taxable upon grant if:

- It has tangible, quantifiable value that the executive has in effect received, and

- There is no substantial risk of forfeiture.

The economic benefit doctrine was formalized in IRC section 83, governing when transfers of "property" are taxed.

409A accelerates income taxation and imposes penalties on executives covered by informal deferred compensation funding arrangements.

Section 409A also penalizes certain officers and top-paid employees of any public company that maintains a tax-qualified DB plan if the employer sets aside assets to pay deferred compensation in specific circumstances: while in bankruptcy, within six months of terminating an underfunded plan or while the plan is less than 80 percent funded under "at risk" funding rules.

Plan Design

In designing an elective deferred compensation plan, decisions on certain key features are needed:

- **Eligible deferral sources.** Which elements of compensation are allowed to be deferred? Base salary, annual incentive, cash-based long-term incentive and/or restricted stock units?
- **Deferral period.** What is the period for deferring compensation? Will payments be triggered at termination, retirement, death, disability, change-in-control or on a specified date? When will payment be made after the relevant trigger?
- **Form of payout.** What are the permissible forms of payment? Lump sum or installments? If the trigger is an employee's termination, the form of payment must be the same for each year's deferral.
- **Investment options.** Deferral accounts are usually credited with a return that can be fixed, based on a variable rate or floating rate (e.g., prime rate, U.S. Treasury bill rate), or tied to a hypothetical investment alternative (e.g., mutual fund).

These design decisions are also important for nonelective deferred compensation plans (e.g., SERPs).

Potential Disadvantages

Despite their many advantages, NQDC plans also have drawbacks. Disadvantages to consider when evaluating such plans include:

- **Current tax deduction unavailable to employer.** An employer cannot claim a current deduction for any NQDC amounts until the employee receives the amount as income.

- **Unfunded plan.** Deferred amounts under an NQDC plan are merely an employer's promise to pay the employee in the future. Because these amounts must remain subject to the claims of the employer's creditors in the event of insolvency, a company's obligation to pay may become an empty promise if it becomes insolvent.
- **Restricted access to money.** In general, participants do not have access to deferrals until the selected payment date or event.
- **Possible higher tax rate.** The applicable tax rate when payments are received may be greater than when funds are deferred, reducing the overall return on the deferrals.
- **Risk of tax penalty for section 409A violation.** If the employer fails to comply with the operational and written documentation requirements of section 409A, the executive will owe ordinary income tax earlier than expected, plus a substantial tax penalty.
- **Securities law registration.** An employee's interest in an elective deferred compensation arrangement is considered a security, subject to registration under federal securities and state blue-sky laws, unless an applicable exemption applies. Most deferred compensation plans are exempt from U.S. Securities and Exchange Commission (SEC) registration, but may need to be registered in certain states where employees reside.

An executive's opportunity to defer compensation can be an effective recruitment and retention tool, so employers should consider making available nonqualified plans that are tailored to their particular circumstances. Executives usually appreciate being able to defer compensation in excess of the statutory limits. Before proceeding, an employer should understand the financial implications of the postponed tax deduction for the deferred compensation. An employer also must ensure that its nonqualified arrangements comply with the requirements of IRC section 409A and are designed to be tax effective for eligible executives.

Performance-Based SERPs: An Alternative Approach to Executive Benefits

In designing executive compensation programs, a key objective is to align the interests of executives and shareholders. Efforts have centered mainly on current compensation and wealth-building opportunities, such as stock compensation and other LTIs. Retirement benefits, on the other hand, typically have been viewed as a reward for long service rather than as a motivator of executive behaviors. In the current era of increased scrutiny of executives' total pay packages and greater shareholder activism, employers may want to include executives' retirement benefits in the mix of performance-based rewards.

Simply stated, a performance-based SERP places one or more performance conditions on an executive's accrual of benefits. SERPs are extremely flexible; there are many ways to design such a plan and various performance conditions that can be appropriate.

Performance Conditions

A fundamental principle of a performance-based SERP is that some criteria other than the passage of time (e.g., achievement of a measure of performance) must occur for a retirement benefit to be accrued. One approach is for the employer to establish the same performance measures as used for the executives' incentives, such as revenue, profitability or cash flow targets. Alternatively, an organization may choose to personalize the performance measures, such as achievement of individual sales targets, improvement in a business unit's profitability, or other personal goals upon. The performance measure can even be an event, such as a predetermined milestone in product development, emergence from bankruptcy, or completion of a transaction (e.g., initial public offering). In determining which performance measure(s) to establish, an issue is assessing and setting the degree of difficulty for attainment. How high should the bar be set? The decision is based entirely on the employer's goals for the SERP regarding the executives' behaviors that the employer wishes to motivate.

As executives achieve the performance measures determined under the SERP, objectively judged positive results should occur. Shareholders and other stakeholders presumably would be pleased that the executive group as a whole is accomplishing its goals or, in the case of personalized performance measures, that the executive is generating positive results for the organization. Such favorable occurrences can create an environment in which stakeholders are better able and more willing to accept the executives' rewards as reasonable.

Applying the Performance Conditions

In a performance-based SERP, application of the performance conditions falls into two categories: benefits accruals and vesting.

Benefits Accruals

If performance dictates whether a benefit is accrued in a given year, the SERP would operate in exactly the same way as a traditional SERP, except that at the end of the performance period an objective measure of performance determines whether that year's benefit accrual is added to the total accrual.

For example, if the DB SERP pension amount is calculated as 2 percent multiplied by final salary multiplied by years of service, then whether the performance goal is achieved could determine whether that year of service would be added to total years of service in the participant's benefit formula. If a DB SERP pension is calculated as 60 percent of final pay, prorated by years of service divided by 15 (not greater than one), then the achievement of the performance goal could determine whether that year of service would be added to years of service in the formula.

A DC SERP operates even more simply if performance measures are applied to benefit accruals — simply add the annual account allocation, or not, based on whether the performance goals are achieved.

Of course, rather than an all-or-nothing accrual entitlement, a proration of the accrual can be applied in either a DB or DC design.

Vesting

Achievement of performance targets also can dictate whether an executive attains a vested (non-forfeitable) right to collect the benefits that have accrued under the SERP. Essentially, vesting is a design overlay on top of the pattern of benefit accruals under the SERP. In designing a SERP, vesting can be done according to a schedule, phasing in over some number of years, and/or can begin at some age; alternatively, vesting can occur 100 percent (so-called "cliff" vesting) at some defined age or service point in time. Depending on the employer's goals for the SERP (i.e., in terms of retaining executives), the vesting schedule can be structured for earlier or later vesting in an executive's career.

For example, a phased-in vesting schedule might be 20 percent vesting per year beginning at age 55, subject to the achievement of personal performance goals. It is important to consider, when establishing the vesting criteria, that vesting of nonqualified benefits generally triggers taxation to the executive of the value of the vested benefit, unless a timely and legally compliant deferral election is made by a participant (or automatically occurs under the plan's terms).

Financial Considerations

The economic value of a pension benefit is based on the ultimate value of the benefits to be paid. Therefore, depending on the nature of the performance measures applied to the accrual or vesting of the SERP benefits, the economic value of the plan may or may not change. If, however, the performance measures instituted under the SERP truly provide for an uncertainty regarding whether some (or all) of the pension will be received by the executive, then the economic value of the pension will decrease, manifesting itself in one of the following ways:

- To the executive, it may mean that the perceived benefits provided by the SERP may decrease or the actual benefits payable under the SERP will decrease, each in comparison to a SERP without performance measures.
- To the employer, cash required to fund the SERP benefits may decrease, and accounting expense also may decrease.

Employers designing a performance-based SERP should consult their actuaries on quantifying these financial impacts.

Use of Performance-Based SERPs

Employers may want to add performance measures to the design of their SERPs to motivate certain behaviors among their executive team.

With proper design, the approach can be very effective. As is the case with most nonqualified arrangements, there can be a great deal of flexibility in developing a performance-based SERP. The various design features should be considered in conjunction with the other incentive-based pay and benefits plans sponsored by the organization to ensure that the performance-based SERP complements, rather than duplicates or conflicts with, other programs.

9
Executive Nonretirement Benefits and Perquisites

By Steven Sabow and Marie Dufresne

Though not as prevalent as in the past, special executive health and welfare benefits and perquisites can be important adjuncts to executive pay packages. Perquisites of various kinds are found in most U.S. companies and are very prevalent outside of the United States. Whether offered in cash or in kind, perquisites cover a broad range of services and benefits — personal use of corporate aircraft, financial planning, company cars and physical exams being among the most common. Typically offered to a select group of employees, executive health and welfare programs (e.g., death, disability, injury, paid time off) usually are add-ons or extensions to existing plans available to all employees.

Perquisites today are in decline. Shareholders and institutional investors continue questioning the reasonableness and costs of perquisites because there is no obvious link with performance. Tax law requirements can result in some or all of the perks' value being taxed as income to the executive. More significantly, in its major overhaul of the executive compensation disclosure rules in 2006, the U.S. Securities and Exchange Commission (SEC) lowered the financial threshold for aggregate perquisite disclosure for named executives and directors, thus giving a much clearer picture of the extent of perquisite use in publicly held companies.

Health and welfare plans, which are found principally in large companies, also may trigger additional taxes to executives. Nonetheless, they represent value to executives and, like perquisites, should be reviewed to ensure that they use company funds efficiently and align with executive compensation and corporate strategies. Health and welfare benefits and perquisites that clearly benefit both the company and the executive without engendering unacceptable criticism, such as those affecting the health and safety of the employee, likely will continue to be used, while others will be reduced or eliminated.

This chapter:

- Analyzes perquisites in large U.S. companies, with a discussion of which perquisites are the most costly to the company, which are likely to be discontinued and which may survive.
- Discusses the trends in executive health and welfare benefits, including the various kinds of executive life insurance, short- and long-term disability benefits, health-care benefits and vacations.

Executive Perquisites

Executive perquisites (perks) have been under fire for many years, so it was no surprise that the SEC targeted them in its 2006 reworking of the executive pay disclosure rules.

Companies now must break out perks that have an aggregate value in excess of $10,000, while the prior rules only required disclosure of perks that were worth more than $50,000 or 10 percent of cash compensation. Because most companies limited their perquisite disclosures to what was required, pre-2007 proxy statements did not furnish a true indication of the prevalence of various perks.

Hay Group research has found that most companies now are disclosing all perks, even if they total less than $10,000 in value. Of course, some organizations follow the reporting requirements precisely and do not disclose the smaller perks.

Prevalence of Perks

Looking for developing trends related to executive perks, Hay Group examined the proxy disclosures of large public companies regarding CEO perks furnished in recent years. Almost all of the sample organizations provided at least one perk to their executives. The most common perk was personal use of the corporate aircraft, followed closely by financial planning and company cars. Other notable perks, in declining order of prevalence, were physical examinations, supplemental life insurance, home security, tax gross-ups, spousal travel and club memberships.

Why Focus on Perks?

In dollar terms, perks are a very small slice of the pay pie. Then why have perks drawn such criticism from investors and corporate watchdogs? The press needs to grab readers' attention and often focuses on outliers — examples from corporate America that are at an extreme (i.e., the largest or smallest amounts). While these examples typically are not representative of the entire sample, they can make interesting news and great headlines. (See "The Outliers.")

Companies Discontinuing or Eliminating Perks

With investors gaining a better look at executive perks in post-2006 disclosures, many corporate boards have re-examined the perks

---

The Outliers

Where companies reported a substantial amount of CEO perk value, Hay Group reviewed the text to look for outliers. Aside from the use of corporate aircraft, the largest perk values were for the cost of home security, tax gross-ups, supplemental life insurance, a company car and driver, personal and spouse travel, and financial counseling. The smallest perk values, all under $1,000, were for the cost of physical examination, health club memberships, personal entertainment, airline club membership and gifts.

Personal Aircraft Usage

Personal use of the corporate aircraft, when provided to senior executives, typically is the most costly executive perk. The value of executive perks appears in the "All Other Compensation" (AOC) column in the proxy's Summary Compensation table, along with the value of discount stock purchases, company contributions to defined contribution (DC) plans and company payment of insurance premiums. The median value of a CEO's personal use of the corporate aircraft most recently was approximately 50 percent of the AOC total value.

Unusual Perks

Hay Group looked specifically for descriptions of unusual perks, but it appears that larger companies have deliberately discontinued using perks that tend to stand out. There are still perks that involve the use of corporate facilities (e.g., company barbershop, boats, hunting and fishing clubs, company helicopter) and those that involve organizations providing company products or product discounts (e.g., tire program, theme park use, merchandise discount program).

furnished to executives. As part of the process, some employers have decided to discontinue selected (or even all) perks. In fact, since that time most companies have reported the discontinuance of at least one perk. The perks most frequently eliminated were, in decreasing order, tax gross-ups, country club membership dues, financial planning and supplemental life insurance. A handful of companies disclosed that no perks were provided, while a few significantly reduced all perks. Typically, companies have not cut back on most security-related perks for the CEO, such as personal use of the corporate aircraft or personal use of the company car and a security driver. These security-related perks became very common after the terrorist acts of Sept. 11, 2001. Many companies specifically disclose that these perks are primarily for security purposes.

Will Perks Continue Declining?
Because the safety of senior executives is critical for U.S. companies, companies appear likely to retain perquisites that enhance executives' safety. Similarly, because it is in the interests of both companies and their senior executives to manage the health of such executives, physical exams are likely to survive.

On the other hand, companies probably will continue curbing various club memberships (e.g., country clubs, health clubs, airplane clubs), free sporting and entertainment event tickets and tax gross-ups, as they are finding insufficient benefit to justify the criticism received from groups such as proxy advisers and the media.

From time to time during the past two decades, cafeteria perks or perks allowances appeared on the verge of becoming popular. The approach involves granting an executive an annual dollar amount that the executive allocated among a select group or menu of executive perks. While few companies report perks allowances, recently several companies have decreased or eliminated allowances and replaced them with a one-time salary increase. Of course, critics are quick to point out that this approach may have an adverse cost effect for the company as base pay increases also raise the costs of items based on salary, such as annual bonuses, target LTI amounts, life insurance and retirement benefits.

Executive Health and Welfare Benefits

Executive benefits and perk programs are designed to attract and retain key employees and frequently are designed specifically for certain executives. While retirement benefits have received much attention, the focus here is on the nonretirement benefits components, often referred to as health and welfare programs. This terminology groups together the benefits received for certain specific life events: death, disability, illness, injury and paid time off, each addressing common health and welfare needs.

Executive health and welfare benefits are rarely examined because they usually follow the "same for all employees" approach that is found at a majority of organizations today. "Top up" benefits are found in less than one-half of U.S. employers, with the prevalence rising as the size of the organization increases. Clearly, cost is an issue, as most of these benefits are provided at little or no cost to the executive. But the real value of any extra benefits may not be appreciated because the covered executives, like most employees, only focus on these benefits when they actually are needed.

From an examination of health and welfare benefits, some insight was gained into the trends observed regarding these benefits. Because executives should consider their health and welfare needs as carefully as their retirement and post-employment requirements, this section concentrates on the "why" as much as the "what" for each key coverage area.

Death Benefits

Executive term-life insurance comes in many forms and designs, with each serving a variety of purposes. The typical life benefit provides coverage often based on a percentage of salary above that provided to all other employees. This benefit may be implemented because the basic coverage levels have caps or upper limits that preclude the executive from coverage of a full multiple of salary. For example, a two times salary basic plan with a maximum of $400,000 would clearly create a shortfall in intended benefits for anyone making more than $200,000 a year in salary. Thus organizations may create a separate insurance class for the executives with higher limits or purchase individual coverage for the additional amounts. In either case, because it only is intended to make up for lost benefits, the full cost usually is paid by the firm.

While many other forms of life insurance are available to executives, all involve more permanent coverage instead of the typical term insurance.

Split-dollar life is a form of whole-life coverage under which the cost of premiums may be split between the employee and the employer; they typically split the proceeds. These policies can enable an executive to afford substantial additional personal insurance. Also, the cash value of these policies sometimes is used to fund deferred compensation or other retirement vehicles. However, few organizations still offer these policies because U.S. Treasury regulations limit the potential tax advantages and, with respect to public companies, the Sarbanes-Oxley Act of 2002 banned executive loans under the collateral assignment version of split-dollar.

Key-person life is an individual policy owned totally by the employer and is provided by only a very small percentage of employers. The most common reason for the coverage is to protect the employer against the sudden loss of a key executive. Other purposes include funding for retirement income and increasing the individual's estate. The organization pays the full cost of the policy and receives the full proceeds.

Disability Benefits

Short-term salary continuance and/or accumulation-of-days programs like paid time off (PTO) provide further coverage for executives. In salary continuation programs, this often takes the form of a 100-percent of pay benefit for the entire short-term disability period or an additional number of days (generally about a week) in a PTO bank.

Special long-term programs are provided by about one-third of organizations, with the majority of the cost covered by the employer. Where employers provide these extra benefits, the larger organizations lead the way. In addition, more than two-thirds of the health-care industry provides these additional disability benefits, perhaps because of their health mission.

The design of these plans is intended to increase the level of coverage through various approaches, including:

- Shorter waiting periods for commencement of benefits
- Higher monthly maximum benefits
- Higher percentage of salary benefits (typically up to 70 percent of base pay)
- The definition of disability based on only the executive's current occupation
- Easing the maximums or expanding definitions all increase the value of this benefit if and when an executive incurs a disability.

One key item executives need to remember is that whatever portion of the premiums are paid by the employer, that same portion of the benefit, if received, also is taxable income.

Health-Care Benefits

Due to the scope of health-care coverage commonly provided by U.S. employers for all employees and the tax-free nature of these benefits, few special executive health-care benefits are offered. Those furnished to executives usually focus on simple additions that have no tax impact because the taxes would be assessed on the full actual medical costs, not just the premiums.

In about half of companies, executives have initial waiting periods for eligibility waived so their coverage begins with the start of employment. An annual physical examination used to be another key executive benefit, as companies and executives each understood the importance of maintaining a healthy executive team. However, as health-care reform has taken effect, all employees have annual physicals covered at 100 percent under preventive-care mandates. Thus, except for a few situations in which the executive can obtain these physicals at high-end clinics, this no longer is seen as an executive perquisite.

Finally, very few organizations offer a formal medical expense reimbursement plan; their scarcity likely reflects the high cost of the premiums. To avoid tax implications, these plans must be fully insured and provide for reimbursement of medical expenses incurred by the executives and their dependents in excess of the amounts covered by the underlying basic plans. Most core plans are designed to cover catastrophic costs, so these reimbursement plans really provide coverage for the first-dollar type co-payments and deductibles in the base plans up to the annual out-of-pocket maximums.

Executive Vacations

"Executive vacations" do not mean luxury suites or fabulous resorts — rather they refer to having more time away from the job. This is a much more critical benefit outside of the United States; our European colleagues really do take significant time off each year. However, in the United States, only about one-third of organizations provide additional vacation days to executives.

For those that do, it typically takes the form of an additional five vacation days and/or waiving the service schedule so the executive receives the full number of vacation days regardless of tenure with the organization.

Usually, U.S. executive compensation and benefits focus on retirement and LTIs. However, all executives need to understand their full suite of health and welfare programs and make sure their individual and family needs are met, just as they are expected to achieve the goals of their organizations.

10
Stock Ownership Guidelines

By Megan Butler

Shareholders, the business media and institutional investors all favor the notion that executives should own a significant number of shares in the companies they manage or oversee. Share ownership guidelines have been around for some years and now are found in many companies across U.S. industry. Their origins can be found in the risk-free nature of traditional stock options. Less prevalent, but noteworthy, are shareholding requirements.

For executives, share acquisition through stock option awards has no financial downside. If the options are underwater, they are not exercised and the executive loses nothing; when they are in the money, executives tend to exercise and sell the shares immediately, thus capturing an already known financial gain while relinquishing share ownership. Shareholders, on the other hand, must wait — sometimes for years — before they realize a similar gain and run the risk of seeing their investment shrink. Hence the question: Do stock options truly align executive and shareholder interests?

Ownership guidelines attempt to reverse this deficiency in stock options by requiring executives to achieve and maintain a certain level of share ownership — usually a multiple of salary — for a designated time period. The level of required ownership increases with rank in the organization. Despite the favorable optics of mandated executive share ownership, some question whether it truly is needed. In up-market times, guidelines usually are easy to achieve and can seem superfluous when senior executives already own shares far in excess of what typical guidelines require. On the other hand, in times of market downturn, guidelines can be difficult to achieve, especially for recent hires.

This chapter:

* Discusses the pros and cons of stock ownership guidelines and describes an approach for establishing an ownership guideline program. In addition, it describes typical aspects of using such guidelines (including which shares qualify, shareholding periods and time frames for fulfilling guidelines).

* Outlines alternative approaches currently gaining attention under which executives are required to hold shares for a specified period or until (or even beyond) retirement.

Use of Share Ownership Guidelines

The majority of U.S. public companies use some form of share ownership guidelines for executives. Implementing these guidelines publicly demonstrates a board's desire for executives to share in the same rewards and risks as shareholders.

Ownership guidelines typically only apply to executives down to senior managers. Most commonly, share ownership guidelines are expressed as a percentage of base salary, with greater requirements for higher-level jobs within an organization. Table 10-1 illustrates typical share ownership guidelines as a multiple of base salary; however, there is a wide variance in the level of ownership requirements.

Usually, participants are given a reasonable time period — typically five years — to obtain company shares and meet the set ownership levels. Once the required level is reached, participants are expected to maintain those levels throughout their employment with the

TABLE 10-1

Typical Share Ownership Guidelines	
CEO	5x
Direct reports	3x to 4x
Key executives	2x to 3x
Senior managers	1x to 2x

company. Company stock that the participant owns outright and vested shares in employee benefits plans commonly are included for purposes of meeting the guideline, although unexercised stock options usually are not counted.

Potential Concerns with Share Ownership Guidelines

Although share ownership guidelines are viewed positively by the investment community and encouraged by corporate boards, they are not without issue:

- In a rising stock market, the required ownership level can be trivial in comparison to the amounts earned from company equity programs, allowing employees to sell substantial amounts of equity while still satisfying the established ownership guidelines.
- Conversely, if the share price does not appreciate, employees are faced with purchasing shares using their personal resources or relying on the company to ease its enforcement of the guidelines; neither alternative provides a positive result.
- Timing also can cause problems. Depending on the time of hire, share ownership guidelines may not be equally difficult for all participants to achieve (i.e., new hires could have difficulty complying due to higher exercise prices than tenured employees).

Many company executives believe that consistent equity award grants and responsible behavior around equity disposition (e.g., limited sales) are sufficient, making share ownership guidelines obsolete.

Net Shares Retention Alternative to Ownership Guidelines

In view of some of the potential concerns with share ownership guidelines, companies have explored other approaches to consider in lieu of, or in tandem with, share ownership guidelines. A net-shares retention plan is an alternative that can increase executive share ownership levels, create a retention tool and strengthen the alignment of interests between executives and shareholders.

The key feature of a net-shares retention plan allows a participant to build share ownership while permitting diversification. This approach has been gaining popularity, including its use in combination with share ownership guidelines.

When a participant exercises his/her stock options, has the vesting restrictions lapse on a time-vested restricted stock award, or receives an earn-out of performance shares, the individual may sell enough shares to cover payment of the exercise price and resulting taxes. The participant is required to hold a specified percentage of the net shares for a designated period of time. The participant may sell the remaining net shares and the funds to diversify his/her personal portfolio. (See Figure 10-1.)

The holding requirements typically range from 25 percent to 75 percent of the net shares. A typical holding period is three to five years, although some companies may require executives to hold the specified net shares until termination.

With each exercise, vesting restriction lapse or earn-out, the participant builds his/her share ownership position while having the opportunity to diversify personal assets. Shareholders are protected from executives cashing out completely after short-term run-ups in the stock price.

Paying for Long-Term Performance

Some organizations have adopted hold policies requiring executives to keep a significant portion of their stock awards until retirement and, in some instances, into retirement. The focus of hold policies is to tie executive equity-based compensation — the primary

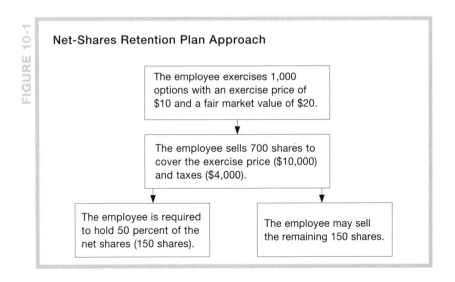

FIGURE 10-1

Net-Shares Retention Plan Approach

The employee exercises 1,000 options with an exercise price of $10 and a fair market value of $20.

The employee sells 700 shares to cover the exercise price ($10,000) and taxes ($4,000).

The employee is required to hold 50 percent of the net shares (150 shares).

The employee may sell the remaining 150 shares.

component of their pay packages — to long-term performance. There are several forms of hold policies, including:

* Retention ratios
* Long-term vesting
* Temporary holding requirements used in conjunction with traditional stock ownership guidelines.

Retention Ratios

The retention ratio is the most common hold design, requiring that an executive retain a fixed percentage (typically 50 percent to 75 percent) of the after-tax portion of earned equity awards until he/she leaves the company. Although less common, the holding period also can be extended for a period of time into the executives' retirement (i.e., hold through retirement).

The key is that the retention ratio applies to earned equity awards. When an executive receives shares of company stock (e.g., a stock option is exercised, restricted stock vests), a portion of the net shares must be retained for the duration of the executive's career. The net shares apply to the profit or gain shares that remain after the payment of taxes and, in the case of stock options, the exercise price. Because the equity awards already are earned, the executive is not in danger of losing the awards if he/she leaves the company.

For example, a company may require executive officers to retain at least 75 percent of common stock and equity awards (less allowances for the payment of any option exercise price and taxes) made to them while they are employed by the organization. Under this approach, a portion of an executive's net worth is tied to the company's share price. Proponents argue that the approach motivates executives to strive for superior performance of the share price on a long-term basis.

Some companies not only require executives to hold a portion of their equity until they leave the company, but also to hold a portion of their equity into retirement. This approach, while worth noting, is not as common as "hold until retirement" policies and is found mostly in the financial industry, perhaps as a result of increased regulatory oversight in that industry.

Long-Term Vesting

Under the long-term vesting approach, a portion of an executive's equity grant does not vest until retirement. One consequence is that an executive cannot sell a portion of the equity grant until retirement, even if the executive is permitted to exercise unvested stock options. This signifies a notable difference between the retention ratio and long-term vesting approach. Under the retention ratio design, the ratio only applies to earned equity awards and, if an executive leaves before retirement, he/she is not in danger of losing the awards. Under the long-term vesting approach, the awards are forfeited if the executive leaves before retirement age. This feature likely explains why the long-term vesting approach is less common than the retention ratio design.

Temporary Holding

A temporary design, as the name implies, requires an executive to hold his/her equity awards only until the traditional ownership guidelines have been met. For example, a company may require its executive officers to hold 100 percent of their equity awards (net of taxes and exercise price) until stock ownership guidelines are satisfied. After achieving the guidelines, executives would be required to hold 75 percent of equity awards for one year. The temporary design is intended to provide a "stop-gap" until traditional ownership guidelines are met.

Benefits of Hold Policies

Hold policies take share ownership guidelines to another level by tying equity grants to the duration of an executive's career with the company. A company may obtain significant benefits from such policies, including aligning executives' long-term net worth to superior and sustained stock price performance. Hold policies also reinforce executive stock ownership guidelines and support the notion that executives should have a long-term equity stake in the companies they manage. Additional benefits of adopting hold policies include:

- **Focus on long-term performance.** Hold policies encourage executives to take a long-term approach to stock ownership, which arguably aligns their interests with those of shareholders. In addition, hold policies force executives to analyze the effect of their short-term decisions on the long-term company results. If an executive is required to hold a significant amount of his/her wealth until retirement, he/she likely will focus on long-term value creation rather than short-term value and/or excessive risk-taking actions and decisions.

- **Size of equity awards.** There has been growing investor concern that executive stock ownership guidelines have not kept pace with the size of executives' equity awards. Investors may argue that that equity pay packages have increased and there has not been a corresponding increase and/or adjustment to an organization's stock ownership guidelines. Hold policies help support the alignment between the size of equity awards and increase in executive ownership.

- **More effective than traditional stock ownership guidelines.** As mentioned, criticism of traditional stock ownership guidelines is that in periods of rising stock prices, the number of shares an executive is required to retain decreases. Hold policies add another layer to traditional stock ownership guidelines, not allowing an executive to decrease his/her stock ownership level based on rising stock prices. Conversely, hold policies also help alleviate unequal burden between long-tenured and new executives in periods of declining stock prices. New executives will not need to allocate a large portion of their compensation to satisfy guidelines.

- **Investors' pay scrutiny.** With the spotlight on executive compensation and particular scrutiny of C-suite compensation in the aftermath of the financial crisis, hold policies can send a strong message to the public. Equity awards with hold policies help enforce the desired long-term executive behavior and performance.

These policies also aid in counteracting the notion that executives can time a market sale (e.g., an ability to sell equity shortly after vesting could lead executives to focus on short-term prices). Hold policies may mitigate potential short-term swings and/or gains.

Potential Pitfalls

The appeal of retirement-based policies is understandable. Hold polices may cause executives to focus more on the long-term results while addressing investor concerns that executive stock ownership levels have not kept pace with the increasing equity awards. However, hold policies, like many executive compensation provisions, also may create contrary incentives. Potential pitfalls and negative consequences of hold policies can be far-reaching:

- **Encourage early retirement.** Hold policies could potentially encourage executives to retire prematurely. For example, if an executive believes that the company's shares are overpriced and will likely fall in the near future, a hold-until-retirement policy could encourage the executive to retire early and cash out at a higher stock price (subject to any blackout periods and insider trading restrictions). This can be a significant issue, particularly for organizations with high-value executives who may be difficult to replace. In addition, the executives with the largest equity stakes, and potentially the executives who generated the biggest returns for the company, would have the greatest incentive to retire early.

- **Focus on short-term results near retirement.** Executives who have a significant portion of their wealth tied up in equity compensation likely will be very focused on the company's performance one to two years prior to their retirement. That is, a hold policy may create an incentive for executives to focus on short-term company results prior to retirement to ensure that they can cash out at an optimal stock price.

- **Hold beyond retirement.** One way for companies to help avoid this issue is to require executives to continue to hold their equity after they leave the company — namely hold-beyond-retirement policies. This should cause executives to be less focused on the stock price at the time of their retirement. However, the approach could be perceived as unfair to executives whose long-term wealth now would be in the hands of their successors. The hold-beyond-retirement provision could be tempered by requiring the executive to hold the equity only for a relatively short-period (e.g., six months) after retirement, minimizing the potential effects of decisions outside of their control.

- **View of Younger Executives.** Some executives may view hold policies as excessive, particularly younger executives who are not planning to retire for many years. Hold policies may create recruitment and retention issues for executives who are in demand in the market and have the option to move to another company with a comparable total rewards package without the restriction of hold policies.

Shareholder Review

Share ownership guidelines, net-share retention plans and hold-until-retirement policies have been positively received by shareholders, boards of directors and industry watchdog groups and should continue to grow. Hold policies currently are a minority practice in the United States, but increased corporate governance and say-on-pay rules may encourage a wider adoption of ownership policies that include hold until retirement and post-termination holding periods. As compensation committees review their share ownership guidelines and assess whether hold policies are appropriate for their executive officers, they should at the same time review the totality of their companies' executive compensation programs to ensure that all policies and practices encourage and engage executives to achieve common strategic goals.

11
Executive Employment Contracts
and Post-Employment Arrangements

By Bill Gerek

Whether through individual agreements or programs covering select executives, top management at U.S. companies typically have one or more financial protections should certain events occur affecting the status of their employment. Most common are employment contracts, severance programs, change-in-control arrangements and post-employment consulting agreements.

While these arrangements share a long history, particularly in publicly held companies, there is much discussion on whether they are needed. Employment contracts, for example, often simply state the obvious regarding salary, bonus and other elements of pay. Because post-termination restrictions (often the key benefits obtained by companies) can be difficult to enforce, agreements also may unduly favor executives. Change-in-control arrangements may go beyond the key objective of encouraging executives to stay until a transaction has been completed.

Nonetheless, these arrangements have numerous supporters. Companies are justifiably concerned about losing key employees in a restructuring, and employees want financial protection if they are made redundant in a transaction over which they have no control. And, in special circumstances, companies may continue to need the services of key employees once they have retired.

Like all other aspects of executive pay, employment contracts and post-retirement arrangements have recently garnered considerable attention from shareholders, proxy advisory groups and the press. They are concerned about policies that potentially result in windfalls to executives and excessive accounting and tax charges to the company. Moreover, with say on pay shareholders can now voice their opinions on golden parachutes and are likely to use this forum to force companies to revisit their policies and justify their actions.

The important question for a company is what makes sense given its particular corporate culture, business objectives and likelihood of a restructuring or a key executive retiring in the near future. Eligibility, costs and the specific purposes of any compensation arrangements need to be carefully weighed; what other companies do should not be the primary consideration.

This chapter:

- Outlines the reasons for having employment agreements, describes their pros and cons, and discusses the key provisions and issues companies should address in designing and refining their employment agreement program.

- Discusses change-in-control design features, such as eligibility, definition of change in control, single- and double-payout triggers, benefits continuation, equity acceleration and structuring cash payments.

- Describes how to handle unvested equity under various kinds of termination events and the accounting and tax issues that must be addressed. The chapter also analyzes equity vesting acceleration under a change in control, the mounting criticism of excise tax gross-ups, and compensation committee considerations in complying with the proxy vote on golden parachutes under say on pay.

- Suggests possible rationales for post-retirement consulting arrangements, including how payments might be structured and the abuses that often are found in such agreements.

Executive Employment Agreements: Why, When and What

Questions around whether an employer should have an employment agreement with one or more of its top executives, along with the associated practices, often are prompted by a reconsideration of current arrangements with these executives. The focus on good corporate governance in recent years is causing many companies and compensation committees to re-examine the rationale for, and terms and conditions of, executive contracts.

In determining whether and when to use contracts for executives, it is critical to examine an organization's specific facts and circumstances and to understand why employment agreements have been used or are under consideration. At many companies it is helpful to review the basic approaches for executive contracts and then consider the pros and cons of these agreements.

Approaches

The use of employment agreements for executives can vary considerably among companies, often depending on the organization's culture and the views and philosophy of the board of directors, the compensation committee and the CEO. Essentially, there are four basic approaches:

- Some employers do not use contracts at all, instead relying on general policies or more limited agreements to address specific issues such as severance, change in control, confidentiality and noncompetition.
- Other companies limit employment agreements to new-hire situations, especially those in which a sought-after executive is reluctant to join a new and largely unfamiliar organization without the protections of a contract. A related question is if and when either the entire contract or certain executive protections should sunset.
- Many organizations extend employment agreements to some or all of the top team of executives. Certain employers may have a contract with only their CEOs, while others may enter into written agreements with a dozen or so executives.
- A few companies use employment agreements to document their employment relationships with all executives above a certain level (e.g., vice president).

Rationale for Contracts

An executive contract sets out the key terms and conditions of the employment relationship. While contracts typically address salary, annual incentives, LTIs (often equity-based), benefits and perquisites, there is little need for a formal contract if the objective simply is to memorialize these items.

Generally, the most important reasons for an employment agreement are to:

- Specify and make clear what an executive will receive upon various events resulting in a termination of employment (e.g., death, disability, retirement, resignation, resignation for good reason, dismissal and dismissal for cause).
- Address the impact of a change in control of the employer.
- Impose reasonable post-employment restrictions upon an executive (e.g., restrictive covenants addressing matters such as confidentiality and nondisclosure, noncompetition, nonsolicitation of employees and/or customers and nondisparagement).

If properly drafted, employment contracts can help secure the future services of key employees critical to the organization's success. These agreements establish the respective rights, duties, obligations and responsibilities of the parties at a harmonious time; from this perspective they can be likened to premarital agreements.

Arguments Against Employment Agreements

While both the employer and the executive can be well-served by documenting the employment relationship through a contract, another view is that such agreements are either unnecessary or overly favor executives. Arguments sometimes advanced against executive employment agreements include:

- **Pay for failure.** The heightened focus on executive compensation has highlighted instances in which an executive dismissed for poor performance was entitled to large severance pay based on the terms of an employment agreement. This view maintains that any payments would have been more reasonable if no contract had been in place and the executive had to negotiate a severance package in connection with his/her termination.
- **Performance equals security.** Some maintain that the protection provided by an employment contract is unnecessary for a top executive who is doing a good job and that an executive should not have this protection if he/she is not performing well.

However, turnover levels among CEOs and other senior executives (a shorter job "life expectancy") have caused many executives to believe contractual protection is necessary — especially for new outside hires.

Key Provisions and Usage

Severance and change-in-control protections usually are the most critical provisions for executives, while employers seek the benefits of restrictive covenants and clawback provisions.

Both parties receive certainty (assuming the agreement is well-drafted) of the terms that will apply in identified circumstances (especially various termination events). From an employer's perspective, a contract may discourage a competitor from recruiting an executive in jurisdictions that provide for tort damages for interference with the relationship of an executive under contract. An agreement may enable an employer to determine which state law will apply where there are contacts in multiple jurisdictions and, if desired, mandate arbitration of disputes regarding employment matters.

Rather than simply limit the use of executive contracts, an objective should be to improve the contents of executive agreements. A consensus is developing regarding best practices that should be considered for employment agreements. (See "Checklist for Considering a New Contract or Evaluating an Existing Contract.")

Considerations in Change-in-Control Design

In view of corporate governance considerations, special rules affecting nonqualified deferred compensation and broad executive pay disclosure requirements, it has become critical for companies to examine their change-in-control programs. As part of their compensation disclosures, companies are required to identify and quantify all potential compensation payments for named executive officers in connection with any termination of employment, including a change in control.

One result has been increased attention to and scrutiny of change-in-control provisions. Compensation committees must understand the rationale around change-in-control plans to be able to defend

Checklist for Considering a New Contract or Evaluating an Existing Contract

☐ **"Evergreen" renewal.** Evergreen provisions typically call for automatic extension of renewal unless a specified advance notice is given. Procedures should be implemented to review agreements before any such extension becomes effective. In any case, an employer's advance notice not to extend the contract term or renew the agreement should not trigger severance pay.

☐ **Critical definitions.** The definitions of "change in control," "cause" and "good reason" should be particularly scrutinized. In reaction to some widely publicized severance payments to executives who were dismissed or resigned after poor corporate performance, the current view is to expand cause definitions and constrict good reason events.

☐ **Calculating pay.** Where any payments are based on pay, a determination is needed on what amounts should be included. Some companies consider only base salary, while many others use salary plus annual incentive; very few include LTIs, especially because that is viewed as a poor pay practice that can produce excessive payouts. Also, annual incentive can be variously defined, so the method of its calculation should be specified.

☐ **Potential cost of retirement benefits or enhancements.** Shareholder groups may object to provisions that provide "deemed service credit" to increase an executive's retirement package (often coordinated with SERP benefits). Where that approach may be needed to recruit a mid-career executive to make up for benefits foregone at a former employer, the cost should be calculated and understood, with the rationale documented in an effort to counter likely opposition at public companies by proxy advisory firms.

☐ **Severance pay.** Any severance payments should be conditioned on the executive's agreement to reasonable restrictive covenants. Depending on what is permitted (and enforceable) under the laws of the relevant jurisdiction(s), covenants relating to noncompetition, nonsolicitation (of customers/clients and employees), nondisclosure of confidential information and nondisparagement of the employer should be considered.

and justify the plans to shareholder activists as well as for strategic business reasons.

Purpose

Before evaluating change-in-control provisions, it is necessary to understand their objectives. The main premise behind such arrangements is to protect shareholder interests by mitigating potential distractions to key executives regarding their future employment with the company in the event of a change in control.

However, critics of change-in-control arrangements question whether such payments are necessary because many executives

☐ **Overall cost analysis.** The potential costs for all payments directly or indirectly affected by an executive's contract should be determined on a worst-case (most costly) basis. These costs should be reviewed periodically to make sure the compensation committee understands how changes in base salary, for instance, may affect these payments.

☐ **Vesting on a change in control.** Accelerated vesting may be appropriate when there is a non-cause dismissal of the executive following a change in control or the executive would have no continuing equity interest in a merged entity. In other cases, it may be appropriate to continue the vesting or provide for discretion in the board to accelerate vesting as appropriate under the circumstances.

☐ **Trigger event.** Any change-in-control severance benefits should require a "double trigger" for payment rather than simply the change-in-control event ("single trigger"). Thus, there would need to be a change in control and an involuntary termination of the executive within the change in control period (commonly one to two years after the change in control).

☐ **Section 409A.** The potential application of IRC section 409A (regarding NQDC arrangements) should be considered when determining payment provisions. Because there are various exceptions and alternative approaches for compliance, section 409A can affect design and not merely legal language.

☐ **Responsibility for drafting.** The employer should have the contract drafted by its advisers, not by someone representing the executive's interests. The drafting process should be within control of the board. Also, a general counsel should not be put in the position of negotiating contract terms with an executive to whom he/she may report.

already have accumulated significant wealth from the company, especially individuals with long tenure. The counter-argument is that severance is needed to protect the executive from losing his/her job due to an event that is outside the executive's influence. A severance program would be designed to bridge the executive financially for a reasonable period while he/she seeks another job.

At times when the market for talent is particularly competitive, companies also use change-in-control arrangements to recruit executive candidates. A candidate who is considering multiple job offers will consider the potential change-in-control payments in evaluating and comparing the total packages.

Design

In reviewing a company's change-in-control plans, there are several design features to consider:

- **Eligibility.** Most companies limit change-in-control programs to a handful of executives, including the CEO and his/her direct reports. Some companies also include another level of senior management or even a third tier.
- **Definition of change in control.** The following are the most common triggers used for defining a change in control:
  - Acquisition of voting stock (generally ranging from 20 percent to 50 percent)
  - Merger, consolidation or reorganization
  - Change of board composition
  - Sale of substantially all of the company's assets
  - Liquidation or dissolution of the company.

  Most companies use some or all of these triggers in their definitions of change-in-control, the terms of which may appear in agreements, policies and plans.
- **Triggers.** Payouts upon a change in control generally are triggered under three scenarios:
  - *Single Trigger.* Only a change in control need occur.
  - *Double Trigger.* Both a change in control and an involuntary termination (other than for cause) or a constructive termination (i.e., a resignation for good reason) must occur within a certain period (generally one to two years after the change in control). Some programs also are triggered when a change in control is after a dismissal if the change in control event was the result of negotiations underway at the time of the executive's termination.
  - *Modified Single Trigger.* A double trigger is in effect, except for a short (generally one month immediately after the first anniversary of the date of the change in control) period during which a voluntary termination results in a payout.

  There usually is a distinction between the trigger for cash severance under the arrangements and the trigger for acceleration of vesting under equity plans. A substantial majority of plans now use a double-trigger approach for cash severance, while a single trigger remains common (although decreasing in prevalence) for accelerated vesting under an equity plan. Single triggers for cash severance often are criticized based on the view that an executive should not need accelerated vesting and payout if he/she is still employed. Also, modified single triggers have come under attack because they permit executives to resign after a certain period following a change-in-control event and receive payment even if they have has not been actually or constructively terminated.

- **Cash severance.** Most change-in-control arrangements provide for cash severance expressed as a multiple of pay that is paid in a lump sum. Now that separation amounts payable in installments are potentially subject to the deferred compensation rules of Internal Revenue Code (IRC) section 409A, installment payments have become much less common. There may be two or three tiers of multiples that correspond to levels within the organization. Among larger companies, three times pay has been the most prevalent multiple for the CEO, while smaller companies usually provide two to three times pay. Organizations typically provide one multiple less in cash severance to the next level or tier below the CEO.

  Cash severance usually is determined as the relevant multiple of either base salary or base salary plus annual incentive. The most prevalent approach is salary plus annual incentive. There are also variations on how annual bonus is defined, including:
  - *Target.* Target incentive for the year of change in control
  - *Average.* Average incentive paid during a prior number of years
  - *Highest.* Highest incentive paid during a prior number of years.

  Target is the most frequently used annual bonus definition, followed by some form of average incentive.

- **Benefits continuation.** Most companies also provide continuation of health and welfare benefits upon termination in the event of a change in control. The period of continuation usually is coordinated with the period represented by the cash severance multiple. In designing these arrangements, care must be taken to avoid unanticipated income tax consequences to the executive, including consideration of IRC section 409A.

- **Equity acceleration.** For equity plans, companies typically provide change-in-control protection in the form of accelerated vesting of equity awards. While a single trigger remains a common approach, its use has been questioned, and use of a double trigger is increasing in prevalence. A double trigger would prevent an executive from cashing out his/her equity before normal vesting if the individual remains employed.

- **Excise tax treatment.** IRC section 4999 imposes an excise tax on an executive if parachute payments made in connection with a change in control exceed the safe-harbor limit, which must be less than three times the individual's "base amount" (the average of the individual's total taxable compensation paid by the corporation for the five years preceding the year of the change in control). However, the excise tax amount is equal to 20 percent of all parachute payments in excess of one times the base amount. IRC section 280G provides that such "excess para-chute payments" are nondeductible to the employer. Companies address this excise-tax issue in various ways:

  - *Gross-up.* The company pays the executive's excise and related income taxes to keep the executive "whole" so that the individual receives the same after-tax amount as he/she would without the imposition of the excise tax.

  - *Modified gross-up.* The company provides a gross-up only if the payments exceed the safe harbor by a certain percentage or amount (e.g., 10 percent or $100,000). If not, payments are cut back to the safe-harbor limit to avoid any excise tax.

  - *Cut-back.* The company cuts back all payments to the safe-harbor limit to avoid the excise tax.

  - *Valley provision.* The company cuts back parachute payments to the safe-harbor limit only if doing so would result in a higher after-tax amount for the executive.

  - *Do nothing.* The company requires executives to pay any excise tax. While the provision of a gross-up previously was the most common practice, its use has fallen sharply due to criticism by shareholder groups, proxy adviser firms and the media. Once potential gross-up payments were included in disclosures under the U.S. Securities and Exchange Commission (SEC) proxy rules, compensation committees focused on the magnitude of the total potential cost of gross-ups. As a result, cutback and valley provisions have increased in use as many companies have eliminated gross-ups. Compensation committees should regularly review change-in-control programs and confirm the plan design is serving its intended purpose(s). Compensation committees also need to understand the potential payments and costs that could be triggered in the event of a change in control. A sharp increase in the company's stock price or a large equity grant can result in millions of dollars of change-in-control payments.

Handling Unvested Equity Awards at Termination

An executive's employment termination raises the issue of whether unvested equity awards should be forfeited or their vesting should be accelerated or continued. While too often an afterthought in designing equity programs and related agreements, the approach taken can greatly affect the amounts ultimately received by a terminating executive.

When negotiating employment agreements and drafting equity plan documents and individual award agreements, companies should consider how they wish to address various possible termination events. In this period of heightened governance scrutiny by advisory firms and the public outrage over perceived excesses in executive compensation, a company's treatment of unvested equity is becoming increasingly important.

Background and Relevant Termination Events

Like most compensation decisions, the particular facts and circumstances are paramount in the treatment of unvested equity. Where an employment agreement is involved, the executive's views may be part of the negotiation process. The treatment of unvested equity generally is addressed in a company's equity plan document and/ or individual award agreements. A company may include language that gives authority to the board of directors or compensation committee to apply discretion to accelerate vesting in certain cases.

Potential accounting and tax considerations also need to be examined so that the company can structure the arrangements in a favorable manner and avoid inadvertently triggering adverse accounting and tax consequences.

The basic employment termination events are:

- Death
- Disability
- Retirement
- Termination by the company (dismissal) without cause
- Dismissal for cause
- Termination by the executive (resignation) without good cause
- Resignation for good cause
- Termination in connection with a change in control.

Other than death, each company will have its own definition for each of the termination scenarios, but most companies' definitions address common themes. In the following discussion of various termination events, those that often are treated similarly are grouped.

Death, Disability and Retirement

When an executive dies, becomes disabled or retires during the course of employment, there typically is a provision in most equity plans and/or award agreements that allows for either the continued or immediate vesting of all or a portion of unvested awards. One reason for this executive-friendly approach is that none of these events reflects any wrongdoing, poor performance or disloyalty on the part of the executive.

- Most companies do not penalize an executive's beneficiary or estate by instituting a forfeiture provision on the unvested equity as of the date of death. In fact, research and experience finds that most organizations accelerate vesting upon the death of an employee.
- Similarly, most companies do not cancel unvested equity awards that were granted to an employee who becomes disabled during the course of employment. While not as prevalent as upon death, research shows that a substantial majority of companies allow an employee to either continue to vest or fully accelerate the vesting of unvested equity awards.

- Although less common than for death or disability, the majority of companies do not forfeit unvested awards at the date of retirement. When unvested stock options are accelerated in any of these scenarios, there typically is a reduction in the exercise period; the new period commonly is the shorter of the remaining option term or up to one year from the date of acceleration; on occasion companies allow option exercise for up to three years after the termination event.

However, some shareholder groups and their advisers are taking the position that no such acceleration of vesting is warranted in these circumstances. The view is basically that, in an atmosphere that increasingly focuses on performance, these awards have not been earned at the time of death, disability or retirement and that any payment would be a windfall.

Termination by the Company for Cause or by the Executive Without Good Reason

When an executive is dismissed for "cause" (generally including fraud and gross negligence in the definition) or resigns without "good reason" (typically including a material reduction in duties), it is extremely rare for a company to allow continued or accelerated vesting on any portion of unvested equity awards. In these circumstances there would be no reason to allow executives to receive compensation other than what was legally required (generally what was accrued up until the date of termination). The definitions of "cause" and "good reason" need to be carefully crafted to the company's particular situation.

Termination by the Company Without Cause or by the Executive for Good Reason

Considerable debate can be had on the appropriate handling of unvested equity awards when an executive is dismissed without cause or he/she resigns for good reason. An analysis of data indicates that unvested equity awards most commonly are forfeited when an executive is terminated without cause or resigns for good reason. While a dismissal (or good-reason resignation) may not be due to any fault of the executive (especially during an economic downturn), most employers do not view this as sufficient reason for accelerating vesting (at least absent a change in control) and prefer to focus on rewarding and retaining current employees. Some companies focus on "fairness" concerns and see value in recruitment and retention efforts by providing vesting protection to actually or constructively dismissed employees.

Termination in Connection with a Change in Control

Vesting acceleration considerations can be especially important in connection with a change in control. While still a prevalent practice, there is growing sentiment against single-trigger acceleration because it does not promote retention. Where change-in-control protection is determined to be useful, proxy advisory firms and shareholder groups now favor double triggers so that executives who simply quit after a change-in-control event are not benefited.

Accounting Considerations

All share-based compensation is accounted for under Accounting Standards Codification (ASC) Topic 718. ASC 718 requires that all share-based awards granted to employees be accounted for at "fair value." Basically, when an unvested equity award accelerates upon a termination event, the service condition of the original award is not expected to be satisfied because the employee is not expected to render the requisite service. Thus, the compensation cost for the original, unvested award should be zero at the date of the modification as none of the awards are expected to vest. The incremental fair value is equal to the full fair value of the modified award, which represents the total cumulative compensation cost that the company should recognize for the award. On the modification date, the company would reverse the compensation cost previously recognized for the unvested award, if any, and recognize compensation cost equal to the full fair value of the modified award, which is fully vested.

Income Tax Considerations

Three (extremely simplified here) income tax provisions are of particular importance regarding unvested equity upon termination:

- First, unless certain exceptions apply, under IRC section 409A, a publicly-held company may not make any payments of deferred compensation to certain key employees within a six-month period after a separation from service. Both the relevant plan documents and actual administration of the program need to satisfy section 409A to avoid harsh tax consequences for the recipient of any such accelerated awards that are determined to constitute deferred compensation.
- Second, companies need to consider IRC section 280G, as the acceleration of unvested equity on a change in control is valued in determining whether any of certain officers and other "disqualified individuals" has received an "excess parachute payment" that is subject to excise tax payable by the individual as well as the loss of the corporation's income tax deduction. If section 280G is not considered until after a change in control, it may be difficult to avoid parachute tax consequences.
- Third, IRC section 162(m), currently applicable only to the CEO and the next three highest paid executives (other than the CFO), contains requirements for a public company to obtain an income tax deduction for performance-based compensation in excess of $1 million for the year. Under the IRS' view, compensation will not qualify as tax deductible "performance-based" compensation if payment may be made on an involuntary termination of employment or retirement without regard to whether the applicable performance goals are satisfied.

Looking at the Relevant Facts and Circumstances

While it can be helpful to see how other companies handle unvested equity upon various employee termination events, a company's focus should be on what approach best advances its particular objectives. Various factors — including accounting and income tax considerations and views of proxy advisory firms — need to be weighed. Recruitment, motivation, retention and cost may be evaluated differently at different organizations; with an understanding of the key issues and approaches, an informed decision can be made.

Equity Vesting Acceleration Upon a Change in Control

Equity-based compensation — whether in the form of stock options/ stock appreciation rights (SARs), restricted stock/restricted stock units (RSUs) or performance shares — is an integral part of executive LTI programs. A common provision in the governing documents addresses how an executive's unvested interests are treated if there is a change in control of the company. Because a significant portion of an executive's wealth often is tied to the value of equity-based compensation, the conditions for accelerated vesting are particularly important.

As discussed in the section of this chapter titled "Considerations in Change-in-Control Design," most equity plans include either a single or double trigger for acceleration of vesting upon a change in control, with a modified single trigger used at some companies. Thus, upon the relevant trigger, all unvested stock options become immediately exercisable, all outstanding restricted stock or RSUs are immediately vested and are no longer subject to forfeiture, and all performance-based shares would be vested and paid in accordance with the governing document.

A Trend Toward a Double Trigger

Use of a double trigger approach for equity acceleration on a change in control has been on the rise in recent years. Single triggers are viewed negatively by many shareholders, investors and proxy advisors. Some shareholders believe that the use of a single trigger creates a windfall to corporate executives while failing to retain them after the acquisition of the company is complete. While certainly not exhaustive, Table 11-1 highlights some notable advantages and disadvantages of single- and double-trigger acceleration.

Implementing the Elimination of a Single Trigger for Equity Acceleration

If a company decides to eliminate the single triggers for the acceleration of vesting on equity-based compensation, it must address the practicalities of how best to implement the change, taking into account anticipated employee reaction, expectations for some quid

TABLE 11-1

Single and Double Triggers: Pros and Cons

Single-Trigger Approach	
Advantages	Disadvantages
• Allows certain executives to share in the value they have created for shareholders. • Provides for a built-in "retention award" that can eliminate the need for a cash retention arrangement through the date of closing. • Does not affect the current stock prices, as outstanding equity awards are treated as a sunk cost by the buyer. • Beneficial when acquiring company is going to terminate the existing equity plan or does not convert the unvested equity of the acquired company into its own stock.	• Can be viewed as a windfall for executives who would not be terminated by buyer. • No retention value after the closing of the transaction. • Incentive for executives to only focus on near-term stock price of the company. • Acceleration generally constitutes a parachute payment under IRC section 280G.

Double-Trigger Approach	
Advantages	Disadvantages
• Viewed by corporate governance and shareholder advisory groups as the preferred approach — a best practice. • Acts as a key retention tool for senior executives who are instrumental to the integration process. • Alleviates the need for additional retention incentives in the form of cash or additional equity. • Aligns executive and shareholder interests due to the long-term value of the acquiring company. • Protection for the executive in the event of termination of employment due to a change in control. • Not necessarily considered a parachute payment under IRC section 280G.	• Executives, unlike shareholders, may not immediately share in any increase in value of company stock (or acquirer's stock). • Potential loss of income to the executive if unvested awards are not converted into the acquirer's stock.

pro quo, and any contractual rights under current awards and agreements. Some companies may determine to make only prospective changes — whereby any future programs and agreements will have double triggers — but leave existing arrangements unchanged until they expire. Others may choose to negotiate with executives to give up the single triggers, perhaps in exchange for some other benefit.

Impact of IRC Section 280G

An important factor to consider when determining the treatment of equity in change-in-control scenarios is the potential exposure to the golden parachute ramifications of IRC section 280G. As brief background, section 280G denies an income tax deduction to a corporation for "excess parachute payments" made in connection with a change in control. Section 4999 imposes a 20-percent excise tax on any person who receives compensation that, under section 280G, is deemed to constitute an excess parachute payment.

As part of the complex calculation to determine if any person has received excess parachute payments, the accelerated value of unvested equity awards is taken into account. This accelerated value is determined under different methodologies depending on the type of equity vehicle but, in many cases, represents a significant portion of the total value an executive is deemed to receive upon a change in control. When a single-trigger acceleration approach is used, all unvested awards are immediately vested and must be taken into account for purposes of the section 280G calculation.

If the value of equity acceleration (when taken into account with all other payments contingent upon a change in control) triggers an excess parachute payment, then the company will lose valuable income tax deductions. To compound matters, if an executive is grossed up for any excise tax that may be imposed, this gross-up protection could potentially cost the company 250 percent to 300 percent of the initial excise tax, as these gross-up payments are considered additional excess parachute payments that become subject to the excise tax as well. These excise tax gross-up provisions are extremely costly to shareholders when taking into account the amount of cash that is required to cover the gross-up payment and they must pay additional income taxes on compensation deemed to be nondeductible.

When the double-trigger acceleration approach is used, there is no immediate value under section 280G because unvested awards are not necessarily accelerated upon a change in control. However, if in connection with a change in control an executive is terminated by the acquiring company without cause or the executive resigns for good reason, then all unvested equity is immediately vested and such acceleration generally is calculated in the same manner as the single trigger. Thus, a double-trigger approach may result in a parachute payment while the single-trigger approach clearly will constitute a parachute payment.

While the discussion around the merits of the single- versus double-trigger approach continues, one thing is certain: Double-trigger acceleration provisions are being considered and implemented by more companies than ever before.

Parachute Excise Tax Gross-Up Considerations

As mentioned, excessive amounts payable on a change in control may be subject to a loss of tax deduction to the company and an excise tax on the employee under the golden parachute provisions of IRC sections 280G and 4999, respectively. Over the years many corporations determined that a gross-up for the effect of the parachute excise tax was the preferred approach for working around the excise tax.

Excise tax gross-ups have attracted negative attention and been criticized as poor or problematic pay practices. With the advent of say on pay and golden parachutes, combined with the increased influence of shareholder advisory groups, compensation committees must carefully consider issues resulting from the use of excise tax gross-ups. In this process, it is helpful to examine why many companies have been using gross-ups for senior executives.

Inequity of Parachute Excise Tax and Argument for Tax Gross-Ups

In determining the amount (if any) of parachute payments subject to the 20-percent excise tax on excess parachute payments, the relevant income tax regulations start with a disqualified individual's base amount. The base amount is the average — for the five years immediately before the year of the change in control — of an employee's box 1 income from Form W-2. If the aggregate present value of all payments made to an executive that were contingent upon the change in control at least equals three times the base amount, then all payments made in excess of one times the base amount are subject to the 20-percent excise tax.

"Example: Parachute Excise Tax Calculations and Comparison" illustrates how the excise tax can be unfair. While this example may be extreme, it highlights the potential inequity of the excise tax:

- Executive A took all of the cash he could from the company and did not align his interests with those of shareholders. As a reward for "cashing out" every year, A pays $0 in excise tax.
- On the other hand, Executive B did everything that a company and shareholders would like — deferred cash and did not exercise stock options, thereby cementing her long-term interests with those of the company. By doing the right thing from a corporate governance perspective, as well as taking less cash annually, B gets hit with an excise tax bill of $1,555,000. (Of course, many executives postpone exercising stock options simply in hopes of maximizing their ultimate returns.)

This example illustrates why excise tax gross-ups became prevalent in senior executive employment agreements. The gross-ups leveled the playing field for similarly situated executives who may have acted differently with respect to stock option exercises and deferrals of compensation.

Example: Parachute Excise Tax Calculations and Comparison

Executives A and B each earn $1 million in base salary and receive a $2 million bonus for each of the five preceding years. In addition, both A and B could exercise stock options worth $500,000 per year.

Executive A exercises all of his stock options every year during the five-year period, while Executive B does not exercise any of her stock option awards. Also, A does not defer any of his base salary or bonus while B defers 25 percent of both base salary and bonus on an annual basis.

In the year of a change in control, both A and B receive a $10 million golden parachute package. The table below illustrates the components of the parachute excise tax calculation for each executive and compares the tax due for each executive.

	Box 1 W-2 average	2.99* x base amount	Parachute payments ($10 million) greater than 2.99* x base amount?	Subject to 20% excise tax	Amount subject to 20% excise tax	20% excise tax
A	$3,500,000	$10,465,000	No	No	$0	$0
B	$2,250,000	$6,727,500	Yes	Yes	$7,775,000	$1,555,000

*2.99 used as short-hand approximation of calculating just below three times the base amount.

Mounting Criticism and Pushback Against Excise Tax Gross-Ups

Many shareholder advocacy groups and various business media have become increasingly critical of excise tax gross-ups. Their argument is that gross-ups are a poor or problematic pay practice that shareholders should oppose by voting against programs that contain them — an opportunity provided by say on pay (as discussed in Chapter 14). Where a say-on-pay vote is unavailable, shareholders may express their displeasure by casting "withhold" or "against" votes regarding compensation committee members (and, in certain instances, other directors) who approve arrangements with these gross-ups. In addition, the presence of this type of perquisite will negatively influence a company's scoring on various governance ratings.

The general public seems to agree; in an age of high unemployment and stagnant wages, an executive who leaves with millions of dollars in severance benefits — and millions more in tax gross-ups — may be depicted as a poster child for excessive compensation. Because excise tax gross-ups are considered additional parachute payments subject to the excise tax (as well as regular federal and state income taxes), it typically costs a company 2½ to 3 times the initial excise tax to gross-up the payment to make the executive whole on an after-tax basis.

As a result of enhanced disclosure rules, companies are required to estimate termination payments under different scenarios as of the last day of the reporting year. Even though these scenarios are calculated and disclosed in a company's proxy statement, the average investor does not understand how the calculations are derived, but does know that these payments and related gross-ups are very expensive. This negative attention — and particularly the threat of a negative say-on-pay vote and/or withhold or against vote recommendations on compensation committee members — has led many companies to review their attitudes toward golden parachute payments and the associated excise tax gross-ups. Many boards have made or are considering eliminating excise tax gross-ups altogether, often by restricting golden parachute payments so that they are cut back to ensure the IRC section 4999 excise tax is not triggered.

Compensation Committee Considerations

Say on pay raised the stakes for compensation committees regarding the use of excise tax gross-ups. Compensation committees no longer deal only with the public scrutiny and proxy adviser oversight. As previously noted, public companies generally now are required (under the Dodd-Frank Wall Street Reform and Consumer Protection Act of 2010) to provide shareholders with an advisory, nonbinding vote on the pay (as described in its annual proxy statement) of its named executive officers. In addition, a separate advisory, nonbinding vote of shareholders is required on golden parachute compensation for a company's named executive officers in connection with an acquisition, merger, consolidation or certain other business transactions.

Compensation committee members need to understand that if any new or materially amended employment agreement contains a parachute excise tax gross-up, they likely will be forced to defend their position to shareholders to rebut a negative say-on-pay recommendation from proxy advisory firms.

As the use of excise tax gross-ups declines, there likely will be an increased search for planning techniques to avoid or limit the potential application of any parachute excise tax. Some approaches may not align with shareholder interests, such as a reduction of compensation deferrals, earlier stock option exercises (followed immediately by sales of shares so acquired), and holding only the minimum amount of company stock to satisfy any stock ownership guidelines. In addition, compensation committees will continue to explore with their advisers various ways of mitigating any potential excise tax though compensation design practices, including consulting and noncompete agreements that can shift compensation from contingent upon a change in control to reasonable compensation for future services.

Post-Employment Consulting Arrangements: Are They Appropriate?

Companies often enter into post-employment consulting agreements with outgoing or "retiring" executives. However, as executive pay is subjected to ever-increasing scrutiny, questions arise: Are these arrangements justifiable? If so, what terms are appropriate?

Sometimes there is a plausible rationale for these arrangements, such as transition to a new management team or passing knowledge on from an outgoing executive. All too often, however, these consultancies simply are a going-away present provided gratuitously by the board without the expectation of any meaningful services from the executive. In the extreme, they can be clearly inappropriate and represent excessive compensation with no pretense of a justifiable rationale. Yet they persist, even appearing in employment agreements negotiated well in advance of actual termination.

In the not-for-profit world, particularly in academia, there have been cases involving an "emeritus" designation of retired executives and professors. These arrangements may include the equivalent full-time salary with far less than full-time responsibilities. Questions can arise regarding whether meaningful services are being provided to the employer. (See "Common Abuses and Issues.")

Common Abuses and Issues

Among the more frequent abuses:

- Compensation rates that are too high (as a percentage of full-time pay)
- Consultancy periods that are too long
- Coverage of spouses under the agreement
- Inclusion of executive benefits and perquisites that would not otherwise be paid to outside consultants
- Arrangements negotiated too far in advance of the consulting period (thereby presuming the need for the executive's services)
- Promises made as an entitlement regardless of the executive's success while active.

These lead to a series of questions:

- Does the payment really represent additional severance?
- Is the arrangement a retirement benefit in disguise?
- Should the amounts be viewed as deferred compensation?
- Whatever the characterization, is it acceptable as such?
- Why doesn't the employer just call it a retirement plan?
- Who actually cares? The board or the compensation committee? Shareholders? The public? The tax authorities?
- Who has the responsibility for determining reasonableness?

Design of Consulting Arrangements

Because a consulting arrangement should be limited to those circumstances in which there is a particular need to retain the executive's services, the design and terms of any such agreement should be customized to the particular situation. (See "Justifications for Consulting Arrangements.") Following is a discussion of key design considerations.

Retainer

A retainer to be available for special projects can be sufficient, but the facts and circumstances should be carefully considered. Even if the executive is expected to be called upon for less than the prescribed time, this does not necessarily affect the appropriateness of the arrangement, but rather is part of the facts and circumstances to be evaluated. In fact, this approach has significant prevalence in post-retirement contracts.

Determination of Value

The value of any post-retirement consulting arrangement to the employer reasonably could be based on a number of alternative theories, including:

- A direct assessment of the value to the employer of assigned consulting projects, regardless of time spent and regardless of results.
- Project results, rather than hours spent (i.e., the "finder's fee" theory). If the value to the employer is sales, this can be a function of relationships and results, not necessarily time. For example, if there was a significant sale negotiated during an afternoon of golf, it was not likely a direct function of time.
- The value of the executive's availability in potential situations.

Structuring Payments

The structure of the consulting payments could be built around:

- A proration of pre-retirement salary
- A dollar retainer amount per year during which the individual's services are available (e.g., a "bench player" that can be called

Justifications for Consulting Arrangements

Clearly there are situations in which a post-employment consultancy is supportable, including:

- Transitions in which knowledge needs to be passed to the new management team

- Proprietary knowledge that must be protected from leakage to competitors

- Special projects that otherwise would require an outside consultant

- Experienced executive is needed to represent the company in relationships with customers, investors, regulators or other special groups

- Outgoing executive might be key to maintaining or further developing business through long-standing relationships

- Changes in control, especially in which the executive's expertise is required on a temporary basis during the post-merger period.

into play if and when needed, but who is barred from "playing" for anyone else during the prescribed time period)

- A consulting arrangement based on an agreed-upon hourly rate, against which the former executive bills time on assigned projects.

Total Compensation Package Approach

What appears to be most important to the IRS — especially for tax-exempt organizations — is the aggregate of the compensation package for post-employment services. Basically, the absence of certain payments (or the provision of lower amounts) can offset "excesses" in other components. To the extent that one or more components of the total package are less than amounts that otherwise would be acceptable, there may be "credits" available to balance any otherwise excessive portions.

In this process, consideration might be given to pay components such as retirement benefits, post-retirement medical benefits, the value of a covenant not to compete (where that covenant has real value to the employer) and severance benefits. This approach can be especially helpful in developing the reasonableness of an executive's compensation under the intermediate-sanctions provisions of the Taxpayer Bill of Rights II (the legislation that restricts executive pay at tax-exempt organizations).

Retirement Benefit

One common approach is for the employer to provide the CEO with a target retirement benefit of an annual life annuity equal to 60 percent of final average pay (base plus bonus). This formula assumes a reasonable length of service with the employer and inclusion of benefits under the company's qualified retirement plan.

If an executive's base plus bonus averaged $1 million for the final three years, such a formula could have a lump-sum present value at age 65 of approximately $3 million. The absence of this type of program could help justify additional benefits on the basis that a major portion of a "normal" executive compensation program was lacking. Under the total package approach described above, an argument could be made that the value of a consultancy agreement is a substitute for the value of a typical retirement program for similar executives.

The Pseudo-Retirement Plan

While in some cases an employer may install a SERP arrangement retroactively just before retirement, care would be needed to assure that there is sufficient rationale for this retroactivity. Because this approach involves crediting service in excess of actual service, a public company would need to consider the likely opposition of proxy advisory groups to that aspect of the program. Another caution exists when the outgoing executive already has a sufficient retirement program in place; a consulting agreement could be redundant.

The Retainer Approach

In another example, a compensation committee and an executive enter into a post-employment consulting agreement on a retainer basis, with the purpose of reserving 25 percent of the executive's time during a five-year period. The compensation committee concludes that there is sufficient value to the organization to have that resource contracted under the terms of the agreement and available to provide a range of duties as needed.

Before considering the amounts actually payable under such an agreement, it should not be unreasonable as a principle for the executive and the compensation committee to enter into such an agreement and for the executive to be paid reasonable amounts.

This assumes that the executive did in fact reserve or otherwise make available 25 percent of his/her time, as required. However, in this case, the five-year duration of the payments generally would be excessive for a management transition or for a noncompetition restriction.

Should We Plan Ahead for Executive Consulting?

One particularly troublesome use of post-retirement consulting arrangements can be when they are agreed to in an employment contract far in advance of any separation discussions. In many cases such use is really just additional post-employment pay for the executive. A compensation committee would have a better reason to consider such an arrangement (assuming it otherwise makes sense) at the time the executive transition is being negotiated. At least then there would be a relationship to performance rather than making commitments to an outgoing executive who may not have been overly successful in his/her active career.

PART II
Governance, Disclosure and Compensation Committee Initiatives

12
Compensation Committee Governance

By Brian Tobin and Dan Mayfield

In recent years, executive compensation and perceived excesses in executive pay have provided fertile ground for legislative and regulatory initiatives, as well as abundant fodder for the press. While most attention paid to executive compensation has focused on the CEOs receiving the pay, it is the compensation committee of the board of directors that ultimately is responsible for the executive pay decisions.

Even the most responsible and diligent committee, however, may make compensation decisions it later regrets, including ones that are forgotten until exposed in a less than favorable light. In the wake of several high-profile severance payments, some compensation committee members involved were quoted as not really understanding the nuances of certain severance and change-in-control programs nor the size of the cumulative awards. Unfortunately, ignorance is no excuse. Sound compensation committee governance initiatives ensure that board members are educated on compensation matters and able to make well-grounded and defensible executive pay decisions.

This chapter:

- Reviews the role and responsibilities of the compensation committee and the need to establish a compensation committee charter and an annual calendar of quarterly committee meetings
- Presents a "governance scorecard" to aid compensation committees in understanding their responsibilities as well as the details of the plans and payouts they approve and monitor
- Offers practical advice on how to conduct the mandatory board and committee self assessment, and the recommended assessment of outside compensation consultants
- Suggests actions to evaluate pay programs for sensitivity to the say-on-pay provisions of the Dodd-Frank Wall Street Reform and Consumer Protection Act of 2010.

Responsibilities of the Compensation Committee

Although some corporate boards may assign certain responsibilities to other committees, the compensation committee generally is responsible for:

- Establishing and periodically reviewing the compensation philosophy for executives
- Establishing and providing oversight of the executive compensation and benefits programs, including base salary plans, all incentive plans, retirement plans, employment agreements, severance arrangements and other pay programs
- Assessing the CEO's performance at least annually
- Establishing, monitoring and reviewing performance targets and results for the executive team
- Approving compensation adjustments and incentive payouts for the CEO and other top officers
- Managing the succession planning process and regularly evaluating the succession plans for the CEO and his/her direct reports
- Recommending compensation for the board of directors
- Communicating with the entire board at least semi-annually on its activities and recommendations
- Understanding the current regulatory environment
- Staying informed on trends and best practices in the executive compensation arena
- Seeking feedback on the effectiveness of the executive compensation program.

Generally, the compensation committee should be composed of three to five outside and independent directors. Given the increased complexity of the executive compensation environment and programs, the chair of the committee in particular should have significant HR and/or compensation experience.

The compensation committee has additional resources to assist it in executing its accountabilities, including senior leadership, internal HR staff and external, independent consultants. (See Figure 12-1.)

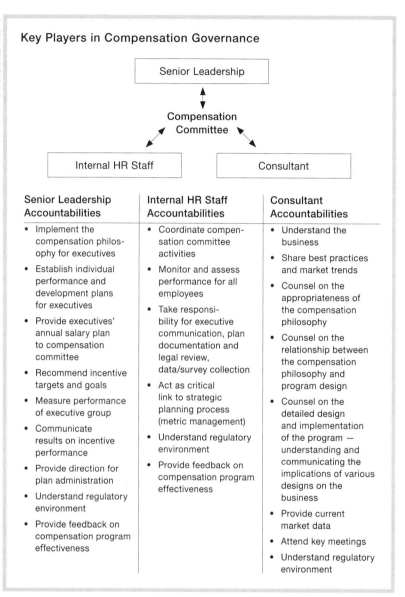

FIGURE 12-1

Key Players in Compensation Governance

Senior Leadership Accountabilities	Internal HR Staff Accountabilities	Consultant Accountabilities
• Implement the compensation philosophy for executives	• Coordinate compensation committee activities	• Understand the business
• Establish individual performance and development plans for executives	• Monitor and assess performance for all employees	• Share best practices and market trends
• Provide executives' annual salary plan to compensation committee	• Take responsibility for executive communication, plan documentation and legal review, data/survey collection	• Counsel on the appropriateness of the compensation philosophy
• Recommend incentive targets and goals		• Counsel on the relationship between the compensation philosophy and program design
• Measure performance of executive group	• Act as critical link to strategic planning process (metric management)	
• Communicate results on incentive performance	• Understand regulatory environment	• Counsel on the detailed design and implementation of the program — understanding and communicating the implications of various designs on the business
• Provide direction for plan administration	• Provide feedback on compensation program effectiveness	
• Understand regulatory environment		
• Provide feedback on compensation program effectiveness		• Provide current market data
		• Attend key meetings
		• Understand regulatory environment

Compensation Committee Charter

The compensation committee is responsible for drafting its charter and submitting it to the board for approval. Charters are critically important for establishing mutual understanding of the board, the compensation committee and the CEO with respect to roles and responsibilities. The charter must be clear and succinct; it should be a living document and reviewed annually to determine its continued relevance. Topics typically addressed in a charter include:

- **Purpose.** Why the compensation committee exists and what its ultimate objectives are
- **Membership and procedures.** Number of members, selection process for members and the chair, frequency of meetings and other governance procedures established by the board
- **Duties and responsibilities.** Specific accountabilities for the compensation committee regarding executive compensation and benefits programs, succession planning, board-of-director compensation, charter evaluation, self-evaluations and so on
- **Reports/communication to the board.** Frequency and content of communications with the board
- **Risk oversight for incentive plans.** Review of company's incentive compensation programs regarding an assessment of potential risks to the company from any such arrangements
- **Advisers to the compensation committee.** Rights and authorities of the compensation committee to hire and use external advisers, including consultants and legal counsel
- **Executive session.** Meetings without the presence of management.

Annual Compensation Committee Calendar

As part of the planning process, the compensation committee should establish an annual calendar of activities to guide it in fulfilling its duties. Most compensation committees should plan to meet three to four times per year in a typical or standard year. Typical items included in the planning process are included in the sample compensation committee calendar in Table 12-1.

The Governance Scorecard

Even without the threat of being pilloried by Congress, the U.S. Securities and Exchange Commission (SEC), other regulatory agencies, the press or a shareholder group, good governance calls for a compensation committee to take a regular, comprehensive look at the practices and programs that make up the organization's

TABLE 12-1

Sample Compensation Committee Calendar

First Quarter Meeting	Second Quarter Meeting	Third Quarter Meeting	Fourth Quarter Meeting
• Review (and approve) incentive payments for the fiscal year just ended • Finalize input on Compensation Discussion and Analysis (CD&A) and proxy disclosures • Annual planning • Develop the compensation committee's plan/calendar for the coming 12 months • Identify special studies to be conducted	• Perform compensation committee self-assessment • Review compensation committee charter • Confirm consultant annual agreement • Board communication	• Review results of any special studies conducted during the year • Review and approve board compensation for the coming year • Review the total executive compensation structure for the coming year, including base pay ranges and incentive targets • Review status of executive succession plans	• Performance and base-pay review • Evaluate CEO job performance for the year just ended • Review (and approve) base pay changes (if any) • Review (and approve) incentive goals for the coming year • Board communication

executive compensation system. Clearly, the explanation and rationale now required as part of the Compensation Discussion & Analysis (CD&A) in the annual proxy have encouraged compensation committees to be more aware of pay programs, but a full review may be more enlightening than expected.

One approach to the process is the "governance scorecard" — a series of rated elements that together focus on key issues in the current executive compensation landscape. Although the specific elements may differ by company, the general elements of a scorecard address some fundamental questions. (See Table 12-2.)

Objectives of Governance Criteria

The evaluation categories and rating criteria should be designed to provide the compensation committee with a structured review of the key elements in plan philosophy and design from the perspective of an external, independent observer (e.g., shareholder, analyst, regulator).

TABLE 12-2

Sample Governance Scorecard

Category	Criteria
Governance	• Is the compensation committee well structured and following practices that would be considered appropriate? Does the compensation committee operate effectively and independent of excessive management influence? • Does the compensation committee have appropriate access to independent advice? • Is the compensation committee's charter and compensation philosophy appropriate? • Are the duties and requirements found in the charter actually followed in practice?
Competitiveness	• Are the compensation plans not only competitive with the external market, but also appropriate for the internal needs of the business? • Is the peer group representative of the competitive market? (Does it properly consider the competitive market for talent?) • Are actual awards consistent with the compensation philosophy? (50th percentile? 75th percentile?)
Plan design	• Are compensation plans adequately thought through and appropriately focused on performance? • Is the mix between base and variable elements consistent with a performance culture? • For a public company, are compensation plans approved by shareholders and designed to secure the income tax deductions allowable under the standards of IRC section 162(m)? • Have the potential effects of IRC sections 409A and 280G been considered? • Are benefits and perquisites aligned with good practice and the needs of the business? Have they been re-evaluated recently? • Are there issues of share depletion? Overhang?
Alignment	• Is the mix of pay and plan design aligned with the financial and operational goals of the company? Are the awards appropriate to support business strategy and for both expected and realized results? • What is the degree of anticipated difficulty in achieving goals? (If plans are consistently paying awards in excess of 100 percent of target, are the requirements sufficiently challenging?) • Are there appropriate controls on the use of discretion and judgment in bonus/stock awards? • Is truly exceptional performance rewarded properly? (75th percentile performance equals 75th percentile pay?)
Executive agreements	• Do severance, change-in-control and any other executive contracts and agreements satisfy a legitimate business need? Do they provide adequate protection for executives while aligning with shareholder interests such as the imposition of appropriate restrictive covenants?

The intent is not to judge the programs as "right" or "wrong," but to provide an assessment as to their fit with the business needs of the company, alignment with good business practices, and appropriate concern for shareholder interests. If nothing else, a thorough and structured assessment furnishes compensation committee members with a structured format to conduct a proper review. A committee's ability to focus where to spend time and energy during the review process can help to ensure necessary changes are considered in light of the regulatory, business and economic environments. A simple rating of A, B or C with follow-up explanation and detail as appropriate, or the classic red light-green light approach, provides for a good starting point for discussion.

- **Green light, signaling alignment:** The company has elements that clearly support and emulate best practice and good governance principles.
- **Yellow light, signaling caution:** There are some potential gaps between best practice and the company's approach. However, the gaps are sufficiently limited in scope or severity that they need be addressed only if there is a perceived need.
- **Red light, signaling misalignment:** There is a clear gap between good governance and the company. When addressing changes in executive compensation, these issues take priority.

The evaluation includes not only current plan *design*, but also the *process and rationale* for decisions. Under the SEC's enhanced proxy disclosure rules, the CD&A disclosure of executive compensation arrangements should address the "how" and "why" as well as the "what." The governance evaluation process helps develop the context required in the disclosure.

As the levels of congressional and regulatory oversight and action on matters of executive compensation evolve, boards and their compensation committees could face increased pressure. In this environment, it is critical that a compensation committee avoid any chance of a surprise and take active steps to be informed and make sound decisions.

Board and Committee Self-Assessments

Board assessments are mandatory at all companies listed on the New York Stock Exchange. Many other organizations, even private companies and not-for-profit organizations, have adopted the practice of conducting an annual review of the performance of the board and its committees; this process is especially important for the compensation committee given the developments affecting executive pay. The value in self assessments can be maximized if companies move away from a box-ticking exercise and into a framework that fosters dialogue and discovery. So what are America's best companies doing to improve their annual board and committee assessment processes?

Using Interviews and Focus Groups

Structured director interviews are undoubtedly the most constructive approach to board assessments, both in terms of gathering the insights and perspectives of participants and in terms of the far richer pool of data that can be collected from a confidential interview process. Directors typically find the interview process more engaging than a survey, and the results yield far more workable data, offering different insights and perspectives on key issues.

An alternative to interviews is the use of a focus group in combination with a confidential survey. In this process, directors participate in a roughly 90-minute discussion about the board's performance led by an outside consultant using a structured protocol similar to that used in individual interviews. One downside is that sensitive topics often are avoided, as participants often are less comfortable discussing these in a group setting than in a confidential interview.

Many boards and committees are now adding another component to the assessments — individual director performance. While various methodologies have been adopted as boards have moved gingerly in this direction, the "real deal" is what is known as a director peer review, in which directors provide feedback on each other's performance and receive feedback from their peers. Legal counsel should advise the committee on how it might safeguard the director peer-review process to avoid opening up litigation possibilities based on any negative feedback.

To build a true snapshot of the big picture, boards can incorporate management's perspective into the review process. While not all boards welcome management feedback on their performance, those that do have found it yields some especially useful guidance. Not only can it prevent the board and its committees from becoming insular, but it also can surface important issues and enhance the working relationship between the board and management.

Practical Aspects in Board and Committee Self Assessment

Not all of these concepts and steps are implemented all at once or conducted every year. One key is variety, or finding appropriate ways of looking at the particular committee's performance that bring new perspectives, engagement and value to the process, as well as yielding insights that help maximize the board's and committee's effectiveness and make the committee a true resource to the company.

Assessment of Compensation Consultants

While not required, a recommended best practice is an annual assessment by the compensation committee of any consultant(s) it has retained to assist the committee in navigating the various issues involved in executive pay decisions and board governance. In addition to evaluating the usefulness and timeliness of the information and advice that the compensation committee receives from its consultant, consideration also should be given to any other services the consultant may have rendered for the company and whether they were approved by the committee. The compensation committee needs to determine how well its consultant understood the company, its particular circumstances and pay philosophy, and the role of various elements of compensation in achieving the organization's goals and objectives.

Addressing Increased Regulation Under Say on Pay

The Dodd-Frank Act contained significant executive compensation and corporate governance provisions applicable to publicly traded companies. A set of provisions coined "say on pay" went into effect during the 2011 proxy season. The term refers to a vote by a company's shareholders on the compensation of its executives. In 2011, Dodd-Frank made say on pay mandatory for U.S. public companies; it requires a nonbinding advisory vote of shareholders to approve the compensation (as disclosed in the company's annual proxy statement, including the CD&A, compensation tables, and narrative disclosures) of its named executive officers. Under Dodd-Frank, a say-on-pay vote must be held at least once every three years starting with the first annual shareholders' meeting occurring on or after the effective date (Jan. 21, 2011). A separate vote of shareholders — captioned a "say on frequency" — is required at the same time, and then again at least once every six years, on whether the mandated say-on-pay vote subsequently will be held annually, every two years or every three years.

The say-on-pay and say-on-frequency votes are advisory only and may be disregarded by the compensation committee and the board. However, a negative or relatively close say-on-pay vote puts pressure on compensation committees to review and justify programs and policies that affect the compensation of named executive officers. In the event of a negative vote, compensation members may feel compelled to conform to a standard advocated by shareholder representatives and activist groups in an effort to avoid receiving withhold or against votes when they next stand for election.

Shareholders that vote down management's say-on-pay proposal most commonly do so mainly due to concerns related to pay for performance. A majority of the companies that receive failed votes have negative three-year total shareholder returns. Other typical reasons for companies failing their say-on-pay vote include: executive pay well above the peer median values, generous severance packages, outsized sign-on bonuses, and failure on the part of the company to address low voting support for specific compensation committee members.

The frequency of future say-on-pay votes received significant attention during their first year. Shareholders generally supported an annual frequency and companies listened. In reaction to support by shareholders for annual say on pay, companies shifted their preference from triennial votes to annual votes.

Overall, these new say-on-pay regulations have increased companies' focus and engagement on compensation issues. Several companies made late changes to their compensation programs or filed additional proxy materials addressing investor concerns and proxy advisers' recommendations to win shareholder support. One major outcome of say on pay is increased communication between the issuers and shareholders. Shareholders are reacting positively to the increased communication and are beginning to have increased confidence in executive compensation practices and governance.

Reviewing Compensation Programs in Preparation for a Say-on-Pay Vote

Shareholder groups, proxy advisers and the press, among others, have expressed growing opposition to various aspects of executive pay in recent years. Complaints generally have centered on the view that pay is excessive in some manner — whether in the aggregate or in one or more specific features. Some common areas of focus include:

- Limiting or eliminating various guarantees or commitments (e.g., guaranteed bonuses, severance benefits, change-in-control benefits, perquisites, post-retirement benefits, tax gross-ups)
- Pay levels, design practices and equity usage to be reasonable and consistent with market norms
- Improved alignment with performance, with an emphasis on alignment with long-term shareholder performance.

The implementation of say-on-pay further heightens the attention on any problematic component of executive pay. In the current skeptical environment, a compensation committee and its advisers should evaluate each element of the company's pay program (including its rationale) and compare it against a "hot button" checklist. Following is a sample of areas to examine:

- **Contractual elements.** Existence of employment contracts, severance, change-in-control benefits
- **Pay design.** Peer group, target pay positioning, base salary

- **Annual incentive.** Structure (e.g., percent of salary), metrics, number of metrics, leverage curve
- **LTI.** Types of programs, vesting type (time, performance), metrics, number of metrics, leverage curve, deferrals, clawbacks for all programs
- **Equity use.** Share allocation, burn rate.

This checklist, adjusted for a company's specifics and other relevant considerations, can be used to evaluate individual pay practices and assess the overall executive compensation program. In examining executive pay, the focus should extend beyond the traditional compensation elements of base salary, annual incentives and LTIs. A company and the compensation committee must understand which practices may be especially sensitive in a shareholder vote.

A comprehensive examination of the individual elements of executive pay can be critical in understanding a company's overall executive compensation program. While a CD&A disclosure may describe a company's pay-for-performance objectives, an analysis (including a consideration of the value of all other compensation elements) may show that the program is neither especially variable nor focused on pay for performance. Use of tally sheets should be helpful in analyzing the details of the overall executive pay program.

Working Team

In preparing for the say-on-pay process and accompanying communications, it can be helpful to form a working team that includes those members of the board and management committee who are knowledgeable about the programs or may meet with shareholders and interact with proxy solicitors. In developing this team, a company generally starts with the members of the compensation committee and then considers including:

- A member of the governance committee (depending on the individual's role in board-shareholder communications)
- The CFO
- General counsel

- The head of HR
- A senior executive in investor relations.

Outside legal and compensation advisers also would be consulted.

Communicating with Shareholders

A company should maintain regular communications with its institutional shareholders to gain their insights on the strengths and weaknesses of the executive pay program. Interaction with shareholders can enable a company representative to discuss the rationale supporting the compensation program and to understand shareholder concerns. Critical issues can be discussed and, where concerns are elicited, suggested modifications can be considered. Before launching a communications program, it generally is helpful to develop a formal strategy with investor relations and outside advisers.

Legal niceties of course must be observed both in these meetings and in communications with shareholders. Company representatives should be informed on what types of information and disclosure can be provided. During the process of obtaining input from various shareholders on matters such as proposed equity compensation plans, a company must take care not to run afoul of SEC Regulation FD by sharing material, nonpublic information.

Enhanced Disclosures and Communications

Communication efforts should include appropriate disclosure within the CD&A, especially the reasons for a material compensation program or feature. Ideally this should be supported by rigorous analysis, including the alignment with the business and human capital strategies and business metrics. Companies should consider creating tables, charts and graphs to supplement and clarify the disclosures. Any discussion should consider both the company's use of best practices and any modifications made to controversial programs. Where any material, hot-button feature or program is continued, the reason(s) should be explained. As with all of these disclosures, clear, plain English is recommended to enhance understanding.

Going Forward

While efforts to rationalize pay and enhance communications with shareholders are welcomed, there is some concern that management and board members may feel pressured by say on pay to homogenize their pay programs. Compensation committee members may attempt to attract a substantial majority of "yes" votes by conforming to myriad compensation policy and design guidelines developed by proxy advisers, shareholder representatives, institutional managers and other organizations. In the face of a tide favoring compensation programs that are in compliance with various guidelines and policies, some compensation committees may look to cookie-cutter compensation programs in an effort to avoid criticism. One sign to watch for might be an increase in communications stating that a particular pay component or compensation program is "consistent with our peer group."

At the core, management and compensation committees want pay programs that create human capital advantages in attracting and retaining talented executives and align pay and incentives with the business strategy. As such, companies will continue to strive for appropriate — and at times unique — pay programs that reflect the capabilities of their businesses and executives to drive performance. To the extent that companies color outside of the lines, they need an executive pay strategy that can be clearly conveyed to their stakeholders in an effort to obtain a positive say-on-pay vote.

Encouragingly, discussions about the challenges of say on pay often turn to the opportunities that are presented. Compensation committees generally realize that now is the time to improve both the design of compensation programs to enhance alignment with business performance as well as communications with stakeholders.

13
Compensation Committee Tools and CEO Performance Assessment

By Irv Becker and Dana Martin

One of the important responsibilities of the board of directors is to assess the performance of the CEO; possibly the most important duty of the compensation committee is to make defensible compensation decisions that align executive and shareholder interests while supporting the strategic direction of the company. Ideally, boards and compensation committees should have a wealth of information to fulfill these duties — information that looks at CEO pay and performance from several relevant perspectives.

The reality, however, is that boards and compensation committees often function by responding to specific issues. At one meeting the compensation committee may decide a CEO's salary increase; at another meeting it may determine annual incentive awards; at a third meeting members may discuss severance agreements. The result is a piecemeal approach that often fails to assemble the parts into a cohesive whole. Similarly, in assessing the CEO's performance, boards often tend to focus primarily on financial performance and neglect just as relevant nonfinancial considerations.

Today, many compensation committees recognize the need to take a big picture approach to their executive compensation decision making. They realize that a change in one pay element can influence other pay elements, and that accrued compensation and benefits for a given CEO or top executive may be far greater than they imagined. In demanding more accountability from CEOs and senior management, compensation committees need a more holistic assessment process.

This chapter focuses on the tools that boards and compensation committees can use to help them make more informed decisions regarding CEO assessment and executive pay.

This chapter:

- Maintains that nonfinancial assessment measures in combination with financial metrics can give a more complete picture of CEO performance; there is a discussion of how nonfinancial performance criteria can be gathered and measured in order to approach CEO assessment in an effective manner
- Explains how tally sheets can bring to light the true costs of the executive pay program and offers guidelines for customizing a tally sheet to a company's particular executive pay program
- Discusses four fundamental questions that should be applied in a fitness review to the key aspects of executive compensation (base salary, annual incentives, LTIs, benefits, employment contracts, and severance and change-in-control arrangements) to ensure that they can withstand external scrutiny
- Addresses issues that a compensation committee needs to consider during times of financial instability
- Provides an approach that enables companies to calculate executives' current and future wealth; with accumulated wealth analysis, companies can better align company and executive needs
- Examines issues involved in the claw-back of compensation paid when a financial restatement, fraud or other identified event leads to a finding of unearned or inappropriate payment.

Nonfinancial Evaluation of CEO Performance

It is a truism that in business, the higher you go, the less feedback you receive. Executives are sensitive to that fact, and the best CEOs seek input from others to accurately gauge their performance. Unfortunately, direct reports can easily be intimidated by those senior to them and may not provide honest evaluations of the CEO even when invited, generally due to perceived career risk. An organization's board is in a unique position to provide evaluations of CEO performance, but frequently relies solely upon financial metrics to do so.

The Importance of Nonfinancial Metrics in Measuring CEO Performance

The CEO is responsible for the entire franchise, so quantitative metrics like earnings per share or return on invested capital are good measures of his/her accomplishments. Furthermore, these measures are numerical and objective, not easily open to manipulation and have a major effect on shareholder value. Unfortunately, financial metrics tell only part of the story and are actually lagging indicators of CEO performance. In these days of heightened scrutiny and accountability, boards are increasingly concerned with both what and how results were accomplished.

Indeed, in case after case of corporate malfeasance, a CEO's need to drive financial metrics caused some individuals to cut corners. It is typically only after these mistakes have snowballed that they come to light, all too often destroying shareholder equity and ruining careers in the process. Experienced boards are demanding increased accountability from CEOs for setting corporate culture, demonstrating organizational leadership, building organizational capability and demanding ethical behavior. While publicly traded companies also need to consider the objective, performance-based compensation requirements of Internal Revenue Code (IRC) section 162(m), a board can help meet its oversight mandate by incorporating nonfinancial metrics into its evaluation of CEO performance.

What Is a Nonfinancial Metric?

It is important to distinguish between nonfinancial and nonquantitative metrics. Just because a measure is not financially driven does not mean it is not quantifiable. By establishing benchmarks, boards can clarify what they expect from the CEO to drive financial performance in both the short- and long-term. Through regular and accurate feedback against established benchmarks, boards can support CEOs in improving their performance on soft side competencies that are fundamental to long-term financial success.

Measuring Nonfinancial Factors

Nonfinancial metrics can be established at the beginning of the appraisal process through discussion between the board and the CEO about the business strategy and the implications for CEO evaluation. There should be concrete goals for CEOs who go beyond financial results and address core issues like those described in "Measures of Nonfinancial Performance." At regular intervals, data can be collected to inform the CEO on his/her progress against those objectives. Finally, at a specified time interval, board members should be briefed about goal progress so that they can suggest additional coaching and support as necessary.

There needs to be tangible, measurable targets set for goal achievement in order for the process to work. Fuzzy objectives like "improved executive team morale" are difficult to measure and quantify. Specific goals such as "scores at or above the 75th percentile on the employee engagement survey compared to Fortune 500 norms" provide clearer and more specific targets for the CEO.

Measures of Nonfinancial Performance

Succession: Has the CEO hired and developed a sufficient pipeline of talent to ensure orderly succession should key executives leave?

Values: Has the CEO articulated and embodied a strong values set that serves as the bedrock for organizational performance?

Diversity: What steps has the CEO taken to ensure a diverse, inclusive and fair workplace?

Employee engagement: How connected are the employees to the organization? What do turnover statistics and employee climate surveys reveal?

Strategy: Has the CEO been able to create and align others with a compelling business strategy to take the organization forward in a competitive external business environment?

Structure: What steps has the CEO taken to create the right structure to enable the company to execute the strategy?

Culture: What cultural attributes are evident within the company? Is it the right culture to help execute the business strategy?

Customer satisfaction: Are the company's customers satisfied with the company's products and services? Are key customers being retained?

Organizational capability: Is the human capital of the organization being effectively developed for future success?

Core organization processes: Are key operational processes being improved?

One example of a nonfinancial metric that can be used for CEO evaluation is organizational climate. Research finds a strong relationship between leaders creating positive work climates and organizational performance. Through anonymous feedback collected from direct reports, the CEO can gain a better understanding of how the work atmosphere is enabling or undermining organizational performance.

Feedback from all directions also can be effective in evaluating CEO performance. When using a 360-degree process, however, the CEO should be inclusive in gathering data from a wide range of sources and protecting the anonymity of the respondents. Because the results are highly sensitive, the utmost care needs to be established in data collection and storage and deciding who is privy to the results. Data can be obtained using online data collection tools or through the use of external consultants who can conduct confidential interviews, providing aggregate feedback to the CEO.

Data should be gathered from multiple sources in evaluating the performance of a sitting CEO. The CEO has many constituencies, and it is important to be inclusive when evaluating his/her performance. Look to gather a variety of inputs in providing the most relevant data to help guide performance improvement. The board itself is one of the most important bases of performance-improvement feedback.

The use of several types of measures is advisable in CEO evaluations. A confluence of data points increases the CEO's confidence in the accuracy of measurement. By employing multiple ways of measuring performance, the credibility of the conclusions is enhanced.

CEO evaluation data is sensitive, and the utmost care needs to be taken to ensure the confidentiality and privacy of all involved. At the beginning of the evaluation it is critical to establish who will have access to the data and how it will be used. Keeping the circle small helps CEOs make the best use of the information in building their capabilities to lead.

Additional Considerations for Effective CEO Evaluation

A board needs to approach CEO evaluation in a collaborative and supportive fashion. In that way, directors can effectively provide the guidance and wisdom necessary to guide the CEO through rocky times and build the trust necessary to have impact in improving CEO performance.

The use of an objective third party may be helpful to provide the feedback and/or coaching necessary to assist the CEO in getting the most out of the evaluation data. While a board member who has the ear of the CEO may be effective in furnishing performance feedback, a professional experienced in executive assessment and coaching can facilitate the process.

Effective CEO evaluation is a process, not an event. If feedback is held back until a year-end evaluation, there could be unwelcome surprises that derail the positive spirit that should underlie the entire undertaking. However, if board members are able to furnish input to the CEO on an ongoing basis, the likelihood of midcourse corrections increases.

CEOs are being evaluated continually on their business results by shareholders and employees. By adding nonfinancial metrics to the mix, CEOs can gain a more holistic view of their leadership and tease out the critical factors that contribute to their long-term leadership effectiveness.

Tally Sheets: Adding Up the Cost of Executive Compensation

Due to an increased scrutiny of executive compensation, corporate boards have turned to tally sheets to obtain a comprehensive view of the true size of executive pay packages. A tally sheet is a detailed compilation of all major components of executive compensation, including base salary, annual incentives, LTIs, retirement programs, and various benefits and perquisites.

While the particulars vary from company to company, the essence of a tally sheet is a summary of an executive's total pay package. To present a true picture, a tally sheet should consider not only what an executive receives during employment, but also what he/she may receive upon the various events that may result in a termination of employment. The value of tally sheets has been recognized as an important tool for compensation committees, and their use has become a common (and best) practice. A substantial majority of public companies already are using some form of tally sheets.

Board members at many companies may not have a "big picture" perspective on all elements of compensation, particularly the benefits, perquisites and termination pay that an executive may receive. For example, this can occur where different elements of compensation and benefits packages are addressed at different times, perhaps without considering how a change in one piece may affect another. Tally sheets can provide boards with a holistic and long-term look at each pay component, the relationships among these elements, and the potential future value of each element under different scenarios — particularly those causing a termination of employment.

As previously noted, decisions on executive pay often are made on a piecemeal basis. Compounded with the fact that many compensation committee members serve on a rotational basis, the committee may lack the historical or other perspective to make comprehensive pay decisions. Too often tally sheets have revealed unexpectedly high (even shocking) aggregate pay packages, causing directors to experience "holy cow!" moments. (See "Benefits of Tally Sheets.")

Tally Sheet Guidelines

While any tally sheet has to be tailored to a company's specific programs, following are some suggested basic guidelines on the level and scope of data that should be included:

- A recent history (e.g., three to five years) of base salary, target annual incentives, actual annual incentives, LTIs, benefits and perquisites
- All vested and unvested equity awards
- The current spread values of all outstanding vested and unvested stock options and stock appreciation rights (SARs) and the current value of all other LTI awards
- The estimated size of the next LTI plan payout and any other LTI plan cycles in progress
- The current value of an executive's interest (both vested and unvested) under all tax-qualified retirement plans and under all nonqualified SERPs, as well as a projection of future payouts.

Benefits of Tally Sheets

Understanding the Costs of Executive Terminations
A compensation committee should be aware of the aggregate value of amounts payable to the CEO and other top executives upon termination of employment. These scenarios should include retirement, death, disability, dismissal, dismissal for cause, voluntary resignation, resignation for good reason and termination in connection with a change in control. To simplify the presentation, those termination events that call for the same payouts can, in many cases, be grouped. By understanding what has been promised under executive contracts and various programs, directors can avoid surprise and/or embarrassment. Tally sheets help ensure that compensation committees are aware of the cost and timing of potential payouts, as well as the terms and conditions that trigger payment.

Revealing the True Value of Executive Benefits and Perquisites
Although compensation committees have been accustomed to tallying top executives' base salaries, annual incentive pay and LTIs, they often have overlooked benefits and perquisites. Compensation committees need to know more than the types of benefits provided; they must understand the value of the benefits and perquisites. Before approving executive pay changes, compensation committees should understand the costs, tax treatment and financial accounting consequences of these modifications to their benefits and perquisites program.

Creating Greater Alignment with the Company's Compensation Philosophy
When decisions on various components of an executive's total pay are made at different times throughout the year, the compensation committee needs to consider how each program fits in the company's overall compensation philosophy. Tally sheets look at the compensation and benefits in totality, allowing the compensation committee to determine the appropriate mix by considering relationships among pay components. A compensation committee should test its tally sheets annually against its compensation philosophy and determine whether the pay philosophy is delivering the appropriate value over time.

- The amounts payable on various termination events (as identified). Tally sheets can be valuable tools for boards in making the most appropriate executive pay decisions. Because compensation committees are responsible for executive pay, it is essential that members are fully aware of all elements of compensation. No compensation committee should feel comfortable in approving an executive pay program without understanding its potential costs, especially payments due after employment terminates.

Executive Compensation Fitness Check

Executive compensation increasingly has become a focal point of potential vulnerability. The media, shareholder groups and their advisers, various prominent boards and commissions and Congress all have described executive compensation as a motivating force behind a purported decline in corporate responsibility.

Compensation committees should periodically conduct a "fitness check" to ascertain whether the company's executive compensation programs can effectively withstand external scrutiny.

Fundamental Questions

Four fundamental questions typically are addressed when conducting a fitness check:

1. Are the compensation programs and policies consistent with shareholders' expectations?
   – Do executives' share ownership standards, share retention requirements and stock sale/option exercise procedures align their interests with those of shareholders?
   – Do cash and equity programs encourage no more than the level and nature of business and investment risk expected by shareholders?
   – Are plan designs and approval processes sufficiently transparent?
   – Is the board governance process adequate with respect to compensation?
   – Are executive incentive (both cash- and equity-based) programs, retirement vehicles and deferred compensation opportunities fair to both the shareholders and executives? Are they tax effective?
   – Is the amount of shareholders' equity dilution appropriate?
   – Are the payments, terms and conditions of severance and change-in-control policies appropriate in both favorable and adverse scenarios?
2. Are the programs appropriately competitive and defensible? Are all elements of the rewards and benefits structure:
   – Appropriately positioned?
   – Internally equitable?
   – Externally competitive?
   – Consistent with good pay practices?
   – Consistent with an appropriate peer group?
   – Reflective of scope of business and role/accountability?
   – Appropriately balanced for both short- and long-term rewards and motivation?

- Consistent with an articulated and supportable rewards strategy?
3. Are the programs and payments linked to corporate strategy and business performance?
   - Does the design drive actions and strategies that enhance value while also promoting ethical behaviors?
   - Are the goals and rewards tied to significant improvements in business operations or company finances?
   - Do the rewards encourage no more than the desired level of business risk?
   - Are the arrangements comprehensive and comprehensible?
   - Are the programs consistent with best practices?
4. Are relative executive-rewards levels and relative performance aligned appropriately?
   - Do the history of payouts under incentive programs and the levels of compensation increases correlate to recent business performance and drivers of shareholder value?
   - Are the rewards levels based on proper broad-based and industry-specific peer groups?
   - Does relative total direct compensation correlate to total shareholder return?
   - Does actual pay delivered correlate to a corresponding degree of performance against relevant value drivers (e.g., cash flow, earnings-per-share growth, return on invested capital, market share, new-product sales, customer satisfaction)?
   - Are the number, weighting and reinforcement of rewards measures appropriate?

In addressing these questions, consideration must be given, at a minimum, to five key aspects of executive compensation:
- Base salary
- Short- and long-term incentives
- Executive benefits (including retirement and insurance arrangements)
- Employment contracts
- Severance and change-in-control arrangements.

In addition, a separate review should be conducted of the board's own compensation programs and its governance processes related to executive compensation.

To reinforce an independent perspective, an independent outside consultant should be retained. He/she should report directly to the chair of the board's compensation committee for the fitness check.

Because the specific components of any fitness check must be customized to an organization's circumstances and objectives, the scope of any review varies from company to company.

An Action Plan for Compensation Committees During Economic Uncertainty

Economic instability often affects executive compensation in unforeseen ways. During such times corporate boards — and particularly their compensation committees — should step back and critically assess their executive compensation programs. Outlined below is a proposed compensation committee action plan that can serve as a starting point to discuss current executive compensation issues.

Review of the Recent Past

Question: How has the business and share price performed in the past several months?

Action: It is critical for the compensation committee to have a thorough understanding of how the company is performing on an absolute basis and on a relative basis against comparable organizations. Even if the company has seen a recent decline in its share price, it nevertheless may have fared well in comparison to its peers. Especially during times of economic upheaval, it is important for the compensation committee to receive frequent financial performance updates along with the resulting effect on executive incentive and retirement plans.

Question: What is the company's relative market position in total compensation?

Action: The executive compensation landscape is changing. A company that has seen its stock price fall dramatically may need to deliver significantly more equity to simply maintain similar levels of compensation as prior years; however, this may not be desirable in terms of share usage or potential value of an ultimate award settlement. Boards need to have current market information (proxy information may not reflect current conditions to the reporting lag) and leading edge thinking regarding proper and reasonable award levels.

Issues Arising: Annual Incentive Plan

Question: Is the plan rewarding the right outcomes and encouraging the right behaviors?

Action: An economic downturn is not necessarily the time to discard an incentive plan, but it is the time to ensure the plan is rewarding behaviors that are necessary to maintain the business and prepare the company for when conditions improve. An assessment of the current annual incentive plan against a new business plan, as well as a review of the incentive plan mechanics and other features, builds confidence that the company is driving and rewarding the correct behaviors.

Issues Arising: Long-Term Incentives

Question: Are events (e.g., failure to pay out, poor payouts, underwater options, unvested awards) causing attraction, retention or motivation issues?

Action: As a regular course of action, whether in good or bad financial times, compensation committees need to be aware of the type and levels of long-term incentive (LTI) grants that are made to their executives. Committee meetings periodically should include an LTI grant history and status of each grant to unearth potential attraction, retention and motivation issues.

Issues Arising: Executive Share Ownership Requirements

Question: Is a falling share price creating significant top-up requirements for executives?

Action: Companies often require their executives to hold shares that are equal to a multiple of salary. When stock prices are falling, executives can fall below their holding requirements. The compensation committee should request an updated ownership analysis to determine if a share price decline has produced any concerns and then decide upon the appropriate action.

Executive Pay Decisions: The Past

Questions: Should anything be done to change annual incentive payments generated in the recent past? What are the contractual/legal issues for any retrospective bonus reductions?

Action: The compensation committee needs to thoroughly understand the features and contractual language tied to the incentive plans. Compensation committee members should request a legal review focusing on what the committee can and cannot do regarding incentive payments. Additionally, committee members should benchmark their current practices against other similarly situated companies, including a consideration of risk mitigation concepts such as the possible use of bonus banking, clawbacks and holding requirements.

Executive Pay Decisions: The Future

Questions: Does the company need to adopt any interim incentive plans to deal with its current circumstances? If so, what should their features be? How long should they operate? Should cash and/or equity be used? What performance measures are appropriate?

Action: Interim incentive plans typically cover six months to two years and can be very effective in driving behaviors in turnaround and restructuring situations. Boards should review all viable options to drive and support company performance, including interim incentive plans.

Two Basic Questions

Question: Does the company need to change its business strategy in response to changing market conditions?

Action: If the answer is yes, then does the business strategy include shorter- and longer-term requirements that could be supported or reinforced via the compensation program? A compensation committee facing a business strategy change should consider all potential incentive plans at its disposal. This includes reviewing the flexibility of the company's short- and long-term incentive plans.

Question: Does the company's executive rewards strategy still support its business strategy?

Action: Assuming the company is going forward with a new business strategy, the compensation committee should ensure that the current rewards programs are supporting the strategy; at a minimum, compensation arrangements should not inhibit the strategy.

Starting Points for a Discussion on Executive Pay

Much of the action plan laid out here cannot be completed without establishing an overall perspective on executive compensation in the current environment. Some critical areas for consideration and action by the entire board of directors to guide actions by the compensation committee include:

- Agree upon what success would look like for the company considering current and short-term business conditions.
- Agree upon who the key executives are in this context.
- Agree upon the critical actions and behaviors required from these executives.
- Identify the key areas of business risk and the timeframes over which these may be resolved.
- Identify any new constraints on the company's freedom to act arising from known shareholders' views, regulatory considerations, tax impacts and other legal concerns.

Accumulated Wealth Analysis: Worth Considering?

Compensation committees are only beginning to gain a better understanding of the total wealth potential of all of an executive's past, current and projected future compensation and benefits. Studies have found that an increasing number of companies are taking accumulated wealth into account when making pay decisions. Given the expanded disclosure of executive pay, this trend likely will continue.

Why is accumulated wealth analysis important? From an executive's perspective, accumulated wealth provides security, independence and the funding of retirement objectives. To the extent that accumulated wealth enables an executive to retire, it can open opportunities for identified candidates to develop and move up in the organization.

Overview of Accumulated Wealth Analysis

An accumulated wealth analysis starts with an examination of awards and accruals under all company-sponsored wealth-accumulation vehicles, particularly an executive's equity interests and retirement benefits (including deferred compensation). While companies may develop and conduct the analysis in various ways, the clear goal is to understand the total wealth position/potential of the executive. A key objective of executive compensation is the creation of wealth for those who enhance shareholder value through successful management of entrusted resources. Accumulated wealth can be especially large where total shareholder returns are strong.

Examining Equity

Because the vast majority of public companies deliver a sizeable portion of compensation in the form of equity-based vehicles (e.g., stock options, restricted stock, performance shares), the process includes the consideration of these grants.

- **Gains from past grants:** The analysis begins with ascertaining the compensation an executive has realized from past grants. While vested grants have lower retention value, retained equity has wealth accumulation value that becomes increasingly important as the executive contemplates retirement.
- **Outstanding equity:** Outstanding equity, whether vested or unvested, should be included in the accumulated wealth analysis because such grants have true economic value. One complication to including outstanding equity is projecting the future gains/losses in stock price for the model. This will have a dramatic effect on the value of stock options (i.e., stock options only have value at prices above the exercise price, while time-vested restricted stock retains some value at all stock prices short of implosion of the company). Additionally, compensation committees should consider the mix of vested and unvested awards when making future pay decisions.
- **Future grants:** A consideration of projected future grants provides information regarding the future value of all equity vehicles at retirement. Again, this type of analysis requires modeling

of future stock price, but will often yield that "ah-ha" moment when the compensation committee realizes the potential wealth accumulation assuming continued grants at the current level.

How Much Is Enough?

The obvious use of the wealth-accumulation analysis is to determine how much wealth has been and will be created. It certainly can be argued that an executive with 100 to 200 times salary in accumulated wealth through his/her stock-based compensation does not need further motivation/alignment via company stock performance. On the other hand, one to four times salary is not enough to provide an executive with financial security, nor the ability to retire or change his/her venue in retirement. Also, current compensation and the opportunity for more wealth operate to motivate and retain the executive.

It is in the middle, and not at the extremes, where compensation committees must discuss and develop a strategy around how much is enough. The objective is not to reduce compensation as much as to understand at what point additional wealth is offset by an executive's desire to enjoy the fruits of his/her labor. Simply "turning off the spigot" is not a viable alternative because the executive could choose to work for a competitor that is more than willing to pay going market rates with the full complement of incentive plan awards. Rather, it is important to align rewards with shareholder value as well as executive needs and desires.

Alignment with Shareholders?

Suggestions have been made that the true use of an accumulated wealth analysis should be to ensure alignment in wealth creation of the executive and the shareholders. While shareholders contribute capital, executives contribute "sweat equity" in earning their wealth. Therefore, converting income to wealth should be an objective. In its simplest form, one would compare the value that could be realized based on accumulated grants and cash to actual company performance.

For example, CEO-realized compensation may be examined during
a five-year period and compared to a peer group of companies.
A comparison of total shareholder return would be included in
the analysis. Ideally, realized pay positioning would align with
performance (e.g., pay at the 75th percentile would align with the
75th percentile of total shareholder return).

Revisit Severance Agreements

Severance agreements and contracts often are structured to provide
an executive with a term "insurance policy" to cover loss of income
stemming from the loss of a job. Using the accumulated wealth
analysis can help directors determine if there is a need for such
term insurance going forward. Is there a level of accumulated
wealth that makes the term insurance provided by a severance
agreement unnecessary?

Succession Planning Tool

The use of the accumulated wealth analysis as a tool in succession
planning is an often overlooked application. As companies lean more
toward developing executive talent in-house, they need to understand
and strategically manage the amount of wealth each future leader
has accumulated to date and his/her future earning potential.

In the case of succession planning, the board and the executive team ideally would build up enough ownership over time to
align the wealth creation of the executive with shareholder value
creation, as well as ensure the incumbent stays and performs until
a viable successor can be established.

An accumulated wealth analysis is another valuable input for
compensation committees when managing an executive's total
rewards. As boards are pressed to consider past compensation
decisions when reviewing current compensation, it is expected that
the adoption of this practice will increase among boards and the
application will evolve. Because the accumulated wealth analysis
is fairly new to most compensation committees, they need to be
wary of setting arbitrary caps on compensation and avoid trying to
immediately align with industry norms; rather, a more productive

approach would involve engaging in a dialogue based on the company's and executive's particular circumstances.

Recouping Executive Pay: Clawbacks

Clawbacks have emerged as a seemingly attractive means of redressing "unearned" compensation. As corporate governance groups and shareholders advocated for the adoption of general policies or terms in executive agreements and incentive plans to enable a company to recapture bonuses and other incentive-based rewards in appropriate circumstances, companies increasingly developed clawback provisions suited to their own particular circumstances.

Initially spurred on by fairly narrow recovery provisions in the Sarbanes-Oxley Act of 2002, Congress included clawbacks in the terms for troubled institutions that received U.S. Department of Treasury investments under 2009 legislation. Congress then moved to center stage with the inclusion of mandatory, fairly rigid clawback requirements (subject to relevant U.S. Securities and Exchange Commission [SEC] rulemaking and implementation of stock exchange listing standards) in the Dodd-Frank Wall Street Reform and Consumer Protection Act of 2010 applicable to public companies.

In general, Dodd-Frank contains considerably broader clawback rules than the clawback provisions under Sarbanes-Oxley. For example, Dodd-Frank's clawbacks apply to any executive officer (not just the CEO and CFO), do not require any misconduct (just simply the requisite restatement described in the next section on "Putting Clawbacks in Context"), and cover a three-year (rather than 12-month) period. Public companies subject to Dodd-Frank's mandates also should consider including any additional features or processes that address the organization's particular circumstances or facilitate administration.

As noted, clawbacks were endorsed well before Dodd-Frank as significant corporate governance tools to deter management from taking actions that could potentially harm the company's financial position; a compensation committee may decide to go beyond the strictures of Dodd-Frank in crafting its policy. Compensation committees should keep in mind that the objective is to eliminate — or, failing that, at least recapture — undeserved payouts to executives, not simply those caught by statutory and regulatory initiatives.

Putting Clawbacks in Context

Traditionally, a clawback is a formal policy or a provision in an employment agreement or compensation plan that permits a company, often in its discretion (typically exercised by the board or compensation committee), to recapture cash and/or equity incentive payments from certain employees — generally senior executives — for one or more reasons (set out in the particular program or agreement). Putting aside the statutory and regulatory mandates noted above, a policy or provision may authorize a clawback if:

- An executive has been deemed responsible for fraudulent actions
- Incentive payments were based on misstated financials, especially if the result of fraud or negligence
- An executive has violated enforceable noncompete provisions or other restrictive covenants
- An executive has been responsible for defined actions detrimental to the company.

Clawbacks can be designed to be triggered by any one of these identified events; definitions of covered events and the consequences can vary considerably across companies as long as the mandated events and circumstances are covered. The most common triggers among the largest U.S. public companies are a financial restatement by the company (e.g., Dodd-Frank's "required ... accounting restatement due to the material noncompliance ... with any financial reporting requirement under the securities laws ...") or an executive's ethical misconduct. The next most prevalent event is a violation of a noncompetition agreement.

Even when clawback provisions are included in an executive's employment agreement or an incentive compensation plan, it may be unclear whether a specific event was actually triggered or, except as legally required, whether the clawback should be enforced (e.g., an executive was unaware of the improper activity and it was not within his/her job responsibilities).

Covered Compensation

As clawbacks grew in prevalence (and became the subject of legal mandates), the definition of "covered compensation" became more expansive. Initial provisions focused on cash-based bonuses; recently, clawbacks have broadened to include equity compensation — both vested and unvested stock awards. Research indicates that the vast majority of policies included both cash and equity incentive compensation (e.g., "incentive-based compensation [including stock options awarded as compensation]" under Dodd-Frank) in their definition of compensation subject to clawback. The addition of equity compensation to clawbacks increases the complexity of enforcement; both the impact of income taxes paid by the executive on the original award and the company's stock price at time of enforcement versus at time of award may be appropriate to consider in determining the value to be repaid by the executive.

Board Considerations in Developing a Clawback Policy

Before adopting clawback provisions, boards and compensation committees need to think through both the legal requirements and the possible application of the clawback provisions. Clawback provisions may seem straightforward, but actual implementation commonly surfaces many issues that need to be reviewed and thoroughly discussed.

Which Employees Should Be Covered Under the Provisions?

Recoveries under Dodd-Frank extend to "any current and former executive officer," with a number of practical difficulties inherent in recouping pay from a former officer. The further down in the organization that the recovery provision extends, the more likely the provision will be viewed favorably by corporate governance groups.

Which Compensation Elements Should Be Covered? Should the Provision Only Apply to Cash Compensation or Both Cash and Equity?

As previously noted, Dodd-Frank requires the clawback of any incentive-based compensation; companies may decide to extend compensation recoupments even further. Base salary typically is not covered in clawback arrangements because base compensation is not usually linked to specific performance objectives. Many companies are adopting provisions that directly link their clawback provisions to all performance-based pay, including both cash and equity compensation. Apart from what Dodd-Frank requires, another design consideration is how to implement the repayment of gains generated by stock sales if the stock price was affected by misstated financial information.

Should the Board Have Discretion in Applying the Provision? Or Should a Portion Be Mandated by Pre-established Contractual Provisions?

The issue of discretion in clawbacks is a delicate balancing act. On one hand, discretion allows a board to apply judgment with respect to the scope of a clawback. However, Dodd-Frank requires (within its scope), and corporate governance groups generally support, mandatory clawbacks due to concern that discretion may be applied too freely and clawbacks not enforced sufficiently. To the extent that the application of a clawback is discretionary, particular care is needed to make sure that its scope is carefully defined (and circumscribed) so as not to be subject to discriminatory application.

How Far Back Should Clawbacks Extend?

Many of the earlier clawback provisions adopted the 12-month period applicable under the Sarbanes-Oxley Act. As the scope of clawbacks grew to encompass LTIs, some companies extended their clawbacks to 24 and even 36 months. Dodd-Frank calls for clawbacks "during the three-year period preceding the date on which the issuer is required to prepare an accounting restatement, based on the erroneous data ..." Subject to that mandate, boards need to exercise caution that clawbacks do not extend so far back in time that executives view incentive opportunities and related payments as too high risk to have real value.

Where Should Clawback Provisions Exist?

Some companies have adopted clawback policies that then are incorporated by reference into the relevant plans and agreements. Other companies prefer to add clawback language to all employment agreements and incentive plan documents. This second approach arguably provides companies with a stronger contractual basis for enforcing the clawback in cases of actual violations. Many groups recommend placing the clawback language in the incentive plan documents because at public companies these are subject to shareholder approval and avoid unnecessarily opening up existing employment agreements.

What Does Applicable State Law Provide Regarding the Enforceability of the Particular Clawback Provisions and Their Scope?

Various states, most notably California, have expansive laws protecting employee rights that apply to matters such as the employment relationship, earnings and noncompetition restrictions. While clawback provisions actually required by Dodd-Frank should preempt state law, other (additional) recovery language that causes the forfeiture of compensation can be especially problematic in certain jurisdictions. Before developing broad clawback language and extending it across the country (never mind globally), a company is well-advised to assess the enforceability of key aspects of the provision in all relevant locations and the potential consequences of devising a program that may not be enforceable (whether all or in part).

Looking Ahead

While clawbacks increasingly are viewed as a common sense solution to "undeserved" executive compensation, various facts and issues specific to a company's circumstances should be considered in designing any clawback policy or specific provision. Because U.S. public companies are compelled by Dodd-Frank to adopt clawback provisions, they need to be aware of the factors that can affect the appropriate design. Companies should focus on developing provisions that address legitimate concerns while balancing the need to attract and retain executives.

14
Disclosure of Executive Pay

By Bill Gerek

Executive pay disclosure goes hand in hand with other legislative and regulatory attempts to achieve accountability and transparency in all matters relating to corporate governance. An interesting development in the past few years is that lawmakers, instead of handing over decision making to the usual regulatory agencies, have become active players in governance matters, even setting pay in troubled industries.

In executive pay disclosure, the U.S. Securities and Exchange Commission's (SEC's) expanded disclosure rules adopted in 2006 and 2009 and the Dodd-Frank Wall Street Reform and Consumer Protection Act of 2010 have considerably altered the disclosure landscape. Companies must now provide more detailed tabular information, additional narrative in the Compensation Discussion and Analysis (CD&A), information on the qualifications of directors and their fees, the degree of risk-taking inherent in pay programs, and the rationale behind the company's leadership structure.

The disclosure of so much information in numerous public documents, each with a distinct reporting schedule and format, makes the work of the compensation committee increasingly more difficult and time-consuming. This is especially true when it comes to disclosing equity compensation, comprised as it often is of several different vehicles and overlapping grants over multi-year periods. The actual total value of equity pay granted and realized over time may be quite different from the snapshot that appears each year in the proxy. We believe compensation committees need to collect and analyze data in a way that allows for a more complete understanding and communication of reported values.

This chapter:

- Reviews the purpose of the CD&A, its connection with the new compensation committee report, and issues and actions to make the CD&A a more meaningful document.

- Discusses the key issues of the SEC's 2009 final rules expanding proxy disclosure in public companies, including the requirement to discuss the extent that pay programs might encourage harmful risk-taking, equity awards to directors, and the company's leadership structure.

- Provides a three-part mechanism for measuring executive pay to better understand how pay programs interact over time and facilitate the communication of executive pay programs to shareholders.

- Reviews say on pay, say on parachutes, clawback policies, and other provisions of Dodd-Frank.

Challenges of the Compensation Discussion and Analysis

In 2006 the SEC adopted substantially expanded executive compensation disclosure rules that were described as a "wakeup call" by the SEC's director of the division of corporation finance. Of particular importance is the CD&A section that was added as a required component of annual proxy statements. Companies have been forced to focus not just on the "what" but also the "why" in executive pay disclosure.

Objectives of the CD&A

In its commentary on the CD&A, the SEC envisioned the section as "overview providing narrative disclosure that puts into context the compensation disclosure provided elsewhere" for a company's named executive officers. The expressed objective was to "explain material elements" of these executives' compensation; critical to this process are six questions that should be addressed:

- What are the objectives of the company's compensation programs?
- What is the compensation program designed to reward?
- What is each element of compensation?
- Why does the company choose to pay each element?

- How does the company determine the amount (and, where applicable, the formula) for each element?
- How does each element and the company's decisions regarding that element fit into the company's overall compensation objectives and affect decisions regarding other elements?

At the time of the 2006 rulemaking, executive pay disclosure at many companies had become standardized — often largely boilerplate — and furnished little meaningful guidance on how executive pay actually is determined. In requiring a CD&A, key SEC goals were to encourage much more thoughtful analysis by compensation committees in determining executive pay and to have these pay considerations thoroughly disclosed. Many statements in the CD&A require significant elaboration; it is not sufficient to state that "pay is based on performance" or that "compensation is targeted at the median of comparable (or peer) organizations." Rather, *how* these standards are applied needs to be described, along with relevant policies, factors and regulatory impact.

Relation of CD&A to the Compensation Committee Report

Although the CD&A discusses compensation policies and decisions, it does not address the compensation committee's deliberations because it is not a report of the compensation committee; rather the CD&A is the company's responsibility. However, the 2006 SEC rules also mandated a new form of compensation committee report that requires the committee to state whether:

- It has reviewed and discussed the CD&A with management
- The committee recommended to the board of directors that the CD&A be included in the company's annual report and proxy (based on the aforementioned review and discussions).

Potential Liability Under the CD&A

While the compensation committee report is considered "furnished" to the SEC, the CD&A is a filed document. This technical distinction means that the CD&A is considered to be part of the proxy statement and the disclosures are covered by the Sarbanes-Oxley Act of 2002 certifications required of principal executive officers and principal financial officers. The potential liability was designed to increase attention to the statements made.

Issues to Address in the CD&A

The CD&A is principles-based (rather than rules-based) and the SEC intends that it furnish perspective on the numbers and other executive pay information contained in required tables and elsewhere. A significant challenge presented by the CD&A has been articulating the rationale underlying the components of the executive compensation package for each named executive officer. The SEC's rulemaking provided nonexclusive examples of potentially appropriate issues that might reasonably be addressed in the CD&A; each should be considered in light of the organization's particular facts and circumstances. The CD&A must be comprehensive in scope; a company should describe any compensation policies it applies, even if not covered in the SEC's examples. The discussion also should address post-employment arrangements relating to compensation.

Besides the breadth of its requirements, the CD&A calls for greater depth than had been customary in compensation committee reports. While a CD&A generally should avoid repetition of the exhaustive information presented in tables and other portions of the proxy, it should identify material differences in compensation policies and decisions applicable to individual named executive officers. Considerable thought and effort can be required to determine what should be discussed and then to prepare the appropriate explanation — which must be written in plain English.

Areas that May Require Particular Attention

The examples provided by the SEC include some items that previously received scant attention in most proxy statements. In expanding the scope of executive pay disclosure, the SEC implicitly furnished its views on items that should be considered in executive compensation design.

- The SEC identified the familiar concept of benchmarking as a particular subject for disclosure. Information is needed on the benchmark for any material element of an executive's compensation, including the component companies (peer group) used for the benchmark. This requirement has increased the focus on having an appropriate peer group and choosing reasonable benchmarks. In comment letters from the SEC in the wake of proxy filings under these rules, benchmarking has been one of the main sources of SEC inquiries.

- One example from the SEC suggests discussing how gains from prior option awards are considered in setting other elements of compensation. By identifying the topic, the SEC implies that compensation committees should look at this issue.
- The well-publicized concerns some years ago at dozens of companies regarding the timing (a concept broader than backdating) and pricing of stock options caused the SEC to specifically provide for extensive disclosure regarding the timing and pricing of option grants. Various elements and questions were identified by the SEC for disclosure; these should be considered in determining the appropriate use and design of stock options in a company's executive pay program.
- Another example refers to a company's equity ownership guidelines and mentions any policies regarding hedging an executive's economic risk of such ownership. Many organizations have since developed hedging policies rather than state that they do not have any such policy. As mentioned later in this chapter, hedging policies were addressed in Dodd-Frank and extended to all employees and directors.
- Because the impact of the accounting and tax treatment of a particular form of compensation is one issue that the SEC views as potentially appropriate for discussion, an organization might consider the role played by various regulatory provisions (e.g., the $1 million deduction cap and the detailed regulation of NQDC under IRC sections 162(m) and 409A, respectively, and the accounting impact under ASC Topic 718) in selecting the form and design of awards.

Recommended Actions

The following actions should be useful for most companies:

- Start the process early each year. Every party with responsibility regarding a CD&A needs to appreciate the significant effort that can be required to satisfy the disclosure standards — a narrative approach that considers a lengthy list of issues. A critical factor in managing this compliance process involves having sufficient time to fully vet all compensation issues that might need to be discussed.

- Develop an overall understanding of the objectives and requirements for the CD&A, working with advisers as needed.

- Internal personnel and external advisers (ideally including attorneys, accountants and compensation consultants) should work together and undertake the preparation of a "mock" CD&A. Generally it is helpful to take the company's most recent CD&A as a starting point, but then view every statement with fresh eyes to assess its applicability for the relevant year. New information is added, irrelevant material is deleted, and the whole reconsidered in light of the particulars of the company and its industry as well as relevant legislation and regulations, economic considerations and a host of other factors. A key focus is on clarity, organization and presentation. When the parties actually commence this process, they realize how much is involved in crafting a focused discussion of the appropriate issues for the CD&A.

- The compensation committee should be involved. While a company has responsibility for the preparation and filing of a proxy statement and the CD&A, it is the handiwork of the compensation committee that is being explained in the CD&A. The SEC clearly expects that compensation-committee decisions will be affected by the knowledge that they will be subject to full disclosure.

- Once an organization understands the scope of the tasks involved in crafting the year's CD&A, it should identify any issues that need to be addressed and information that should be included in the CD&A. As instructed by the SEC, each company needs to focus on its particular facts and circumstances. Minutes of compensation committee meetings, reports of internal staff and consultants, and various plan documents and summaries may be helpful to examine as part of this process.

- A draft CD&A should be circulated among the working group for comment. During an iterative review process, all parties should keep in mind the ultimate goals of a clear yet comprehensive overview of the company's executive pay determinations.

Enhanced Disclosure of Executive Pay

The regulation of executive compensation accelerated in 2009 as Congress, the Obama Administration, and various regulatory agencies all added their voices to the debate surrounding sound executive pay practices. Near the close of 2009, the SEC adopted final rules further expanding proxy disclosure of executive compensation for public companies. Following is an overview of these SEC rules and some of the key compliance issues. These rules generally were effective for fiscal years ending after Dec. 19, 2009 for proxy statements and annual reports filed on or after Feb. 28, 2010.

Relationship of the Company's Compensation Policies and Practices to Risk

Under the 2009 rules, public companies must discuss compensation policies and practices for all employees — not just named executive officers (NEOs) — to the extent that risks arising from them are "reasonably likely to have a material adverse effect" on the company. Companies need to identify and then review all compensation arrangements to determine whether there are potential risks that might trigger disclosure. Any problems discovered in the review process then can be fixed or appropriately mitigated.

The SEC furnished examples of situations that could potentially trigger discussion and analysis:

- A business unit of the company carries a significant portion of the company's risk profile.
- A business unit has a significantly different compensation structure than other units.
- A business unit is significantly more profitable than others within the company.
- Compensation expense at a business unit represents a significant percentage of the unit's revenues.
- Compensation policies and practices vary significantly from the overall risk and reward structure of the company.

In assessing the degree of risk, companies can consider any compensation policies and practices designed to alleviate risk or balance incentives (e.g., clawbacks and recoupment policies, bonus banking, stock ownership requirements). The type of disclosure is determined on a case-by-case basis, but may include:

- The general design philosophy of compensation policies for employees whose behavior would be most influenced by the incentive programs
- The company's risk assessment or considerations in structuring its incentive compensation policies
- The ways in which the company's compensation policies relate to the realization of risks resulting from the actions of employees (e.g., through the use of clawbacks, holding periods)
- The company's policies regarding adjustments to its compensation practices to address changes in its risk profile
- Material adjustments the registrant has made to its compensation policies or practices as a result of changes in its risk profile
- The extent to which the registrant monitors its compensation policies to determine whether risk management objectives are being met.

Risk-related disclosure has its own section and is not included in the CD&A. Importantly, as stated in the final rules, the SEC does "not require a company to make an affirmative statement that it has determined that the risks arising from its compensation policies and practices are not likely to have a material adverse effect on the company." In view of this limitation on the disclosure that is required, companies have been split on whether they should take the next step to voluntarily make such an affirmative statement that they maintain no such unreasonably risky compensation programs.

Reporting of Equity Awards to Executives and Directors

The full grant-date fair value of stock option and share awards is reported in both the Summary Compensation Table and Director Compensation Table. Rules under FASB ASC Topic 718 require that compensation expense be recognized for financial reporting purposes, which affects the calculation of total compensation used to determine a company's named executive officers. Companies had to update values shown in the stock award, option award and total compensation columns for prior years for each named executive officer. Disclosure of grant-date fair values of individual equity awards also continues in the Grant of Plan-Based Awards Table.

Disclosure Regarding Fees Affecting Independence of Compensation Consultants

The new disclosure rules require a company to disclose the fees paid to a compensation consultant if the consultant furnished consulting services related to executive or director compensation as well as other services to the company. However, fee disclosure is not required if the fees paid to the consultant for additional services did not exceed $120,000 during the company's fiscal year. When disclosure is required, it must include:

- Aggregate fees paid for executive and director compensation consulting services
- Aggregate fees paid for nonexecutive compensation consulting services
- Whether the decision to engage the consultant for nonexecutive compensation consulting services was made or recommended by management and whether the committee or board approved the other services, if the consultant was engaged by the compensation committee.

Disclosure on the Qualifications of Directors and Nominees

Under the disclosure requirements, a company must discuss the particular experience, qualifications, attributes or skills that qualify an individual to serve as a director for the company, based on the company's business and structure at the time the disclosure is being made. However, the rules do not require disclosure regarding the specifics that qualify the individual to serve as a committee member. Disclosure is required for all directors, even if they are not standing for re-election in the applicable year, and should include:

- Any directorships at public companies held by each director at any time during the past five years (instead of only disclosing currently held directorships)

- Certain legal proceedings involving any director or executive officer during the past 10 years (instead of five years)
- Whether and how diversity is considered when identifying director candidates.

The SEC has not defined "diversity"; rather, each company is allowed to define it as it determines to be appropriate for its particular circumstances (e.g., experience, skills, education, race, gender). If a policy on diversity exists, the company must disclose how the policy is implemented and how its effectiveness is assessed.

Discussion of Company Leadership Structure

A company is required to disclose whether and why it has chosen to combine or separate the CEO and board chair positions, along with the reasons why the company believes that this board leadership structure is the most appropriate for it at the time of the filing. If the same person serves as CEO and chair, the company needs to disclose whether and why the company has a lead independent director and the role of the lead independent director in the leadership of the board. As discussed later in this chapter, Dodd-Frank confirmed this requirement through a statutory mandate.

In addition, the new rules require companies to describe the board's role in the oversight of risk (which may include credit risk, liquidity risk and operational risk). For example, a company may describe whether the entire board reviews risk or if there is a separate committee. Further, a company may find it helpful to discuss how risk information is communicated to the board or relevant committee members.

Expedited Reporting of Results of Shareholder Votes

Traditionally, final results of shareholder votes have been reported in a Form 10-Q or 10-K. Reporting now is required on a Form 8-K within four business days of the meeting.

The Continuing Challenge of Appropriate Disclosure

The 2009 rules:
- Responded to some criticisms of the 2006 overhaul of the SEC disclosure rules relating to executive compensation

- Addressed various executive compensation issues that have become important in recent years
- Generally expanded the scope of required disclosures.

Companies are faced with the challenge of accurately explaining their programs and policies in a way that is sufficiently detailed yet understandable and meaningful to investors and other interested parties.

Measuring Executive Pay: The Equity Compensation Challenge

The 2009 changes in proxy disclosure rules caused a shift in the method and outcome of future years' executive compensation reporting. The reported numbers that tend to be the focus of media, pay critics and analysts do not always capture the true story of executive pay.

Understanding Reported Values of Executive Pay

The complex structure of executive compensation, dominated by various forms of equity and cash-based long-term incentives (LTIs), can lead to significantly different interpretations of pay. These differences result from the interaction of varying approaches to data collection, analysis and reporting. Ensuring that all relevant data is collected for incorporation in the analysis, applying meaningful analytical tools to construct pay models, and reporting the information in a way that recognizes the complexity of pay practices all are essential for board-level decision support. Increased disclosure requirements, governance pressures and continued media attention make it imperative that pay values are well understood and clearly communicated — internally and externally.

Effect of Prior Year's Compensation Actions

Special circumstances underlying a previous year's equity awards can be misinterpreted the next year. In 2009 many companies acted to address the results of a depressed stock market, increased market volatility, poor business results and the effects of those conditions on executive pay. These special, often one-time actions held potential for misinterpretation — either because they might be deemed part of "annual" pay or, conversely, because they might be excluded from pay calculations altogether. Such decisions made during the data collection process can lead to a flawed analysis as true pay levels resulting from these items are not represented properly. A particular executive's compensation often can only be interpreted properly by understanding pay actions on a before-and-after basis.

For example, companies that implemented stock option exchange programs canceled many years of stock options and re-granted some or all of those at a more favorable price. Merely reporting the Black-Scholes value of the re-grant as an element of 2009 pay oversimplified the total compensation implications. Some of those companies excluded officers from their programs yet took other action — such as skipping or deferring the normal annual grant — that also needed to be considered. A company whose compensation peer group consists of several companies that made these types of pay decisions in 2009 may have found that its executives' pay is deemed to be "high" without recognizing these dynamics.

These complexities highlight the need for heightened attention to a three-faceted approach to executive equity compensation interpretation — collection, analysis and reporting.

Data Collection

Discussions of executive compensation focus primarily on single-year values, forming the root of many misunderstandings. But executive equity awards often are developed as part of a multi-year plan. SEC proxy disclosure rules recognize this through the required three-year reporting format for the Summary Compensation Table and the multi-year aggregations in other tables. A common example is when an executive receives a large new-hire equity grant, often two to four times the size of a typical annual grant, and then receives no equity award the following year(s). The single-year approach often leads to the conclusion that there has been a pay cut or an elimination of LTI awards when pay in year two is compared to that of year one.

Much of the important detail is contained in footnotes and narrative in the proxy statement, without which the tabular figures may be misinterpreted. In addition, many pay actions not captured in the tables are nevertheless disclosed in the CD&A section or appear in Form 8-K filings subsequent to the issuance of the proxy statement. Given the dated (look-back) nature of tabular information, these additional sources are critical to understanding the true current market for executive pay. The complexities of executive equity compensation have long required a multi-year, multi-source perspective and the economic turmoil certainly increased the importance of this approach.

Data Analysis

While the valuation of equity instruments receives much attention, the variations in fair value that may result from volatility or expected life assumptions are less significant than the effects on deemed value from a series of decisions that guide the equity compensation calculation. Such analysis often is bypassed and the fair value resulting from the reporting process — typically what appears in SEC filings — is accepted as the pay value without any further consideration. Compensation committees and executives need to understand these dynamics to ensure effective pay decisions.

The volatile equity markets in recent years resulted in equity grants with an unprecedented variation of values relative to business fundamentals and significant intra-year variations in relative grant values. For example, looking back to 2009, assume two companies whose share prices directly track the Nasdaq index both granted stock options in 2009, the first in early March and the other in early September. The first company reported grant-date fair values approximately 50 percent lower than the second company, but by the end of 2009 provided intrinsic value that was 260 percent greater. Variations of this magnitude are unprecedented in the history of executive pay and cannot be ignored. An unusually large number of companies awarded stock options in February through April 2009 near the market low, and in many cases those grants quickly accumulated value far greater than the artificially low Black-Scholes value that was reported in SEC filings. Ironically, many of those companies granted a larger number of shares to offset the lower fair value at the time, exacerbating this effect.

These dynamics require that companies understand not only what was granted (i.e., stock options, time-vested shares, performance-based shares, cash LTI) and how much was granted, but when it was granted. In addition to understanding award type and timing, the emergence of performance features requires attention to the effect of performance contingencies or accelerators, thresholds and targets, absolute versus relative performance measures, and the interaction of time-based and performance-based conditions. Also, as companies add stock ownership guidelines and share retention requirements, the risk-reward balance has changed. Thoughtful analysis is required to understand the real effect on executive pay value resulting from the interaction of these features.

Data Reporting

With proper data collection and analysis, pay can be reported in ways that provide a meaningful picture of executive pay practices over the past years. A single snapshot of pay is not adequate for telling the story in this complex environment. Merely viewing pay as a single number may lead a compensation committee to reach flawed conclusions about the company's competitive position in the market. Scenario-based pay projections — incorporated into tally sheet and wealth accumulation analyses — will provide the compensation committee and the executive team with a point of view consistent with other business decision processes.

Pay Granted, Earned and Realized

A greater scrutiny of pay values introduces a need for the multi-dimensional view of pay, with at least three possible pay views to be considered. This approach requires taking pay analysis beyond a grant-based focus to a dynamic view of the life cycle of executive pay — when granted, earned and realized.

A significant change made in 2009 to the revised proxy disclosure rules altered the equity incentive figures in the Summary Compensation Table from an "earned"' to a "granted" basis. The fair value of all equity awards made during the reporting year are deemed to have been what was "paid" to the executive for that year rather than what was accrued for accounting purposes. There are lengthy and complex arguments around which of these two methods is preferable, and why, but sound pay analysis does not force an "either/or" decision. It is important to understand what was granted, the incremental amount earned, and — as media organizations often do — the pay realized over a period of time to obtain a true picture of executive pay.

While no single analytical structure will make sense for all companies, compensation committees and executive teams should:

- Think through the three data processes (collection, analysis and reporting) in the context of three alternative views of pay (granted, earned and realized) and

- Ask a series of questions to ensure a comprehensive approach. Table 14-1 illustrates the types of questions that may help guide a year's analyses and decisions.

TABLE 14-1

Data Processes of Collection, Analysis and Reporting

	Granted	Earned	Realized
Collection	Did we capture all of the grants and actions taken last year? Have we properly categorized "annual" pay actions	Did many of our peers grant during the market lows? How is that affecting reported grant value and fair value?	Were there significant realization events that created compensation not captured in the typical proxy and survey formats? Have we compared vested but unexercised in-the-money option gains?
Analysis	Have we explored the stock price patterns of our peers and reviewed scenario-based pay values?	Have we analyzed competitors' changes in vesting schedules, acceleration provisions, and holding requirements to understand changes in earnings opportunities?	Have we conducted an historical analysis of realized pay to understand how this may be affecting current grant patterns?
Reporting	Have we accounted for new hires, promotions, terminations, founders and special qualifications of incumbents?	Are we considering risk-adjusted differences in pay values: options vs. time-vested full-value awards vs. thresholds and targets on performance awards?	Do our tally sheet and wealth accumulation tools capture realized value including post-vesting accumulation?

Many emerging tools — tally sheets, wealth accumulation models, "walk away" value calculations and scenario-based analysis — address some of these issues. A methodical approach can help a company understand the tools being used and the rationale for using a tool to the exclusion of others. It can be helpful to view these alternatives in this three-by-three analytical framework to capture the issues surrounding the collection, analysis and reporting of equity compensation data and recognize alternative measurement points of grant, earning and realization to ensure a clear understanding of market pay levels and practices.

Further Executive Pay Disclosure Under Dodd-Frank

While broadly targeting the financial services industry, including provisions that address consumer and investor protection, Dodd-Frank contains important executive compensation and corporate governance provisions that apply to most public companies regardless of industry. To a considerable extent, Dodd-Frank leaves the specifics of the new requirements to rulemaking by the SEC and the national securities exchanges and associations (securities exchanges).

Most of the executive compensation provisions of Dodd-Frank add new disclosure requirements for public companies. Following are the basic terms of key executive compensation and corporate governance disclosure provisions enacted by Dodd-Frank. The effective dates of the various parts of the act are critical, with certain changes effective on enactment (July 21, 2010), while other provisions are only to take effect either after a transition period or after the regulatory authorities have promulgated rules fleshing out the statutory mandates. Dodd-Frank undoubtedly is having a substantial effect on executive pay processes at most public companies.

Say on Pay

Resolving a long-running debate on whether and how to obtain the views of shareholders on executive pay, Dodd-Frank requires a public company to provide shareholders with a nonbinding vote to approve the compensation of its named executive officers. A say-on-pay vote must be held at least once every three years, which started with the first annual shareholders' meeting occurring after Jan. 21, 2011 (i.e., six months after the date of enactment). As of the same effective date, and at least once every six years thereafter, shareholders must be afforded the right to vote on whether a say-on-pay vote occurs once every one, two or three years.

A company's say-on-pay vote covers the compensation shown in its CD&A and Compensation Tables (including narrative disclosures). Effective communications with shareholders is especially important in connection with a say-on-pay vote. Before a vote a company should make an effort to address potential shareholder concerns with the goal of obtaining strong majority approval. After either a negative vote or one with a narrow approval margin, feedback can help the company understand shareholders' concerns so that they can be addressed and to limit the possibility of strike suits.

Advisory or not, a failure to respond effectively to a high level of dissatisfaction may result in "withhold" or "against" votes regarding the re-election of compensation committee members.

Say on Parachutes

Executive compensation payments and other benefits triggered by a change in control of the organization (golden parachutes) are common at U.S. companies. However, well-publicized examples of particularly large payments to executives sparked controversy over the authorization of what some perceived to be overly executive-friendly arrangements. The initiatives regarding say on pay ultimately led to the related requirement of disclosure and a nonbinding shareholder vote regarding executive compensation arrangements related to proposed change-in-control transactions — coined "say on parachute" votes. The disclosure for a say-on-parachute vote is required in any proxy for a shareholders meeting at which shareholders are asked to approve an acquisition, merger, consolidation or proposed sale of all (or substantially all) of the company's assets. A say-on-parachute vote is not required if the parachute arrangements already have been subject to such a vote, although the conditions imposed by the regulations regarding this provision will limit its utility.

Compensation Committee Consultants and Other Advisers

Two critical and related issues involve the ability of a compensation committee to engage compensation consultants, legal counsel and other advisers, and the independence of any advisers so retained. Dodd-Frank contains separate provisions that authorize a compensation committee to retain a compensation consultant, independent legal counsel and other advisers, with the committee to "be directly responsible for the appointment, compensation and oversight." A company is required to provide appropriate funding, as determined by the compensation committee, for any advisers so retained. With respect to compensation consultants (but not the other advisers), proxy disclosure is required regarding whether the compensation committee has retained a compensation consultant, whether that consultant's work led to any conflict of interest, the nature of any conflicts and how those conflicts are being addressed.

With respect to independence, a compensation committee "may only select a compensation consultant, legal counsel or other adviser ... after taking account the factors identified by the [SEC] ..." The SEC was directed to identify factors that affect independence, including five general ones listed in Dodd-Frank.

Pay-for-Performance Disclosure

Dodd-Frank requires the SEC to craft rules that require a public company to disclose in the proxy statement for its annual shareholder meeting a "clear description" that "shows the relationship between executive compensation actually paid and the financial performance" of the company, taking into account any changes in the value of the company's stock and any dividends and distributions. The disclosure may include a graphic representation of the required information.

CEO Pay Ratio Disclosure

In an effort to address the debate about internal pay equity, Dodd-Frank imposed its potentially most burdensome provision by requiring the SEC to amend its regulations to mandate a new compensation ratio pay disclosure. The required disclosure (applicable for various SEC filings, not simply a company's annual proxy statement) consists of three items:

- The median of the "annual total compensation" of all of the company's employees except its CEO
- The CEO's total annual compensation
- The ratio of the two former numbers.

Under the SEC rules, the components of total compensation are those disclosed in the Summary Compensation Table of a company's annual proxy statement. Applying this definition to all employees can be extremely time-consuming (including a need to determine the value of equity grants, pension compensation, perquisites and various other forms of compensation for a company's entire global workforce). A company with many employees in low-wage countries likely will find that its pay ratio is significantly higher than at an otherwise comparable company whose employees are concentrated in high-wage countries.

Clawback Policy

Under rules to be established by the SEC, Dodd-Frank requires public companies to develop, implement and disclose what is commonly called a "clawback policy." The required policy must address the company's recovery from current and former executive officers of incentive-based compensation based on certain financial information where there has been a required accounting restatement due to material noncompliance with a financial reporting require-ment. At a minimum, in the event of a restatement, a company needs to recoup any excess incentive payments (including stock option gains) that were paid based on inaccurate information in the previous three years.

In general, the clawback rules under Dodd-Frank are considerably broader than the clawback provisions of the Sarbanes-Oxley Act. For example, Dodd-Frank's clawback provisions apply to any executive officer (not just the CEO and CFO), do not require any misconduct (just simply the requisite restatement), and cover a three-year (rather than 12-month) period. Companies should review the features of any current clawback provisions that they may have implemented.

Consideration should be given not only to the Dodd-Frank requirements, but also to any additional features or processes that address the organization's particular circumstances or facilitate administration.

Employee and Director Hedging

Dodd-Frank calls for the SEC to require each public company to disclose in its annual proxy statement whether any employee (not just an executive officer) or board member is permitted to purchase financial instruments "designed to hedge or offset any decrease in the market value of equity securities" granted as compensation or otherwise owned by such employee or director. Because equity hedging strategies can enable an employee or director to limit the effect of holding requirements commonly imposed on top executives and directors, the provision aims to shed light on any such actions and indirectly encourages companies to bar or limit such hedging. SEC rules already called for the disclosure of policies regarding hedging even before Dodd-Frank, so the main effect of the legislative provision seems to be the extension of such disclosure to all employees as well as directors.

Disclosures Regarding Board Chair and CEO Structures

The SEC is directed by Dodd-Frank to issue rules requiring a public company to disclose in its annual proxy the reasons why the company has chosen either the same person to serve both as board chair and CEO or two different people to serve in those positions. Basically, Dodd-Frank provides a legislative mandate for what companies already were required to do under the SEC's proxy disclosure rules.

15
Risk in Executive Compensation

By Jeffrey Bacher and Sara Wells

The crises in the financial services industry put a spotlight on executives who reaped huge profits from excessively risky financial deals. As a result, the U.S. Securities and Exchange Commission (SEC) now requires public companies to consider whether any of their compensation plans create risk-taking incentives and, if so, to disclose in their annual proxy whether a materially adverse effect on the company is reasonably likely. Risk management, not traditionally within the purview of the compensation committee, is now an important item on the committee's agenda.

Incentive plans encourage executives to aim for the maximum rewards permitted under the plan. While these plans seldom resemble the bonus arrangements that figured so prominently in the financial crisis, risk is, nonetheless, a necessary element in executive pay. How should companies and their compensation committees go about taking on the added burden of risk-reward analysis and ongoing monitoring? What are the red flags that alert boards to a high-risk situation?

The best way to do this is through a balanced, fact-based approach that allows for a prudent exposure to risk without compromising sustainable long-term growth. The results, however, should not be so balanced that the creative spirit is curbed. Companies will not derive benefit from a watered down incentive program in which the business needs and priorities unique to the company are not underlying factors. While risk-adapted incentive plans will require a decision process that will be more thorough and complex, boards and management will gain from internal effectiveness and enhanced external defensibility.

This chapter:

- Addresses the key questions compensation committees need to ask in determining if compensation programs potentially pose a business risk. There also is a checklist for risk assessment and a discussion of the role compensation systems in the financial industry downturn.
- Discusses how a balanced approach to risk addresses pay elements and mix, long-term incentives (LTIs), performance measures, goal setting and payout structures.
- Offers an approach to benchmarking executive pay that supplements the usual two-dimensional snapshot approach with a third dimension that provides an in-depth analysis of executive pay under various scenarios over time.

Risk in Executive Compensation

The ongoing economic crisis has focused attention on the design of certain executive pay incentives as promoting overly risky behavior in attempts to earn especially large payouts. As a result, the assessment and management of risk in executive compensation is the subject of various legislative, regulatory and corporate governance initiatives that are intended to limit excessive risk. In designing and evaluating executive pay programs, risk now is a critical factor.

Some Background

According to a common definition, "risk" involves the possibility of suffering harm or loss in the pursuit of an objective. The issue of risk in compensation programs typically has centered on the downside of the equation — the probability and consequences of failure. However, executive compensation programs historically focused on the positive side with little regard for the potential negative outcomes. Business decisions should be made to create an appropriate balance between risk and return — not to maximize both. During difficult times, shareholders look to the board of directors for guidance on these difficult issues.

Following the debacles at Enron and WorldCom, there were concerns that the boards of these companies (and no doubt at many others as well) did not fully understand the complexity of the company's financial structure. As a result, the Sarbanes-Oxley Act of 2002 was enacted to force corporate boards to address weaknesses in financial controls. In fact, one of the most significant effects of the statute was to require that a qualified financial expert be included as head of the audit committee at a public company. This, in turn, drove significant changes in board composition, qualifications and compensation.

More recent financial difficulties have directed blame in a different direction — failed risk oversight by the board. Risk management failures have been viewed as a leading cause of recent economic problems. A consensus has developed that one of the drivers of overly risky business decisions was the highly leveraged design of pay programs in the banking and financial services sector.

In the past, the management of risk generally was lodged in the audit committee or the full board. As a result of the current focus on the effect of incentives on behavior, compensation commit-tees need to evaluate executive compensation in a new light and address the age-old link between risk and reward.

Going Forward

The issue of determining performance risk and factoring in time horizons adds complexity to the design of executive compensa-tion programs. Some suggest the use of long holding periods for equity awards to focus on the creation of long-term value. Other techniques may involve fail-safes such as bonus banks or claw-backs, so that organizations can recoup some of the incentive pay they have disbursed if a longer time horizon shows performance results actually were poor.

In aligning pay incentives with risk management, compensa-tion committees need to monitor compensation programs and any potential link to risky behavior. To properly manage risk, companies also must provide greater authority to risk managers.

Programs that have features similar to the following are consid-ered high-risk and suspect in the new compensation environment:
* Low salary relative to incentive (e.g., 10 percent salary/90 percent incentive mix)

- Focus on annual performance rather than long-term sustained results ("swing for the fences" behavior)
- Uncapped upside
- Excessive use of stock options
- Use of multi-year recruiting guarantees.

Other quasi-regulatory bodies also are becoming involved. As part of its evaluation of business strength and financial condition, Standard & Poor's added an enterprise risk management assessment.

Certainly there is a need to be more aware of the potential risks in designing compensation programs. Compensation committees should undertake a formal evaluation of compensation policies and practices to determine their potential effect on enterprise risk. While few compensation plans promote the level of risk that was built into Wall Street's incentive structure, there are other elements of risk that can harm the company short of bankruptcy, a forced sale or a total collapse. To name a few:

- Exposure to criticism/public image with shareholders and customers
- Difficulty with proxy voting on proposals regarding executive compensation and/or share availability
- Board embarrassment, particularly regarding severance arrangements
- Risk of unintended payments (payments made for performance that were not earned or are wildly disproportionate to the value created).

Key questions for a compensation committee involve both philosophy and design.

Do Plans Reflect Strategy?

Are the metrics aligned to promote balance between short- and long-term objectives? Many banking practices were entirely focused on short-term behavior and results. Going forward, this is viewed as inappropriate in most cases.

Does the Compensation Committee Understand All Potential Scenarios?

For example, has there been a conscious and detailed analysis of all executive compensation plans (severance and change-in-control payments as well as incentives) to understand the complexities and potential consequences of certain events and decisions? The use of tally sheets enables compensation committees to approach executive compensation decisions by evaluating the overall combined exposure to the company from all sources. Further, the compensation committee should take a careful look at the possible behaviors and business decisions that would trigger large payouts. A common example might be plans that could encourage executives to look for risky acquisitions to promote top-line growth at the expense of returns. Similarly, change-in-control payments may be so rich as to drive strategy, regardless of whether they are in the best interests of the shareholders.

Is There Too Much Weight on One Metric?

Good plan design suggests that there be balance in the metrics selected (e.g., a combination of growth, profitability and sustainable returns). The risk here is that too much emphasis on one issue can significantly detract from, or even impede progress on, other important performance metrics.

Are the Plans Diluted with Too Many Metrics?

Is there a risk that the plans are so balanced that they fail to provide direction or proper weighting to strategic objectives?

Is the Leverage in Executive Compensation Reasonable?

In at least the financial services sector, the traditional view of executive compensation was that "high risk, high reward" was a good thing. Plans in many cases were designed with significantly escalating rewards for performance. While there may be sound reasons for high levels of award opportunity in some cases, events have demonstrated the need for compensation committees to evaluate the risk of promoting excessive and risky business activities in search of the "big score."

Are Controls in Place to Mitigate Risk in Executive Compensation?

Checks and balances to consider include:
- Clawbacks for payment in prior years that ultimately were shown to have been unearned or based on financials that had to be restated

- Consideration of "bonus banks" to smooth out the variability in annual payouts and provide the company with a vehicle for reversing previously "earned" bonuses
- Multi-year performance periods (three years or more) rather than excessive focus on short-term gains
- Holding requirements on shares/meaningful ownership guidelines (even up to and after retirement)
- Caps on plan upside to limit the potential for unexpected or windfall payouts.

Once a thorough assessment of compensation is completed, the compensation committee can evaluate the effect of plan features relative to the risk factors involved. In speaking about risk in October 2008, John White, then head of the SEC Corporation Finance Division (but expressing his own views), phrased the risk disclosure issue:

> *"Ask yourself this question: Would it be prudent for compensation committees, when establishing targets and creating incentives, not only to discuss how hard or how easy it is to meet the incentives, but also to consider the particular risks an executive might be incentivized to take to meet the target — with risk, in this case, being viewed in the context of the enterprise as a whole?"*

What Changes in Executive Pay Arrangements Are Occurring (or Are Likely to Occur) as a Result of the Focus on Risk?

While most executive compensation plans are not a threat to the business, there have been some changes in the overall framework of best practices in executive pay design.

- **Shift to a longer-term focus in plan design and a more rigorous alignment of payment to the timing of the result.** In reference to the risky acquisition strategy noted earlier, rewards may be matched to the timing of expected corporate benefits, not at the close of the deal.
- **Changes in plan design that reduce the impact of single metrics.** It is not uncommon to find similar measures used in both short- and long-term incentives. Although neither plan may be excessive in itself, the double usage may concentrate risk and create problems.

- **Greater consideration of both absolute and relative performance measures.** Over-reliance on one or the other can result in unintended payout results.

- **Greater use of modeling tools so that compensation committees can better understand the potential effect of compensation decisions.** Had the directors at financial companies better understood the disastrous effects of a down economy combined with high leverage, the painful consequences at many companies might have been limited or even avoided.

- **Greater attention to plan caps and more modest leverage in plan design.** Companies have recognized the usefulness of compensation committee discretion — especially negative discretion — in plan awards to address not only what was achieved, but also how it was attained.

- **A continuing re-evaluation regarding the use of stock options.** Stock options are a form of compensation with high potential returns, but with no real downside prior to exercise. Research indicates that stock options are declining in prevalence and this trend can be expected to continue.

- **More consideration of compensation risk as part of the overall board risk-assessment process.** This has been the central theme in the current focus on risk in the compensation process.

A concern in the current focus on risk is that it may have a negative effect (hopefully temporary) on the creativity and entrepreneurial spirit that has propelled U.S. business success. There needs to be a continued emphasis on taking reasonable risks and aligning the rewards with the gains produced.

Risk Assessment: Initial Process and Checklist

Risk and reward are the two ends of the compensation spectrum. Compensation committees have continuously tried to balance these components — risk (in the form of stretch goals) and reward (enough to make the risk worthwhile). But how much is too much? The SEC now requires all public companies to evaluate their risks from compensation arrangements.

The new rules require that every publicly held company discuss in its annual proxy statement whether any of its compensation plans or practices (for executives and nonexecutives) create risk-taking incentives that are reasonably likely to have a material adverse effect on the organization. From a practical viewpoint, the result is that every public company needs to examine each of its compensation programs to:

- Be assured that no such potential risks exist, and
- Fix or otherwise mitigate any potential risks that may be uncovered.

Because many compensation committees have not historically examined broad-based rewards programs, the learning curve on these programs may be substantial.

One of the most important and immediate challenges for organizations and compensation committees is developing a process to assess and then manage the possible risks posed by the compensation programs they maintain or oversee. As part of the initial process, it is useful to develop a checklist to guide the analysis. However, any process and checklist needs to be tailored to a company's specific circumstances — real thought and analysis are needed, not simply a "check-the-box" compliance mentality. The initial process for assessing risk involves:

- Creating a project team (which might well include a senior risk officer, inside and outside legal counsel, a senior HR or compensation officer, and a compensation consultant) to assess the level of risk for each of the distinct compensation programs to be reviewed against a key set of criteria.
- Collecting and reviewing the organization's existing written and unwritten pay policies, practices and plan documents as well as similar items pertaining to the company's enterprise risk management.
- Conducting the compensation risk assessment and identifying for the compensation committee the risks that the organization faces that could threaten its value or have a material financial, operational or reputation effect on the company. Identify the features of the organization's executive and nonexecutive compensation policies, practices and supporting management processes that could induce executives and employees to take those risks.

- Analyzing the results of the risk assessment and discussing how to mitigate and manage any such excessive risks, and/or establishing a process and timetable for revising those compensation and incentive programs that contain excessive risks.

Checklist for Risk Assessment

Table 15-1 is a sample checklist containing generally relevant criteria for use in assessing the risk profile of compensation programs. To determine the risk exposure of each program, consider determining the potential cost under a worst-case scenario and the probability of such scenario. It is helpful to characterize (or rank) potential cost and risk on a grid as high, moderate and low, at times using a red, yellow and green "stoplight gap analysis" as a visual means for characterizing and addressing levels of risk.

Review

The financial industry crisis spawned an increased focus on potential risk in compensation programs. Companies, regulators and advisers all are attempting to address the various factors that contribute to risk in compensation programs, but many important issues still must be addressed. For instance (and most basically), there is no universal definition of what is meant by "risk." While the SEC has eased the reporting burden for public companies by limiting required disclosure to risks that are "reasonably likely to have a material adverse effect on the company," the core issue remains.

Ultimately companies will receive more guidance (and hopefully more clarity) from the SEC (and perhaps from the courts) on their compliance efforts. Upon review of a company's proxy statement by the SEC (perhaps as part of the SEC's triennial reviews), a failure to show the company conducted a risk assessment in compliance with these rules could prompt queries on specific programs. Aside from any input or feedback from the SEC, ideas are exchanged among companies and their advisers. Reasonable approaches also are developed after considering information disclosed in filings during the most recent proxy season. In any case, the initial process

TABLE 15-1

Risk Assessment Checklist	Risk Managed Effectively	Caution	Risk Not Managed Effectively
		(Check One)	
Alignment and balance in performance metrics			
Is there risk in division or subsidiary reward performance metrics not aligning with corporate reward metrics?			
Is there a risk in one financial measure dominating employee focus at the expense of other key performance measures?			
Is there a risk in short-term measures dominating employee focus at the expense of long-term performance measures?			
Overall:			
Corporate financial protection and use of hurdles			
What is the degree of risk in team and individual goals requiring incentive payouts in a year when the corporate entity did not meet baseline financial or profitability goals?			
Are hurdles appropriately set that balance corporate protection and reasonable probability of an incentive payout?			
Overall:			
Alignment of pay with market competitiveness			
What is the degree of risk in organization pay levels and target earning opportunities not aligning with marketplace practices?			
Is there risk in eligibility criteria not being consistent internally?			
Overall:			
Effect on motivation and engagement			
What is the degree of risk in current incentive plans not providing optimal motivation and results?			
Are employees aware of and committed to the principles behind the intent of the incentive plan?			
Overall:			
Appropriate use of management discretion			
What is the degree of risk in the use of management discretion in incentive plan payouts where the criteria may or may not directly align with corporate performance?			
Are the principles and rules of discretion consistently known and applied?			
Overall:			
Plan effectiveness			
What is the degree of risk in incentive plans not being perceived as effective and motivational by managers and employees?			
Overall:			

and checklist provide a solid starting framework for a company's compensation plan risk assessment.

Executive Pay for Sustainable Performance: Restoring Investor Trust in Financial Institutions

The 2008 financial crisis exposed financial services companies that did not effectively manage risk. Bear Stearns, Merrill Lynch and Lehman Brothers, three titans that had weathered the Great Depression, World War II, and Sept. 11, 2001, could not survive the economic turbulence. In the aftermath of the recession, survivors must redesign risk management and employee rewards to ensure sustainable performance. Investors will increasingly require that executive pay be tied to sustainable performance measured by economic profit to take account of both total capital deployed and risk.

Despite unprecedented fiscal and monetary interventions by governments and central banks, the global economy remains highly volatile. Uncertainty in markets persists because investor and creditor trust was breached in a way that had not been experienced in generations. While governments, central banks and regulators took aggressive actions to combat the painful symptoms of "frozen credit" and "toxic assets," the approaches were reactive and insufficient. Resolution can only occur by addressing the root causes of the breach in trust.

A Concentration of Risk

Financial emergencies requiring government intervention have been a pattern in the sector. In the recent past we have seen Greek, Russian and Latin American sovereign debt defaults, the reinsurance spiral and Lloyds of London failure, the collapse of Long Term Capital Management (whose principals were supposedly the experts on risk!), and the U.S. savings and loans debacle. Most recently, a handful of countries in the European Union have taken turns in sparking new financial crises. A common factor has been the concentration of risk in a few areas that appeared to be producing high returns without providing adequately for the possibility of a disaster. The concentration of risk often has been disguised by the recycling of the same risks among industry players. Rewards programs that pay out a substantial proportion of nominal profits (or even of revenue) have operated to encourage this process, as short-term revenue and nominal profits tend to be highest from the highest risk investments — for so long as the risks do not materialize. Even companies that recognized the risks were afraid to change their reward systems for fear of losing out in the war for talent.

The Transparency Challenge

Investors now are demanding from management greater transparency, accountability and long-term performance sustainability than ever before. But transparency in financial services is a difficult goal to attain. Financial instruments are pioneered daily, and it is difficult to adequately describe the complexities of a single transaction, let alone a diverse global portfolio. The credit default swap market illustrates the problem, as it took the dramatic and sudden decline in the housing market to expose the riskiness of the assets. Timeliness is challenging because asset values change on a tick-by-tick basis. Determining the effect of a single change in the bid/ask spread of a highly leveraged asset can be misleading if not presented with great care. The continuing debate on marking-to-market focuses on this issue, and is further complicated by the significant claims attached to any one asset at any point in time.

Finally, the issue of risk-adjusted performance in financial institutions is difficult because there are three categories of risk in financial institutions: credit, market and operating risk. While Basel II, or the Revised International Capital Framework, has provided a useful standard for "value at risk" and "risk-adjusted return on risk-adjusted capital," even the savviest investors can find these calculations difficult to interpret. Furthermore, transparency and timeliness are critical to these measures having any utility at all from an investor perspective.

Keeping Rewards in Context

Rewards systems have certainly contributed to the problem and need to be radically overhauled. However, changing rewards so that executives suffer if there is a financial crisis is not the whole solution. Financial crises are infrequent, so they only affect the executives in place at the time; they are also generally (almost by definition) not anticipated, so the possibility of a collapse tends not to affect executive behavior. Therefore, in addition to changing rewards:

- Financial services companies need to improve their risk assessment and ensure that they are not betting the company on a single investment or on investments that are likely to be correlated in an economic or financial crisis. Given the long timescales, this has to be a governance and regulatory responsibility, not driven by rewards — although part of top executive rewards should be for doing this well.

- Companies also need to build up reserves against the inevitable losses from time to time, as insurance companies do. Arguably the excess of the risk-adjusted required return over the risk-free rate is an "insurance premium" that should be reserved against future losses, not paid out in bonuses (or dividends).

Achieving Risk-Adjusted Rewards

Executive rewards must be based on measures of corporate performance that take account of the risks to shareholders' capital inherent in the business strategy. Notwithstanding complexity, investors will no longer be satisfied with the "too complicated" excuse on risk-adjusted performance management.

Corporate performance must be assessed based on a broad framework of interrelated metrics that influence current expectations. To succeed, the framework must first and foremost be economically sound. The "performance mathematics" must ensure that as levers are pressed, expected values are achieved and perceptions influenced accordingly. Second, it must be comprehensive and balanced. As Peter Drucker reminded us, "we manage what we measure." History is replete with pay-for-performance issues stemming from improvement in "measured" revenue growth offset by "nonmeasured" expansion in assets or risk. And finally, it must be easy to implement. If it cannot be readily understood and tracked by all stakeholders, it will not work.

Two measures that should be considered to tie executive pay to performance are total shareholder return (TSR) and economic profit (EP). TSR is a strong de facto measure of long-term corporate performance, despite the difficulties of defining a peer group to measure relative performance and the potential effect of short-term price fluctuations.

EP is fundamentally the return on capital deployed net of its risk-adjusted cost. It is an essential measure because it ensures that return is calculated in the context of both the scale of capital deployed and its inherent riskiness. While this is a more complicated calculation for financial services companies because these companies are essentially "spread" businesses, EP can be superior to other metrics like earnings per share (EPS) and earnings before interest, tax, depreciation and amortization (EBITDA) because these do not consider risk and capital deployed.

However, TSR and EP must be managed through a performance framework. Figure 15-1 is an example of a performance management framework that connects TSR and EP with actionable enterprise operating metrics. From a board and investor point of view, the framework provides a holistic approach that enables effective assessment of performance in the context of executive pay.

While this approach is not immune from the aforementioned issues of comparability and complexity, it is a useful paradigm for establishing a standardized approach to performance management.

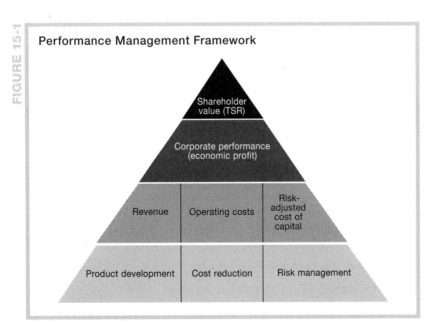

FIGURE 15-1

Performance Management Framework

Investors made their voices clear in 2008; a failure to tackle the problem will no longer be tolerated. The restoration of trust begins with executive pay for sustainable risk-adjusted performance.

Designing Incentive Plans in Today's Risk Environment

Incentive plans recently have come under increased scrutiny, sometimes even cast as the villain in organizations' rewards programs. In particular, incentive programs have been cited as a cause of excessive risk-taking for short-term gains at the expense of long-term sustainable performance, which can ultimately contribute to business failures. However, incentive plans are essential for linking pay with performance, placing needed emphasis on critical near-term and long-term business priorities, and motivating employees to achieve challenging goals. Based on studies and work with clients, Hay Group has found that balance is a key to designing incentive plans that accomplish these objectives, but also mitigate unhealthy risk.

The primary objective of a balanced program is to ensure that no single compensation element is driving a specific outcome at the expense of other key outcomes. Where do we look for balance?

- Pay elements and mix
- Long-term incentive elements
- Performance measures
- Goal setting
- Incentive payout design.

Pay Elements and Mix

We begin by looking for balance in the overall mix of compensation elements. Not only do we assess the competitiveness of each element of pay, but attention also is focused on the mix of pay. How much is being delivered in fixed versus variable pay? What is the ratio of short-term compensation versus long-term compensation? And how much is delivered in cash versus equity?

Many of the answers depend upon the roles and levels within the organization. For executives, a large percentage of the total pay mix is typically delivered in long-term, variable pay. Because many positions below the executive level do not have the same line of sight to long-term results, fixed base pay typically becomes a larger portion of the mix as one travels down in the organization. Similarly, the focus generally is more on variable annual incentives rather than on long-term programs in moving down from the senior-executive level.

A growing number of companies are delivering a portion of annual incentive earnings in the form of deferred stock or "banking" the bonuses for payout at some point in the future based on future performance. These features further reduce the incentive for risky behavior to achieve unsustainable short-term gains.

Long-Term Incentive Elements

There are several choices regarding LTIs, each serving a unique purpose with its own set of advantages and disadvantages. Stock options and stock appreciation rights link directly to shareholder interests and are of value only when the share price increases; however, these can be a temptation for inappropriate risk-taking to achieve the increases. Time-based restricted stock provides opportunities for ownership and serves as a retention device, but can be viewed as a giveaway. Performance-based share and cash plans align with critical strategic performance, but it can be difficult to set challenging yet realistic long-term goals in light of market uncertainties.

When it comes to managing risk, once again balance generally is the best approach. Research has found that most large public companies are taking a portfolio approach to LTIs, making grants in two or even three vehicles.

Performance Measures

Performance measures are arguably one of the most difficult aspects of incentive plan design. Choosing the right metrics in the right combination can stymie even the best of experts. There are some general rules, however, when it comes to managing for risk and, not surprisingly, a critical one is about balance.

Incentive plans, whether short- or long-term, that use multiple metrics (particularly more than one financial/operating metric) reduce the risk of driving performance of one metric to the detriment of other measures that are important to the long-term success and viability of the company. Metrics that present a balanced view of how the organization is performing are favored, particularly combinations of profitability, growth and sustained return measures, and reduced reliance on top-line growth measures. Additionally, it is important to consider qualitative measures that emphasize strategic priorities.

From Hay Group's work with *Fortune* magazine, we know that Most Admired Companies place a greater emphasis on the balance of performance measures and measures that encourage cooperation and collaboration.

Goal Setting

Another challenge in the design of an incentive program is being able to forecast company performance (especially for periods longer than a year) and setting goals at the right level. If performance goals are not set appropriately, there can be negative consequences.

Generally speaking, goals should be challenging, but attainable. If goals are set too high, we see two alternative unsatisfactory outcomes:

- Executives may not be motivated if they perceive there is little likelihood of achieving the targets.
- Executives may take excessive risks to try to reach very difficult goals.

Conversely, if goals are set too low and the incentive plan is paying out more frequently and at higher levels than is intended, the company is at risk of paying incentives for mediocre (or even poor) performance and not achieving an appropriate return on its investment.

There are two basic approaches companies can use in setting standards:

- **Absolute.** Goals are set based on the company's year-over-year performance and/or budgets. An internal approach requires a strong planning process and is difficult in industries in which external events can have a dramatic effect on results. Performance goals are usually effective when there is rigor around the goal-setting process and the goals are based on the company's strategic and operating objectives.

- **Relative.** Goals are focused on how a company performs relative to its competitors or peers. A relative or external approach measures the company against direct competitors that are affected by similar macro-economic factors and compete in the same market or with the same products. This approach mitigates the risk of setting the goals too high or too low. However, the approach can sometimes result in unintended payouts: If a company outperforms the majority of its peers, it is nevertheless possible that it produced negative value for shareholders, including negative profitability or negative total shareholder return.

Plans that allow management and the compensation committee to use discretion in determining achievement of results, and ultimately the corresponding payouts, further mitigate risk. Plans that are entirely formulaic are viewed as contributing to the potential for risk and unintended, negative consequences for the company. More and more, companies are also including clawback features (even beyond the strictures of the Dodd-Frank Wall Street Reform and Consumer Protection Act of 2010) to recoup incentive awards that may be deemed in the future to be based on unearned performance results or financials that later were restated.

Incentive Payout Design

In designing incentive arrangements, one critical item is the structure of the relationship between performance and payouts. Typically this is a range, from threshold to maximum, with incremental pay for incremental performance. To mitigate risk, the program should have upside and downside potential. All-or-nothing plans, whereby a participant receives a fixed award for achieving a target level of performance, but nothing for just missing the target, are viewed as contributing to potentially risky behavior. Additionally, the slope of the line (i.e., the relationship between performance levels and the associated payouts) can vary. Flatter slopes that require greater performance for incremental payouts are generally more appropriate in today's risk environment, but must be balanced so that stretches in performance are not unrealistic.

One of the most important features in the payout design, when it comes to risk, is limiting the upside potential with a predetermined maximum level of performance and payout ("capping" the plan). Caps prevent windfall earnings that may not represent achievements attributable to management or may be from unsustainable levels of performance. Another important feature that mitigates the risk of a company making payouts when it cannot afford to do so is a financial trigger. The trigger typically is established as a minimum level of corporate-wide profitability (or similar measure) that must be achieved before any incentive payouts can be made. The cap and trigger can work in tandem to provide balance in the overall payout structure and mitigate potentially risky scenarios.

Be Careful Balancing

So, balance is good. But can there be too much balance? The key is to achieve balance in the areas where the risk outweighs the benefits. Beware of watering down your overall program and losing focus. Achieving balance at the expense of putting in the right program that will motivate and retain your people could reduce the return on your investment.

There is no one right way to design an incentive plan. There are a variety of plan designs that work well in different companies for different reasons. The organization's rewards strategy, and the purpose and intent of the incentive programs, should guide the design of the plans to ultimately drive performance.

Benchmarking Executive Pay: The Third Dimension

It can be reasonably argued that making decisions on executive pay is one of the most important responsibilities of the board, and in particular is the most important responsibility of the compensation committee. If nothing else, decisions on executive pay are certainly one of the most visible, and can be one of the most controversial decisions made at the board level. Each year the annual proxy of a public company must disclose how much each of the top five executives is paid, how the incentive compensation plans work, and why each element of pay was included. Further, after the market collapse of 2008, a new element was required with respect to the proxy — an assessment of the risk level built into the incentive plans in order to disclose, as previously noted in this chapter, whether any incentive plans that "are reasonably likely to have a material adverse effect on the company." "High risk, high reward" was no longer considered a reasonable compensation strategy (if it ever was).

Executive pay has always been a subject of interest in the popular press, and following each proxy season the leading newspaper in virtually every major city across America publishes a story on the most highly paid CEOs in the area. The data may not always be accurate, but is almost always the source of serious discussion and shareholder activism.

What's more, beginning in 2011, public companies were required to provide shareholders with an opportunity to vote on the overall executive pay package via say on pay. The vote is advisory and nonbinding and, in theory, could be ignored by the board. But what responsible board could ignore the will of the shareholders? And if it did, how long would the shareholders continue to elect them to the board? Shareholder activist groups are already taking an active role in shaping the votes, and in some cases shareholders have filed suit against the company and against individual members of the board as a result of failed say-on-pay results. Nonbinding indeed!

The Problem

So given this environment, boards — particularly compensation committees — must be certain that they are following a rigorous, fact-based approach to decisions on pay. As part of this process, most committees engage an independent third party to provide data on market pay levels, short- and long-term incentive plan design and provide advice on what may be appropriate for their company. The core of this information typically is a detailed proxy study that compares the value of the package offered to company executives relative to the value provided to executives at a select group of peer companies.

The common analysis of executive pay follows a two-dimensional approach.

- The first dimension is simply the value offered to peer group executives — base salary, annual and long-term cash incentives and the grant-date fair value of equity grants. This dimension provides a snapshot of what was paid.

- The second dimension provides the committee with the "mix" of pay elements — how much of the value was provided by cash, stock options, restricted shares, performance shares, restricted stock units and other incentive vehicles. This dimension can be illustrated by a pie-chart that can illustrate how much of the executive pay is fixed (base salary, restricted shares) and how much is performance-based, at-risk.

But in looking at this market snapshot, are committees getting a full and true picture of the competitive landscape and the potential risks inherent in any compensation plan? The authors think not.

As a simple example, assume two executive pay packages as set out in Table 15-2. In looking at this data, the casual observer may conclude that these executives are paid the same, when clearly the realized value of what they will earn as their equity grants mature may be very different based on factors such as market change and performance.

Although the grant value of equity is the same (in dollars) based on the concept of fair value, the number of shares used for an option grant will typically be greater than that of a restricted

TABLE 15-2

Comparison of Composition of Pay Packages

	Executive 1	Executive 2
Base	$1,000,000	$1,000,000
Target annual incentive	$500,000	$500,000
Option grant	0	$1,000,000
Restricted share grant	$1,000,000	0
Grant date price	$10	$10
Total value	$2,500,000	$2,500,000
Pay mix	40/60	40/60

share grant. For this example, assume an option on three shares deliver the same fair value as one restricted share, which means:
- Executive 1 would receive 100,000 restricted shares
- Executive 2 would receive 300,000 stock options.

As the share price changes over the term of the award, the value to the executive differs substantially. Thus, assuming both grants will be fully vested after three years, Table 15-3 illustrates the different outcomes of two executive compensation packages depending on the level of the change in the price of the company's shares.

Clearly, these alternative grant strategies do not produce the same effect, and as an issue of good corporate governance, compensation committees need to be aware of the effect that plan design can have on value. Specifically, as an enhancement to the traditional proxy analysis, good corporate governance might suggest that these committees also look at the volatility of potential outcomes — the third dimension.

What Is the Third Dimension?

The third dimension is a method of evaluating not just the snapshot, but the potential outcomes of plan design given a number of different stock performance scenarios over time. Using data provided in company proxies, a careful analysis can determine the effect of plan design on each executive's total compensation (base

TABLE 15-3

Comparison of Outcomes of Pay Packages

	Executive 1	Executive 2
	100,000	300,000
Potential price change	Shares' value	Options' value[1]
95%	$950,000	$0
100%	$1,000,000	$0
110%	$1,100,000	$300,000
120%	$1,200,000	$600,000
150%	$1,500,000	$1,500,000
200%	$2,000,000	$3,000,000

[1] Value expressed as actual realized value, not Black-Scholes

salary, annual and long-term incentives and retirement benefits/ deferred compensation). Data can be provided for the named executive officers both in the absolute and relative to peer companies.

The Range of Outcomes
Figure 15-2 provides an array of potential outcomes expressed in dollar values highlighting the potential exposure of the company to unexpected costs, as well as the potential values of the compensation plan relative to competitors.

Why Is This Analysis Critical to the Compensation Committee?
As discussed, the simple answer is that it provides the committee with an in-depth look at executive pay over time, not just the snapshot approach common to most compensation reports. In addition, having this data is consistent with the general trend in compensation disclosure requirements for more analysis and consideration of "what if" scenarios. Best practice already expects that the committee will look at tally sheets to review executive pay in its totality. How much better to add performance scenarios and outcomes?

It also provides the committee with a more robust illustration of compensation risk for the required disclosure in the annual proxy statement. Too much risk and leverage creates an incentive for risky (and ethically challenged) behavior from executives. Too little risk and leverage may create a competitive disadvantage and/ or internal dissatisfaction with the alignment of executive rewards with the results delivered to shareholders.

One of the drivers of the economic downturn of 2008-2009 was presumed to be related to risky incentive design in the financial services industry. More importantly, following the collapse in the financial services industry, many compensation committee members confessed that they had not fully grasped the potential impact of outcomes in highly speculative compensation plans. The volatility analysis suggested would have gone far in providing committees with full disclosure and may have helped prevent disaster.

Finally, a "volatility of outcomes" is not yet required as part of the proxy disclosure rules. But the trend is clearly in the direction

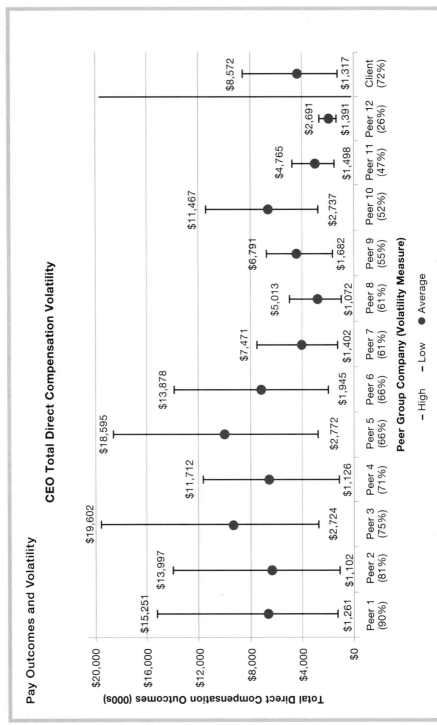

FIGURE 15-3

of more disclosure regarding the relationship between pay and performance. Shareholder groups are demanding visibility and Dodd-Frank requires that companies illustrate how the company performed regarding pay versus performance. Can it be long before progressive, well-governed companies begin showing not just what happened in the prior year, but what *could* happen? If nothing else, it provides a proactive defense for committees against legal action by disgruntled shareholders.

16
CEO Succession Management

By Ron Garonzik, Jeffrey Kirschner and Katie Lemaire

The media, shareholder activists and other governance watchdogs pay considerable attention to CEO and executive pay. Some would argue, however, that choosing the right CEO and top management team is even more important than determining how much they are paid. For this reason, these conversations often are held together and the compensation committee of the board is charged with making CEO succession recommendations.

CEO succession planning has undergone two major changes in recent years. First, boards of directors are far more engaged in CEO succession management, including preparing for the possibility of premature departure, than a decade ago when this process was largely driven by the CEO. Second, the norm in boards of public companies is to have a robust succession management process rather than just having a succession plan. As a result, directors are taking a more hands-on role in guiding the selection and development of candidates for the CEO position.

A Hay Group study of 150 of the world's largest companies, conducted in conjunction with *Fortune's* Most Admired Companies research, indicated that 75 percent of boards favor internal candidates to outside hires absent unusual or turnaround situations. This obliges boards to make sure they have a feasible pool of internal talent with the skills and experience needed to succeed as the next CEO. Moreover, they must implement development programs to groom top talent for potential leadership. Simply identifying a list of "high potentials" and giving them increased board exposure is not enough to ensure successful succession. Boards need to have in place a clearly defined process of CEO succession in advance of the actual search, one that includes developing internal and external search mechanisms.

This chapter:

- Discusses why CEO succession planning is one of the most important responsibilities of the board of directors and details some of the common mistakes boards make in planning for a CEO replacement.

- Offers a five-step process based on current and future business needs to assist CEOs and boards in developing a proactive succession program. This process should be put in place well in advance of any anticipated CEO departure and includes advice on how to identify and assess potential candidates, how to identify and remedy gaps in a candidate's skill set, and how to manage the transition into the new position.

Importance of CEO Succession Management

Few decisions can be more devastating to a company than picking the wrong CEO. At the same time, the rapid pace of change in corporate America coupled with increased scrutiny from multiple constituencies has resulted in shorter average tenure in the CEO position. A decade ago, CEO tenure of 10 years was not uncommon. Now, the average global CEO tenure is about seven years, and two out of five CEOs fail in their first 18 months. CEO failure can be incredibly costly — CEO turnover in the United States costs a minimum of 2½ times direct compensation in immediate severance and replacement costs. Additional negative outcomes can include backlash in the financial markets, internal disruption, loss of key talent, misguided strategic direction, inability to meet performance objectives and bleak results for shareholders. The CEO may simply be misfit with the corporate culture, providing leadership that fails to foster team spirit. Hiring an internal candidate is no guarantee against choosing the wrong candidate.

Despite the increased attention given to succession, most directors today admit that their boards could be far more effective in CEO and executive succession management. A study of 800 board members across the United States conducted by the National Association of Corporate Directors (NACD) found that only half felt that their boards were effective in CEO succession management.

Many corporate experts maintain that selecting the new CEO is the single most important task that the board has. The steps outlined here furnish directors with the comfort of better information and a process that provides the level of due diligence shareholders deserve in this all-important decision.

Step 1: Identify the Future CEO Role Requirements

Effective succession management begins by proactively identifying how anticipated changes in the firm's strategy and organizational structure will affect the requirements for the CEO. Given the importance of this work, all board members should have input into developing this role profile. The resulting discussion can help to clarify role requirements for all parties and align the board in a common direction.

The first step is to ensure that the board is aligned on the three-to five-year strategy. If it is not aligned on the company's strategy, the board can hardly be aligned in terms of the requirements of future corporate leadership. For example, the requirements for a CEO managing a primarily domestic business with international operations requires far different capabilities than managing one that depends on its growth from emerging markets. As another example, CEOs of companies that plan to go public require quite different capabilities than those that remain private.

Additionally, when a company has a highly effective CEO in place, it is extremely useful to assess him/her as part of the development of the future CEO profile. This process can surface key attributes and capabilities that have made the CEO successful in leading this particular company, thus yielding practical insights that can be used in developing the future CEO role profile. While the next CEO should not be a clone of the current one, understanding which of the current CEO's capabilities helped foster his/her success can help determine which of these attributes will be equally important in future leadership. The CEO typically finds the assessment process illuminating both from the standpoint of his/her own leadership and in mentorship of future CEO candidates. The output of this effort is a robust CEO role profile that prioritizes the key position requirements, as trade-offs nearly always will be required and it is important for the board to agree on which requirements are "nice to have" versus essential in future corporate leadership.

Development of future CEO role requirements is the anchor of CEO succession planning. Once the board has agreed upon the future CEO role requirements, this should become the core metric against which all candidates are evaluated and developed. Yet, too often these critical aspects of CEO succession planning are glossed over only to surface at the 11th hour, disrupting the board's decision making and sometimes even forcing a less desirable compromise hire that may have been avoidable.

Step 2: Identify Potential CEO Candidates

One of the biggest challenges that boards face is whether to consider internal versus external CEO candidates. The decision depends on multiple factors, including the quality of available internal talent, future business challenges, the availability of qualified external talent and the desire to retain current senior executives. After the board has a clear picture of the internal potential successors, informed decisions can be made about whether it is necessary to conduct an outside search for a new CEO.

Identifying the potential internal CEO candidates is not as easy as it seems, given the limited view that the most board members have of executives. (See "Common Errors Companies Make in Succession Planning.") A critical success factor in identifying potential candidates is to control for the discontinuous shift in accountability in moving from their current senior executive positions to CEO. Public company CEO jobs, in particular, come with a sudden increase in high-stakes external interactions in which most executives (except for the CFO) have little prior experience. CEO candidates need to be identified based on their ability to manage competing internal and external priorities. These jobs tip the scale decidedly in the direction of managing the external environment and accountability areas that cannot be delegated to others — in particular, balancing

Common Errors Companies Make in Succession Planning

Pick the CFO or General Counsel as the Logical Candidate
Because the board is usually very familiar with the CFO or general counsel, they are often on the top of the list for CEO succession. However, in each of these staff roles, the candidates often lack the leadership and fundamental operational experience necessary to lead large organizations and make business trade-off decisions.

Pick Who You Know
What is familiar is not necessarily what is best for shareholders. Just because board members may have had a successful experience at another company with a CEO candidate does not mean he/she is the best choice for the specific situation at hand. A careful consideration of the role requirements for the target position is the best way of ensuring the success of the new CEO.

Pick a Celebrity CEO
Everyone wants a famous leader with a demonstrated track record to be their CEO, but what works for one firm might not be appropriate at other companies. Celebrity CEOs are a little like sports stars: By the time they have achieved acclaim, they may not be at the top of their game. Additionally, what works for one top executive team might not be best for another; team chemistry is a critical success factor for CEOs. Identifying the future needs of the business and selecting against a clearly defined model offers the greatest likelihood of long-term fit.

Pick the President of the Largest or Most Successful Operating Group
Enterprise leadership is a different leadership challenge than running an operating unit. Having the skills to address multiple constituencies, managing the relationship with the board of directors, and facing off against the investment community are but some of the external-facing capability areas that presidents need to develop before ascending to the top spot.

Let the Search Firms Handle It
Search firms have broad knowledge about potential CEO candidates, and they can be very helpful at surfacing qualified external talent. However, their core competence is neither in creating strategically anchored role profiles nor in assessing talent against the desired characteristics. Long-term business relationships between search firm professionals and CEO candidates may result in conflicts of interest that can be difficult to untangle.

the needs of multiple constituencies and stakeholders (e.g., analysts and the investment community, shareholders, government and regulatory bodies).

Step 3: Objectively Assess Potential CEO Candidates

Once the board agrees on the future-oriented CEO profile, top internal candidates for the CEO position should be assessed to determine their current degree of fit with the requirements. Clearly,

it is critical to evaluate candidates against the requirements identified for the future CEO position — not merely to consider their
performance in their current roles.

CEO succession decisions should not be made solely on the basis
of the board's previous familiarity with company executives. An
outstanding CFO, general counsel or functional leader does not
always have the skills and capabilities required to become CEO
of the same organization. Perhaps most importantly, measuring
candidates against the role profile can help identify gaps and
longer-term risk factors that can be targeted in creating tailored
leadership development plans for top internal candidates.

Too often, board members get only a narrow view of company
executives through presentations at board meetings and interactions a company dinners. While many board members are good
judges of character, proper due diligence on one of the board's
most important decisions should involve multiple considerations:

- The CEO's view on the candidates
- Board members' perspectives
- Formal executive assessments by a professional third party calibrated to the future CEO requirements
- 360-degree feedback from within the company
- Performance on stretch assignments for candidates with regular
  check-in points with the board.

By gathering multiple perspectives, the board obtains a more
complete picture of candidates and, therefore, has better information for decision making. At the conclusion of the executive
assessment, reports are generated about individual capability and
potential relative to the CEO profile. Feedback often is provided
to the candidates in a one-on-one development planning session.

Objective assessments against the CEO profile allow the board
to measure all candidates against common criteria, diminishing the
influence of familiarity in final decision making. Moreover, tools
such as behavioral ("critical incident") interviewing can provide
a more level playing field in making comparisons between the
capabilities of external candidates with those from inside the organization. In our client work, Hay Group often is asked to conduct

a job analysis of external candidates to go behind their titles and examine the key components of their jobs so that the board can gain greater insights to fairly compare the capabilities of outside versus inside candidates before making a choice.

When boards feel compelled to conduct an outside search as proper due diligence, it is critical to use the same platform to compare inside and outside candidates, starting with common CEO role requirements. Moreover, outside searches need not all go to a formal assessment process if internal candidates appear to be making good progress; a silent search or benchmarking study may give the board the comfort it needs.

Ideally, capability assessments should be conducted several years in advance of an anticipated CEO transition event so they can be used to identify top talent and create plans for further development in relation to the future CEO role demands. However, they also can be used closer to the time of an actual candidate decision. While such assessments should never substitute for the board's own judgment in CEO selection, they invariably provide useful insights that boards can incorporate into a more robust view of the candidate pool.

Step 4: Identify and Manage Succession Risks

For imminent succession needs, boards should evaluate the top candidates against the requirements of the job and the potential risk — for both the organization and the candidate. Contrary to longer-term evaluation, this requires a laser-like definition of the suitability of a candidate against the role requirements. Given that no fit is perfect, this allows the board to identify the risks each candidate poses and any development needs that, if appropriately addressed, might minimize those risks.

Risks are not created equally. Gaps in critical knowledge and skill areas often can be addressed through education and on-the-job experiences designed to provide professional development. But gaps in required leadership often become more difficult to address the later they are identified and the higher the individual is in the organizational hierarchy. For instance, CFOs with no history of leading business delivery teams often lack fundamental leadership competencies that are core to line management roles — the ability to translate strategic objectives into clear implementation goals, leading large organizations and providing direct feedback in a manner that enables team members to enhance their performance (rather than coming across as overly critical). Business leaders often fine-tune these leadership capabilities over years through trial and error. The absence of such capability can pose serious risk without focused efforts to provide leaders with the opportunity to develop and refine these skills.

For longer term situations, targeted development plans — often involving skill building, business exposure or both — can be created for the most promising internal candidate to address gaps. Running a global business, having formal exposure to more parts of the organization or taking on a key matrix role are examples of the types of development steps that may be put into place. For such stretch assignments to work, the CEO should be held responsible for ensuring the accountability of candidate progress against the plan and should furnish regular updates to the board.

An additional possibility could involve restructuring the office of the CEO to take advantage of the strongest capabilities of the best candidate, while leveraging the capabilities of additional parties. For example, partnering a strong finance or legal professional with an equally adept operational leader may result in a stronger team and help to ensure continuity and stability within the organization.

Step 5: Manage the Transition

Once the board has identified the best candidate and addressed the risks he/she (and the organization) faces along with any capability gaps, a comprehensive on-boarding plan should be developed that is tailored to the specific situation (e.g., Is the current CEO leaving voluntarily or involuntarily? Is the CEO candidate a logical successor or a "dark horse" candidate who may not be as known to investors and all leaders?). This plan should include not only a development plan for the individual, but also the specific accountabilities that the board has in making the transition successful, as well as the outgoing CEO, if appropriate. If there is a planned transition, there is much more opportunity to manage these risks than if there is a sudden CEO departure. Contingency plans should be in place to manage multiple succession scenarios involving planned or untimely departure of the current CEO.

Current CEO succession planning processes vary widely, ranging from informal discussions to well planned and executed strategies. For some CEOs, the succession planning process starts from the first day on the job. Unfortunately, many major corporations fail to take a sufficiently rigorous approach, resulting in a thin slate of internal candidates or creating an urgent need to hire externally, creating unnecessary risks for the board and the organization. By bringing same level of objectivity and metrics to succession planning that the company does for strategic business planning, the board can reduce risk and fulfill its fiduciary responsibility to shareholders.

17
Board Compensation

By Robert Dill and Timothy Bartlett

A series of legislative and regulatory reforms, coupled with increased scrutiny from shareholder advisory groups, have resulted in an expansion of the duties and responsibilities for outside (nonemployee) directors at publicly traded companies. Factors such as increased time commitments, potential exposure to liability and a reduced pool of candidates with the necessary levels of independence, experience and expertise have all contributed to the continuing growth of directors' total compensation.

In reaction to well-publicized corporate scandals at prominent companies, the Sarbanes-Oxley Act of 2002 ushered in the current era of governance and oversight responsibility for all directors and led to significant changes in compensation design and total compensation levels for outside directors. More recent legislation and rulemaking — including enhanced proxy disclosure rules, expanded governance and compensation standards under the Dodd-Frank Wall Street Reform and Consumer Protection Act of 2010, and new listing requirements applicable to companies traded on national securities exchanges — have affected the structure of director pay programs while overall total compensation levels have remained relatively stable.

Other developments affecting board makeup and board pay include:

* Pressure on many companies to separate the CEO and board chairman roles

- The feasibility of creating a "lead director" to enhance board independence in cases when the CEO and the chair are the same person.

Similarly, as corporate boards look to demonstrate that the compensation of their nonemployee directors is aligned with the long-term interests of shareholders, director stock ownership guidelines and holding retention/requirements are likely to become more important in the evaluation of the company's pay programs.

This chapter:

- Reviews trends and best practices in director pay programs, explains how board members are chosen and paid, and discusses the concept and role of the lead director. Recommendations for allocating the cash and equity elements of director pay are offered.

- Addresses director stock ownership guidelines including common approaches to determine share ownership, compliance and stock holding/retention requirements.

- Contrasts the roles of CEO and board chairman and provides reasons why a company might want to separate the two positions. Various approaches to compensating a non-CEO chairman are presented.

Director Compensation Practices

In recent years director pay has shown modest increases versus the more substantial increases that followed passage of Sarbanes-Oxley. This stability is most likely explained by the financial and economic landscape where boards have been naturally reluctant to significantly increase their compensation while employees face pay reductions, salary freezes or layoffs. Once the economy is on track, director pay levels likely will begin reflecting the new demands and expectations of outside directors as well as the complexity of their roles.

Board Compensation Trends and Developments

Although total compensation levels and mix may differ across industries and in relation to company size, traditionally the compensation package for outside directors at publicly traded companies has included:

- Annual cash retainer
- Committee chair cash retainer

- Lead director cash retainer
- Meeting fees (board and/or committee)
- Benefits/perquisites (e.g., matching gift programs, supplemental insurance benefits)
- Equity compensation.

Director pay commonly has been linked with company size, with larger companies awarding higher cash retainers and total compensation to directors.

While similarities exist when comparing current trends to historical director pay practices (i.e., level and mix of pay continue to differ across industries; total compensation levels are correlated to company size; the use of annual cash retainers and equity awards are the primary elements of director pay) several new developments regarding the structure and form of director pay are evident in the current marketplace.

Elimination of Board and Committee Meeting Fees

The elimination of fees paid to directors for attendance at board and/ or committee meetings has been a growing trend for serveral years. Where the use of meeting fees has been discontinued, companies are providing increases to annual cash retainers to compensate directors for meeting preparation and attendance. Companies that use this approach commonly cite the benefits associated with the simplification of the design and administration of their director compensation programs and the removal of the need to define what constitutes a meeting for fee-payment purposes. Among companies that have retained meeting fees for directors, a minority approach is to provide for payment of meeting fees only after attendance at a pre-defined number of board or committee meetings.

Increased Focus on Work and Pay at the Committee Level

Recent regulatory changes have continued to increase director responsibilities and oversight resulting in more work being performed at the committee level. Companies traditionally have provided additional cash retainers to the chair of a standing board committee (e.g., audit, compensation, nominating, governance) in recognition of the additional duties and time involved in chairing a committee. This practice continues, with the audit committee chair earning a premium over the other committee chairs. While increases in compensation committee chair retainers are common in the current environment of enhanced scrutiny on executive pay practices, it remains to be seen if these changes will serve to close the gap between chairs of the audit and compensation committees.

Another recent development at the committee level is an increase in the number of companies that pay additional annual cash retainers to non-chair members of the committees instead of meeting fees. Where used, the cash retainer amounts are paid in recognition of the workloads for non-chair members and the added responsibilities related to risk management.

Shift to Full-Value Equity Awards and Change in Determination of Equity Awards Size

Mirroring the recent trend with executive pay, director compensation programs have increasingly moved toward full-value awards (restricted shares or common stock) to deliver equity-based pay, with stock option use becoming a less prevalent practice. For director pay programs, the decline in stock option grants may be due in part to a concern that options could encourage inappropriate risk taking, as these awards deliver value only where there is appreciation in the share price.

Another significant change to equity-based director pay is the method used to determine the size of equity awards. In recent years and likely in response to volatility in company stock prices, an increasing number of companies are moving to an approach in which the size of the director equity award is equal to a fixed dollar value and away from an approach in which the equity award is based on a fixed number of shares.

Vesting Periods for Equity Awards Reduced to One Year or Eliminated

In recent years, the majority approach has been to vest annual full-value equity awards within one year of grant. As companies move to declassify their boards in response to pressure from shareholder advisory groups, this trend likely will continue as companies use vesting schedules of one year or less to align the vesting term with the directors' annual service period. Similarly, a short vesting period for director annual equity awards can be viewed as a "best practice," as it is thought to maximize director independence because a continued service relationship is not required for a director to receive compensation.

Equity Election and Use of Deferral Programs
As director compensation levels have increased, so have the number of companies that allow directors to elect to receive additional equity awards in lieu of cash retainers or meeting fees. This practice serves to further align director interests with those of shareholders and assists directors in meeting required stock ownership levels in place at a majority of companies. Similarly, a common practice at larger publicly traded companies is to require or permit directors to defer all or a portion of their cash compensation or equity awards. This practice is supported by shareholder advisory groups that encourage companies to require that directors defer equity awards through or until retirement.

Director Stock Ownership Guidelines and Holding/Retention Requirements
While various types of stock ownership guidelines and holding period/retention requirements are common for senior executives, such standards are less widespread for directors. However, boards are increasingly determining that the use of director stock ownership guidelines and holding/retention requirements can contribute to the goal of aligning the interests of nonemployee directors at a publicly traded company with those of its long-term shareholders. Recent economic uncertainty and greater focus by shareholders and advisory groups has generated pressure to improve the alignment of director and shareholder interests, and has led to the increased use of stock ownership guidelines and holding/retention requirements.

Stock Ownership Guidelines: Overview and Common Approaches

Stock ownership guidelines for nonemployee directors generally are designed to require the attainment of a sizable target equity ownership stake within a specified period of time. The most common design approach is to define the applicable stock ownership goal as a multiple of the director's annual cash retainer. The ownership multiple used (on a fairly universal basis) is the same for all directors, which differs from executive stock ownership guidelines that commonly apply different multiples based on an executive's level at the company.

While a multiple of the annual cash retainer is the most prevalent method, a minority of companies define target stock ownership levels for directors as a fixed number of shares or a specific dollar value of shares. Recent stock price volatility has resulted in an increased use of the fixed number of shares approach (the least volatile type of ownership guideline) to lessen the effect of significant short-term swings in share price.

Similarly, to address the issue of fluctuating share ownership targets resulting from change to stock prices, some companies that use a multiple of annual cash retainer to define stock ownership levels have chosen to combine this method with the fixed number of shares approach. In so doing, companies typically define the target stock ownership levels as the lesser of a fixed number of shares or a specific multiple of a director's annual cash retainer.

Determining Share Ownership

In determining which shares/equity awards are taken into account to determine achievement of the stock ownership target, common practice is to include all shares owned outright or beneficially (e.g., held in a trust account) and unvested restricted stock, but to exclude vested and unvested stock options. This way of handling the issue is consistent with the most prevalent share counting approaches used to determine compliance with executive stock ownership guidelines.

Compliance

When designing and adopting director stock ownership guidelines, boards should define what will occur in the event a director does not achieve the required ownership level by the applicable deadline. Common approaches to address this situation include:

- Requiring the director to retain all (or a majority) of the net shares acquired following a stock option exercise
- Providing that all (or a portion of) future cash retainers and meeting fees be paid in shares of company stock that cannot be sold until the guideline is met.

In addition, some companies define compliance with their director ownership guidelines to include situations in which a director has achieved the required ownership target, has not sold any of his/her stock, but has fallen below the applicable multiple of annual cash retainer as a result of a downward movement in share price.

Holding/Retention Requirements

Holding/retention requirements are commonly used by companies in conjunction with stock ownership guidelines to reinforce a meaningful commitment to stock ownership and shareholder alignment through the retention of equity that otherwise could be sold. Generally speaking, holding requirements are enforced for a specified period of time (e.g., three years after exercise of stock options), while retention requirements are enforced for an indefinite period (i,e., until retirement or stock ownership guidelines are met).

Holding/retention requirements typically require nonemployee directors to retain a specified percentage of the shares they acquire through the exercise of stock options and/or vesting of restricted stock awards. These requirements are commonly used along with stock ownership guidelines, with different holding/retention requirements applicable to directors before and after the achievement of targeted stock ownership levels.

Pre-Ownership Guideline Achievement

These holding/retention requirements are applicable to directors during the share accumulation period prior to achievement of

Issues That Have Affected Board Member Selection and Pay

- The imposition or lowering of a limit on the number of boards on which a member may sit has reduced the talent pool.

- Increased obligations, time commitments and risks for directors have caused some candidates and former members to decline board seats.

- There is a shortage of top-quality candidates and a need to replace some board members with independent directors or persons with a specific expertise (e.g., accounting expert).

- A requirement under Sarbanes-Oxley stipulates that the board have a "financial expert" as a member.

- Due to concern regarding potential liability for questionable practices, many boards have been forced to examine their governance structures and independence levels.

- A call for an independent "lead director" has evolved substantially in recent years, prompted by the concern that both the chair and CEO roles often are held by a single individual. Many believe that this arrangement concentrates too much power in the hands of one person and impedes board independence.

- The board has a unique governance role, and directors should be compensated differently than executives:

  - Directors should be compensated for exercising their fiduciary oversight responsibilities, not for the company's performance.

  - Equity should be aligned to shareholders; thus, full-value shares (e.g., time-vested restricted stock) are appropriate to eliminate decisions involving undue risk.

  - Retention should not be a key strategy for board members — it can be important to avoid entrenchment of directors and to allow the board a fresh perspective.

  - Directors should not be offered benefits (e.g., retirement payments, life insurance, health insurance or perquisites).

- The scrutiny placed on financial statements since the Sarbanes-Oxley legislation and concern over executive pay (the Dodd-Frank Act and more information available under expanded proxy disclosure rules) have placed extraordinary demands on a committee chair. Board members at some organizations now are being paid through new or enhanced committee chair fees for meetings with auditors, legal counsel and executive compensation consultants prior to regularly scheduled committee meetings, as well as for the additional time involved in scrutinizing and approving information being presented at their committee meetings.

- Institutional Shareholder Services has adopted a policy to withhold votes from compensation committee members of companies with poor/problematic pay practices, at least in cases in which there is no opportunity to express such displeasure through the say-on-pay vote for the year; other advisory groups have similar policies.

- Today's investors demand high standards of corporate governance and an especially well-informed and active board.

required equity ownership under a company's stock ownership guidelines. Typically, policy requires directors to hold a large percentage of equity awards received (e.g., net shares after option exercise, vesting of restricted shares, common shares granted outright) until such time as stock ownership targets are met.

Post-Ownership Guideline Achievement

Although infrequently used, these holding/retention requirements apply to nonemployee directors that have achieved target stock ownership guideline levels. A typical policy requires a director to hold all (or a significant percentage) of the equity granted under a directors' pay package until retirement from the board.

Nonexecutive Chair Pay Practices

Organizations that transition to a nonexecutive chair structure must establish the appropriate compensation (both level and composition) for the newly defined role. To attract the right person, organizations must compensate the individual appropriately.

Reasons for a Nonexecutive Chair

First, it is important to understand reasons why a company may separate the chair and CEO roles:

- **Independence.** Some believe that having a nonexecutive chair provides greater independence from management in terms of board leadership. A nonexecutive chair can serve as a check and balance on a CEO. Although separation of the chair and CEO roles creates greater independence, it is not a requirement for effective board leadership. Many effective boards have an arrangement in which the CEO and chair roles are combined and a new leadership role (lead director) is created to provide a focal point for the independent work and independent functions of the independent directors.
- **Tradition.** While uncommon in the United States, some companies have a history that dictates that the chair title be held by a separate individual.
- **Transition.** A CEO may be too inexperienced or too new to the company to be given the chair title.

- **Time considerations.** A determination may be made that the CEO should spend his/her time managing the business, and the chair should spend his/her time managing the board and its corporate oversight functions.

The decision to combine or separate the chair and CEO roles is a company-specific decision. Companies should not rely on typical market practices or governance experts in making the decision about whether the roles should be separate or combined. Governance experts typically agree, however, that all companies should appoint an independent lead director when the chair and CEO roles are combined or when the chair is affiliated (e.g., a former CEO with the company).

Essential Qualities of a Nonexecutive Chair

There are several qualifications that should be satisfied by a nonexecutive chair:

- High integrity, accomplishment and emotional maturity
- Strong leadership capabilities and the ability to lead the board's oversight and advisory roles
- Respected by all directors and senior management
- Runs meetings effectively (i.e., draws out different viewpoints and knows when to intervene to keep discussion on track)
- Good listener (i.e., keeps a finger on the pulse of the board)
- Demonstrates independence of mind
- Has the courage to step up to challenging issues, including director or CEO performance issues.

Not only should a nonexecutive chair have superb personal qualities, but knowledge of the company's industry and the company itself can be especially helpful. If company experience is lacking, upon taking the job the nonexecutive chair must strive to learn the business, the people and the company's issues from the bottom up.

Of particular importance, a nonexecutive chair should have the time available to properly discharge the duties involved. The amount of time needed varies in each situation and depends on the complexity of the organization and its issues.

Pay Practices for a Nonexecutive Chair

Recent market data have yielded observations on approaches and practices in nonexecutive chair compensation:

- The ratio of nonexecutive chair compensation to that of other board directors ranges from roughly 1.25 to 2.5, with a median ratio of 1.7. The pay package for the nonexecutive chair position does not approach the pay levels of an employee chair.
- The compensation for a nonexecutive chair who was never the CEO is generally higher than those who are former CEOs of the company.

Setting Pay of a Nonexecutive Chair

In establishing a process for determining the compensation of a nonexecutive chair, a guiding principle should be that the pay should match the commitment and effort required by the (nonexecutive) chair role. There are several approaches and factors that should be considered in setting nonexecutive chair compensation:

- The traditional approach has been to compensate the chair with a fee or retainer that is linked to a daily fee rate.
- A more common method for establishing nonexecutive chair compensation is using a pro-rata amount of the CEO's pay (with a decision needed on whether to include or exclude long-term incentive [LTI] values). This approach considers the perceived value and influence in the company of the individual versus that of the CEO. It also looks at the time required by the role relative to a full-time position.
- Evaluating the complexity and effect of the chair job may be a useful exercise in creating a quantitative relationship between the CEO and the board chair. The chair's pay then can be scaled against the compensation of the CEO.
- Alternatively, broad discretion may be used to set compensation that the company believes is representative of market levels and is equitable based on the services.
- Boards must consider that the more compensation that is given to a nonexecutive chair, the more the perception of his/her independence is diminished.

Today any pay package for a board chair is likely to be scrutinized by the public and shareholders. Regardless of the process chosen, it is important that the decisions can be explained, defended and viewed as supportable under the company's specific circumstances and the requirements of the role.

Comparing the Roles of the Nonexecutive Chair and CEO

The respective roles of the nonexecutive chair and the CEO need to be clear to the individuals serving in them, as well as to the board, senior management and key external parties. "Roles of the Nonexecutive Chair and the CEO" compares the two roles.

What Does a Lead Director Do?

The lead director's primary role is to manage and facilitate a board's governance process and allow the board a measure of independence from the CEO. Other duties of the lead director may include:

- Serve as an objective conduit through which directors can communicate.
- Create a process that ensures each important issue is given both analysis and consideration.
- Act as a useful director recruitment tool, allowing directors to feel more accountable to other board members and shareholders.
- Demonstrate to shareholders, regulators and the public that the board is administering governance processes that are appropriate and defensible.
- Add a visible layer of independence at a company that has a CEO who is also the board chair.
- Help develop other board members, mentor newer members, provide guidance to manage board responsibilities and advance the learning curve.
- Conduct annual outside director performance reviews.

Lead directors may not be suitable for every company. However, in today's environment, most anything a company can do to emphasize board independence and thorough governance will only help build regulator, shareholder, investor and public confidence and trust.

Director Pay Practices in Private Companies

Similar to publicly traded companies, it has become a challenge for many private companies to recruit qualified individuals as directors. While some key differences exist in the responsibilities of board members in the public and private sectors, the basic principles and practices that apply to publicly traded companies also should be observed for private companies. According to Hay Group studies, about three-quarters of private companies provide some sort of cash compensation, while less than one-quarter provide stock as part of such director pay.

When considering director compensation of private companies, total director pay is about one-half of amounts at publicly traded companies. This can be explained by the fact that 50 percent or more of total director pay for publicly traded companies is made up of equity-based awards.

A private company may benchmark against publicly traded companies, but then apply a discount to account for the lessened responsibility for regulatory and other issues not faced in the private sector. Generally, it is better to look at the business approach of paying enough to attract quality directors and make it worth their time to serve on the board.

Director Pay Practices in Tax-Exempt Organizations

Not-for-profit organizations traditionally have not paid their directors. Today, however, with competition for director talent and increased responsibilities for board members, many tax-exempt organizations have found it necessary to pay their directors or are considering doing so. See the section titled "Considerations for Board Pay at Tax-Exempt Organizations" in Chapter 20.

Roles of the Nonexecutive Chair and the CEO

Role of the Nonexecutive Chair

- Plays no role in company operations

- No company officers report to him/her; CEO reports to the board

- Has authority to call meetings of the board of directors

- Chairs meetings of the board and the annual meeting of shareholders

- Chairs executive sessions and debriefs with the CEO

- Sets board agendas and oversees board information packages

- Facilitates discussion among board members on key issues and concerns outside of board meetings

- Serves as nonexclusive conduit to CEO of views, concerns and issues of other directors

- Addresses any board or director performance concerns

- May represent the company with external stakeholders at the discretion of the board and in conjunction with the CEO

- Speaks for the company in a crisis situation when CEO is unable

Role of the CEO

- Leads company operations; officers and employees report to him/her

- Attends board meetings and the annual meeting of shareholders; makes presentations on company operations

- Receives feedback from executive sessions

- Provides input into board agenda items

- Provides content for board information packages

- Communicates with the chair on various issues between board meetings

- Raises with the chair any concerns management may have about board performance, individual director performance and board composition

- Represents the company to external stakeholders

PART III
Executive Compensation in Special Settings

18
Mergers and Acquisitions

By Shawn Hamilton and Matthew Kleger

Although a business transaction undoubtedly can have significant implications for an organization, executive compensation issues are often neglected once due diligence is completed. Executive compensation is seldom a deal breaker, but it can have a substantial effect on the deal structure and future operations of the ongoing organization.

In a merger and acquisition (M&A) situation, management and HR professionals have to consider whether current pay programs are properly structured to retain and motivate executives if a potential transaction looms. In addition, companies must apply increased rigor and vigilance to properly craft incentive programs that satisfy the views and objectives of various interested parties, including shareholders, investment and proxy advisers, regulators, bloggers and reporters, all of whom intensely scrutinize compensation.

Private equity (PE) transactions and spin-offs, like other business transactions, demand considerable preparation; compensation elements that were once a critical piece of the overall system may represent limited or even no value to executives in the new organization. Many companies discover too late that they need to rebalance their compensation programs to reflect the new reality of PE and, in particular, how to replace pre-acquisition stock options.

There are many moving parts in an M&A transaction, many of which are focused on financing and structuring the deal. Compensation programs prior to the deal typically reflect company culture — risk-averse companies favoring fixed compensation vehicles, higher-risk profile companies preferring variable compensation. Compensation systems must be adapted to the new environment, with particular attention paid to equity awards so that the newly combined team retains high-potential performers going forward.

This chapter:

- Discusses retention through the M&A process, focusing on those employees who should be considered for any potential program and recommended practices for setting retention incentives.

- Describes the typical M&A transaction scenario and the steps that can be taken to preserve unrealized option gains. Alternatives to the treatment of stock options in a spin-off are offered, along with and recommended techniques to make executives whole, including preservation of option spread, preservation of economic value and no conversion of options.

- Illustrates how a PE transaction is structured and outlines key issues to consider, including who typically gets equity.

- Describes alternative strategies for integrating performance-based long-term incentives in M&A, focusing on the potential strategies for addressing goal setting, performance measurement and outstanding award cycles pre- and post-transaction.

Retention Through the M&A Process

Savvy managers understand that the stabilizing force of retention pay can work wonders in settling staff members. Applied smartly, this form of compensation can keep key employees focused on business instead of worrying about their future. For purposes of this discussion, retention compensation refers to the practice of encouraging critical employees to stay for a certain period or through (or beyond) a particular event by offering them phased payouts — whether in cash, stock, other enticements or some combination.

Who to Consider for Retention Pay

A common mistake is to spread a retention program like peanut butter, applying it to everybody in the organization. At some organizations retention payments cover employees who do not need any special incentive to stay. While that may be easier than evaluating individual performance, the practice uses up resources that could be better directed to critical employees who may be more likely to leave.

In general, loyalists — employees committed to the organization and particularly to the CEO — do not require any incentive to stay when these aspects of the employer are not changing. The same may be true for staff members with heavy investments in stock options or restricted stock that would be forfeited upon leaving. Of course, deeply underwater stock options lose their retentive hold and may cause employees to seek to re-price them through grants from a new employer. Also, if salaries are competitive within a close range, companies are less likely to see their people depart for a marginal bump in pay. Yet, even fairly satisfied individuals are at risk of leaving should hard times last more than a year. Year two is when a retention plan really needs to kick into action. Just about anyone can tolerate doldrums for some period. But when that person starts to see a pattern of inaction on the part of company leadership or a disruptive event occurs, that is when he/she becomes more drawn to the allure of another organization.

When considering who to compensate as part of a retention plan, a company should focus on individuals or job functions that are critical to running the organization and its businesses, especially those who are more likely to accept headhunters' calls during times of turmoil. These typically include:

- **Executive officers,** particularly those who run multi-functional groups. Because those individuals tend to be higher profile, they also are more likely to be identified and wooed first by recruiters.
- **Operational experts,** such as a knowledgeable, yet unsung IT person who keeps the computer systems running smoothly. What would be lost if that employee left at a crucial time?
- **"Creatives,"** such as a team of designers doing amazing work — and who know it. How quickly could the organization replace them if the group departed unexpectedly?
- **The highly marketable,** such as in-house experts on identification theft and energy usage who are probably taking calls weekly from companies desperate for similar talent. How much is it worth to keep them on board during this hot period for those jobs?

Notice that sales people are not specifically mentioned. Many sales personnel fall within the "highly marketable" category. Otherwise, apart from trying to make sure they are happy overall, reliance is on their compensation plans that tend to have built-in incentives.

Plus, those who make money directly for the company rarely are in the line of fire to lose their positions during times of uncertainty.

Where Retention Compensation Comes into Play

Establishing an equitable and intelligent retention compensation plan involves a consideration of various design and regulatory issues. A company needs to pinpoint the appropriate targets, amount of compensation for a given situation, and the terms of the plan while making sure that tax, accounting, legal and other compliance matters are appropriately addressed.

There are several common scenarios in which some form of retention compensation may prove vital for continuing operations. M&A transactions are obvious triggers, particularly when the firm is being acquired by a strategic buyer, such as a competitor. In that situation, most corporate jobs — accounting, human resources, marketing — within the acquired business are at risk. Retention planning is of less importance when the company is being bought as an investment, such as a PE deal in which the buyer is more likely to leave overall operations intact.

CEO turnover is a driving force that generates uncertainty. Frequently, the new chief executive will hire people he/she knows and trusts, and those new hires will in turn do the same. Suddenly, company leadership has a completely new face, which can be unsettling. Layoffs, bankruptcies, restructurings and elimination of divisions also trigger mass insecurities. In these cases, individuals often can predict they will lose their jobs at some point. Likewise, those who are currently unaffected may begin to wonder when their turn will come up. Less dramatic, but just as draining, a competitor may be expanding and recruiters may be picking off the best talent to fuel that growth.

Smart Practices for Designing Retention Incentives

In setting the levels of compensation in a retention strategy, decision makers should consider some lessons garnered from experience:

- First, time is a major factor in establishing the amount of compensation that is at stake. Keeping a worker for two years of transition will cost more than if the transition only will last six months.

• Second, the person receiving an incentive probably will compare the amount of time it would take to find a new position to the amount of the compensation being offered. Whichever one looks more advantageous will probably win out.

• Third, the compensation has to be in line with other company expenses. How much can the company afford? What's reasonable, given the entire situation?

• Fourth, geography can play a role in determining the appropriate amount of retention compensation. If employees have fewer employment opportunities because of where they are located or, conversely, if they are in a location where they can make a job change by simply going one stop farther on the subway, that will influence how much to offer.

When structuring the terms of the retention plan, there will be variations depending on context. For instance, an M&A situation may put the emphasis on a staff person helping to get the deal done altogether or wrapped up in a certain amount of time. Achieving a specific result is the goal. The payment plan also will vary by role. Executives will probably be satisfied with payouts spaced further apart. A line person will want to see more frequent compensation. In general, the nearer the individual's safety net is to each paycheck, the closer together those payments need to be. High-potential, high-performing people exist throughout an organization. During both healthy and slow economic times, a properly structured retention plan can keep them engaged and committed.

Stock Option Treatment in M&A

Of all the business strategies that companies follow in their quest to increase shareholder value, M&A transactions typically garner the most attention due to the size of the dollars involved.

The same focus on increased shareholder value also has resulted in the widespread use of executive compensation packages with strong links to corporate performance. While declining in prevalence in recent years, stock options still represent a significant portion of the long-term incentive (LTI) component of executive compensation packages at U.S. public companies. However, in M&A transactions, an executive holding stock options is not like the average shareholder.

Due to restrictions typically put on executive stock option grants (i.e., vesting), executives often cannot participate in M&A-driven stock price movements as easily as an ordinary shareholder. Consequently, the treatment of executive stock options is a significant component of an M&A transaction.

An M&A transaction generally transforms two business entities into one. In one type of transaction, a corporation (Target) may be purchased and merged into another corporation (Buyer). In Figure 18-1, Target's equity disappears and its shareholders either receive cash for their shares or become shareholders of Buyer.

Another M&A transaction is a consolidation, illustrated in Figure 18-2. In this case, two (or more) companies consolidate to form a

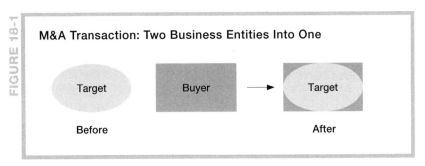

FIGURE 18-1

M&A Transaction: Two Business Entities Into One

Target   Buyer   ⟶   Target

Before   After

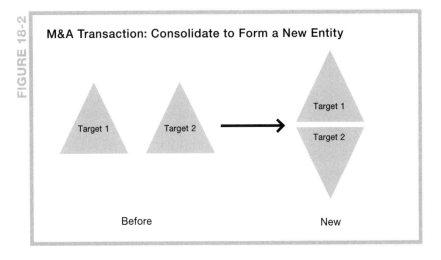

FIGURE 18-2

M&A Transaction: Consolidate to Form a New Entity

Target 1   Target 2   ⟹   Target 1
                                   Target 2

Before   New

new entity whereby the stock of the old companies is converted into shares in the new entity.

A common goal in M&A transactions is the preservation of executives' unrealized option gains at the time of the deal. Preservation of option "spread" (the difference between option exercise price and current fair market value [FMV] of the underlying stock), preservation of economic value and the cash purchase of options are three alternatives by which companies involved in M&A transactions might achieve this goal. In accomplishing these goals, care must be taken to satisfy applicable accounting and tax rules to obtain the desired treatment.

Preservation of Option Spread

Stock options in Target are converted into stock options in Buyer at a rate that preserves the aggregate spread. The ratio of exercise price to FMV must be at least as high as it was under Target's stock option design, and other stock option design features (i.e., vesting) must carry over.

In Figure 18-3, the ratio or exercise price to FMV for Target stock options is 60 percent ($12/$20). Therefore, the exercise price of the Buyer stock options to be issued to Target's executives must be a minimum of $30 (60 percent of $50, the FMV of Buyer's stock). The current aggregate spread is calculated on Target options as $20,000 (2,500 options times $8), and then the number of Buyer stock options to be granted to Target's executives is calculated as

FIGURE 18-3

Example: Preservation of Option Spread

	Buyer	Target
FMV	$50	$20
Exercise price	$30	$12
Spread (FMV minus exercise price)	$20	$8
Number of options	1,000	2,500
Aggregate spread (spread times number of options)	$20,000	$20,000

1,000 ($20,000/$20). However, the use of a below-FMV exercise price generally results in nonqualified deferred compensation (NQDC) and subjects the awards to requirements of Internal Revenue Code (IRC) section 409A.

Preservation of Economic Value

Stock options in Target are converted into Buyer options in a manner that preserves Target's stock options' "economic value" (prospective value of the option at grant). While the calculation is similar to the option spread preservation method, this alternative involves using an option valuation model (e.g., Black-Scholes, binomial) to determine the economic values.

Cash Purchase of Options

In the event Buyer does not have stock issued or does not want to enter into an option exchange, it may purchase all outstanding Target stock options. A cash buyout would compensate Target's executives for any lost future value in their stock options. Cash buyouts of stock options often are used if the target company's stock options are not vested or are underwater (FMV of the underlying shares is less than the stock option exercise price).

Critical Steps in M&A Due Diligence

Due to the widespread use of stock options by U.S. corporations, deciding how to handle unvested stock options held by a target company's executives is a critical step in M&A due diligence. The aforementioned three alternatives represent some of the ways companies handle target companies' unvested stock options.

Stock Option Treatment in Spin-Offs

Especially after a merger or acquisition, a company may decide to sell — or divest itself of — a subsidiary when it is no longer essential to its business model or long-term strategy. A spin-off is a specific type of divestiture in which, rather than being sold, a subsidiary becomes an independent company itself. In a spin-off, shareholders in the parent corporation receive the newly issued stock of the former subsidiary. The result is that the shareholdings of that intact corporation prior to spin-off are preserved through proportionate ownership of the parent corporation's stock and the stock of the newly spun-off subsidiary, as in Figure 18-4.

Stock Option Issues

Often an executive of a spun-off subsidiary will have options on the stock of the parent company. After the spin-off, compensation based on the former parent's stock may not be appropriate and may even terminate by the terms of the stock option awards themselves because the participants no longer will be employees of the issuer or an affiliate.

Spin-offs create interesting questions of "making executives whole" on both sides of the transaction. An initial reaction may be to distribute cash or other consideration to maintain an option holder's economic position.

For example, the company could purchase the stock options from the executives of the subsidiary. However, as a practical matter, this is usually not done because:

• It would require use of cash targeted for other corporate purposes.
• A cash payment would result in an expense to the income statement.
• Cash conversion of the stock options would terminate the stock options and their inherent benefit to the option holder (i.e., the risk-free investment opportunity in the stock).

FIGURE 18-4

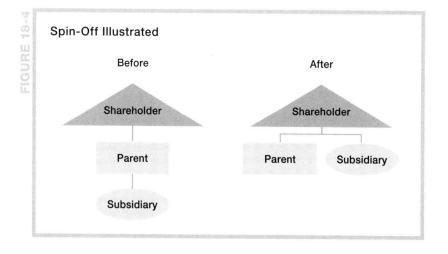

Spin-Off Illustrated

Instead, executives' unrealized stock option gains can be preserved in order to carry over the value of their compensation after the spin-off without the use of cash. Two basic approaches have been used to maintain unrealized stock option gains in a spin-off: preservation of stock option spread and preservation of economic value.

Preservation of Stock Option Spread

To preserve the aggregate spread, stock options in the parent corporation would be converted into stock options in the spun-off entity. In such a conversion, the ratio of exercise price to FMV must be at least as high as it was in the parent options and the remaining stock option term and vesting period must be incorporated into the design of the spin-off's options. Once again, the application of the NQDC rules under IRC section 409A must be considered.

Preservation of Economic Value

Another alternative would be to preserve the economic value of the stock option at the time of conversion. Unlike the stock option spread alternative in which the new stock options are in the money at grant, this alternative results in a grant of new stock options where the new exercise price equals the fair market value at grant to the spin-off. Usually the Black-Scholes (or a binomial) value of a stock option is determined on the date of grant; however, in this alternative, the economic value is determined instead at the time of conversion, or spin-off.

Basically, this method replaces the economic value of discounted stock options (the in-the-money grant in the old parent) with an equivalent economic value for a stock option grant in the spin-off where the exercise price equals the FMV at the spin-off. As a result, the optionee receives more stock options; however, the built-in spread is gone. In effect, the built-in spread on the old stock options is converted into additional shares and more leverage.

No Conversion

Alternatively, a parent corporation may choose to preserve its stock option grants in the spin-off. Under this method, option holders in the parent company continue holding the stock options, though they become employees of the spun-off corporation.

Use of this approach requires a careful examination of the terms of the stock option plan and specific awards to make sure that the term of a stock option is not ended or truncated due to the holder's termination of employment with such entity — a situation that commonly occurs. Otherwise, treatment upon termination of employment may be triggered, resulting in the forfeiture of unvested stock options and only a short period to exercise any vested stock options.

Is Private Equity in Your Company's Future?

The business press focuses considerable attention on PE transactions. One household name after another has been acquired by PE firms. With the size of funds established by some PE firms and the participation of multiple PE firms in certain deals, few companies may be safe from the reach of these investors.

In a typical leveraged buyout (LBO) transaction, PE firms take out debt in the company's name and use about 20 percent of their own assets to fund the purchase price of the transaction. For companies targeted by PE firms, the following primer has been developed on compensation and benefits considerations. In general, these deals are very complex with their own terminology, which can be confusing to the uninitiated. Table 18-1 provides a sampling of common terms. Following are key items to consider in preparation for an LBO/PE transaction:

- **An LBO transaction likely will trigger a change in control for the target company.** As a starting point, typically all deferred compensation, equity and other plans will vest. Depending on a plan's payment trigger, amounts may become either payable immediately or on an employee's subsequent dismissal "with cause" or "good reason" resignation. Consideration must be given to the golden parachute rules of IRC sections 280G and 4999 and the conditions to avoid adverse tax consequences for NQDC under IRC section 409A.
- **Communicate often and early.** Even if there is no actual deal, if your company is "declared" a target by the media, Wall Street or even a blogger, people will begin to develop their own theories

TABLE 18-1

Common Terms in LBO Transactions

Term	Definition
Multiple of money	PE firm's estimate of the return on its initial investment (typically expressed as a 2x, 3x and so on.)
Sponsor	The private equity firm or group of firms taking part in the LBO
Portfolio company	One of the companies that is owned by a private equity sponsor
Liquidity event	An initial public offering, sale or divestiture of a portfolio company
Management promote	Equity plan in the newly private company designed to "promote" the best interests of the new private equity owners
Leveraged common stock	Preferred shares of restricted stock designed to create a tax-efficient vehicle for the management promote
Strip	Equal to option on 10 shares of stock
Buy-in	Direct investment by executives in the newly private company; can be a requirement in order to receive management-promote shares; typically capped in amount available per person and by level in the company (e.g., only available to SVP and above)

about what is happening. Preparing employees with facts and information typically is the best approach.

• **Special severance plans may be necessary.** Employees may begin to receive opportunistic headhunter calls. Even with a communications strategy in place, make sure that employees feel comfortable even if their jobs are eliminated.

• **Inventory all current vehicles that were designed to retain employees and assess their retention ability under the current circumstances.** Make sure that there are appropriate retention "hooks" that hold your most valuable people assets in place before, during and after the transaction. Because many existing retention programs will have vested (e.g., equity, deferred compensation), new plans and strategies may need to be quickly designed, formalized and communicated.

- **Assess and identify all long-term liabilities created by contracts and plans.** Examples include change-in-control arrangements, equity plans, cash LTI plans, retirement plans and severance programs.
  - Revise and/or prepare your compensation philosophy for the new organization.
  - Equity may not be available to employees; what will take its place?
  - PE sponsors typically do not support fixed compensation. Plans that are not directly related to performance and/or nonessential plans may not survive the transition.
  - Update your succession plan. Regardless of how much you prepare, plan and anticipate, your organization will lose some talented individuals. Additionally, executives — flush with gains from recent plan payouts and gains acquired upon the vesting of equity — may choose to pursue a dream rather than re-enlist for another tour of duty.

Once the deal is finalized, there still may remain a need to address various details regarding executive compensation arrangements. Considerable effort should be taken to ensure all compensation and benefits plan details are accounted for in the merger/acquisition agreement. In some cases, certain portions of the compensation packages may be subject to negotiation with the affected executives.

Ownership interests in the newly private entity are often only provided to senior officers. In some circumstances, a cash-based LTI plan can be negotiated for corporate directors and vice presidents who do not participate in the management promote of the newly private company. High-potential as well as mission-critical employees also may be included in a long-term plan with the new company.

Almost all equity interests under the management-promote plan are allocated when the deal is consummated; the remaining shares are held for new hires and targeted retention awards. Sponsors view these awards as one-time grants that will carry management until a future liquidity event (e.g., IPO, sale). Sponsors typically view a deal's horizon as five years or less until the liquidity event. The management promote usually will not have any feature that allows for disposition prior to this event. From the sponsor's perspective, executives need to be tied down for the deal's entire duration. This is a fairly long-term commitment for management given current rates of executive turnover and the lack of a more typical annual LTI grant program.

Table 18-2 provides some additional detail about compensation and benefits issues before, during and after a transaction. In the end, do not underestimate the compensation-related work involved and the complexity of these transactions. Changes will need to be made to many of the current compensation and benefits programs. Communications are critical during this type of transaction; keeping employees "in the know" should help retain them throughout the transaction.

TABLE 18-2

Compensation and Benefits Issues Before, During and After a Transaction

Due Diligence: Pre-Transaction Planning	Deal Announced: Managing During the Transition	Going Forward: Managing the New Organization
• Establish compensation and benefits philosophy - Market, position, mix - Different strategy (executive, salaried, hourly?) • Review change-in-control consequences of existing programs (e.g., acceleration of liability/payouts) • Measure accrued liabilities for programs with a future benefit promise (e.g., defined benefit plan, SERP) • Consider severance and retention plan costs - Buyer will want to know those costs on the front end	• Create total remuneration strategy • Develop base pay plan - Bands/grades/other - Assess impact • Short-term incentives - Metrics, eligibility, etc. • Long-term incentives - Vehicles possible - Tax/accounting consequences • Audit benefit competitiveness • Redesign as appropriate • Identify appropriate vendors (e.g., TPA, outsourcers) • New plan documents, summary plan descriptions, etc. - New owner will want to be involved	• Develop integrated statement of total compensation • Implement new compensation and benefits structure • Determine appropriate severance and retention policy for new organization • Identify administrative roles and duties (both internal/external) • Roll out and communicate

Integrating Performance-Based Long-Term Incentives

Integrating two sets of similar compensation programs can be challenging enough; then consider the potential difficulties when cultures, philosophies and program designs are distinctly different at the combining organizations. It can be daunting to resolve issues such as determining the appropriate compensation philosophy and reconciling compensation plan mechanics (e.g., eligibility, target award levels, award/grant processes, performance measurement, goal setting). If handled properly, these areas can be key drivers of success pre- and post-transaction.

The focus here is on alternatives for integrating two distinct performance-based LTI plans, looking specifically at goal setting, performance measurement and outstanding award cycles during the transition period immediately post-transaction.

Performance-Based Long-Term Incentives

Performance-based LTI plans are becoming more prominent as companies seek alternative approaches to align pay with performance in today's environment with active shareholders. These vehicles can pose unique challenges in connection with an M&A transaction, including:

- Handling outstanding award cycles
- How to set performance targets for new grants, especially when the two integrating companies are performing on different levels
- Length of performance measurement periods.

Successful integration requires the HR team to be acutely aware of the compensation disparities between the two companies. Issues may include:

- How do we reconcile performance-based LTI without providing windfalls or penalizing plan participants?
- How do we adhere to the desired compensation philosophy?
- How can a consistent plan framework be developed, yet be flexible enough to be customized for both companies and their various business units?

Assume that a larger, higher performing company is acquiring a smaller, lower performing company as we try to answer these questions and provide alternatives to integrating their performance-based LTI plans.

Alternative Strategies

Begin by taking inventory of the existing performance-based LTI plans. Due diligence is done to answer the following questions:

- What vehicles are being utilized to deliver pay?
- How many and what types of measures are being used?
- How many award cycles are outstanding?
- What is the typical grant process?

One of the most significant challenges can be handling outstanding award cycles. The acquisition of a lower performing company likely will reduce profitability and may divert company resources and executive focus. Accordingly, executive LTI plans should consider the effect of an acquisition and incentive plans should be aligned with responsibilities. The following strategies could be considered for harmonizing two performance-based LTI plans:

- **No changes to plans or metrics.** This approach is potentially viable when financial performance and pay strategies are very similar between the two companies. The strategy also may work if the target company's performance can be "carved out." The key challenge posed by this alternative is that it does not hold the acquiring company accountable for the acquisition. Shareholders want executives to be accountable for an acquisition as shareholder capital and company resources are being diverted and utilized toward the strategic acquisition. Shareholders will not want to reward executives today for returns (perhaps) realized tomorrow. It is unusual for pay strategies to be aligned well enough to allow performance-based plans to continue unchanged.
- **Terminate all plans and make payouts based on current performance.** This approach requires both companies to annualize performance and pay pro-rata awards based on duration of completed award cycles. The strategy can be appropriate for companies attempting to make a "transformational" change to the business. The combination of two entities may create new collective strategies and synergies, whereby existing goals and

metrics no longer make business sense. Challenges raised by this alternative include retention, loss of upside incentive opportunity, urgency of a replacement plan and planning around potential tax concerns (including compliance with IRC section 409A on plan terminations and section 162[m] regarding performance-based compensation for compensation to covered employees in excess of $1 million for the applicable year).

If awards are paid out immediately, the retention component is lost and participants typically would lose any potential upside opportunity (important if the company is expecting continued strong performance). A replacement plan would need to be developed and implemented immediately to address retention and/ or performance issues. This urgency may result in the development of a reactive plan; such a program often does not contain the design mechanics that generally are desired to retain and motivate key employees, reward high performers or drive the future success of the business. Also, participants may experience negative financial implications, as tax events may have to be addressed at the time of payment.

- **Reset goals in existing plans.** This alternative requires some degree of certainty in setting new target goals. However, setting goals in a stable environment is challenging enough, let alone in a transactional context. Goals and metrics would have to be fairly similar to avoid a complete overhaul of actual metrics and achievement levels. Uncertainty regarding performance expectations makes this difficult to accomplish without creating unintended windfalls or penalties. The year following a transaction is often considered a transition year, with the acquiring company developing a better understanding of the financial outlook and strategic opportunities created by the acquisition. In addition, before making any changes after the start of a performance period, the requirements of IRC section 162[m] would need to be considered with respect to the potential effect on the deductibility of incentive payments.

- **Maintain existing plans with an incentive plan modifier that recognizes the newly acquired asset.** This strategy can be effective when the acquirer is dominant both in the acquisition and in the future development of the combined entity, particularly when goals and strategies are, or will be, aligned. A challenging task might be selecting the modifier level to ensure management is held accountable. This requires making some assessments of target performance, but generally is considered less invasive than other alternatives. Modifier goals do not have to be financial and can be qualitative and focused on strategic or operational matters.

Companies need to consider that modifiers can be equally rewarding or penalizing. One approach in determining the level of the payout modifier is to create a set of strategic objectives (i.e, three objectives), with each one being accountable by business unit or functional heads (i.e., finance, legal, human resources). The modifier level is increased or decreased with the success or failure to achieve each objective (i.e., modifier level can range from -20 percent for failure to achieve any objectives, to +20 percent for successful achievement of all objectives). Once again, the potential effect of IRC section 162(m) would need to be considered.

These alternatives provide high-level concepts on integrating performance-based LTI plans. The alternatives are conceptual and will require further elaboration based upon key objectives of the acquisition, as well as views on compensation and performance management. A transaction potentially can yield many benefits, but they may take several years to be realized and to have significant effect on the company. In any case, the LTI plans should not create a "we versus them" mentality. Employees should participate in and benefit from the best possible culture, brand and philosophy either company has to offer.

19
Initial Public Offerings

By Brandon Cherry and Kyle Holm

In an initial public offering (IPO) a company raises capital by offering its shares to the public via a stock exchange, such as the New York Stock Exchange (NYSE) or Nasdaq. With a more liquid market for a company's shares and easier access to capital come numerous reporting and disclosure responsibilities and an expanded involvement of legal professionals, auditors and consultants.

Companies intending to go public usually are aware that under U.S. Securities and Exchange Commission (SEC) and stock exchange listing rules they will have to disclose detailed information about business operations to investors and the general public. They may not realize, however, that they can no longer rely on the compensation policies and practices in place while they were private entities. While equity compensation — typically but not exclusively in the form of stock options — garners the most attention in an IPO and represents the lion's share of potential financial gain for executives, other compensation elements need to be addressed before and after the company goes public.

Meaningful benefits can be achieved by realigning the executive compensation program in light of the new corporate structure. Not to do so can lead to a perceived lack of security on the part of executives and potentially the loss of needed executive talent. This chapter:

- Addresses the importance of understanding the value of equity compensation in planning for and creating an IPO and discusses factors that may determine equity levels for executives hired before or after the public offering.

- Discusses the issues a company needs to address if it contemplates going public, including complying with SEC disclosure rules, likely changes to the annual incentive plan, equity compensation and dilution levels, and governance.
- Discusses the need to adopt a new compensation philosophy once the company goes public. Comparing pay levels against the competition, reviewing individual pay elements as well as target total cash and total direct compensation, and updating employment agreements are also recommended.

Understanding Equity Compensation Prior to an IPO

Private companies often use their equity as an effective compensation vehicle to attract and motivate key employees prior to an IPO. But equity in a pre-IPO company is subject to much interpretation. Through thoughtful planning and communication, this powerful tool can have a strong perceived value to the recipient, allowing companies to potentially offer below-market base salaries, smaller annual cash bonuses or both.

However, this trade-off between cash compensation and company equity is a delicate balance and should take into consideration the potential value delivered to participants, as well as the portion of the company allotted to participants.

Understanding Value

"A competitor is offering me 100,000 shares; why does my current employer only offer 25,000?"

While a pre-IPO equity grant can have considerable perceived value, employees need to understand where their grants fit in the context of the company overall, as well as the competitive marketplace. The above question is one that compensation professionals often are asked and it can be difficult to answer. While 100,000 shares is more than 25,000, the important question is not necessarily how many shares, but how much of the company is being offered and at what price.

As companies move toward an IPO, financial analysis is used to understand potential share value. By analyzing additional rounds of financing that might occur prior to the equity event, an employee can understand how his/her individual grants will become diluted through each round of financing, as well as see the potential increase in company share price over the exercise price. Even assuming a company proceeds all the way to an IPO, there is no way a company can definitively say what the gain at IPO will be for an individual participant; however, an estimate can be created using the overall market capitalization of the company at IPO and the estimated size of the offering. In the end, educating an equity plan participant on the value of a grant and how that grant relates to the marketplace could be necessary — sometimes 25,000 is much larger than 100,000, as shown in Figure 19-1.

Determining Executive Equity

"As our company approaches an IPO, we need to hire a senior vice president; how do we determine the appropriate equity grant level?"

Chances are, when a private company on the road to an IPO recruits senior managers, the shiniest carrot will be the equity award. A qualified, high-performing senior manager is not contemplating a move to a startup because the company has a generous pension plan or offers above-market base salaries. The equity grant is the lure and the question is: "How much is enough?" Unfortunately the answer is: "It depends." The important factors to consider are industry, size, potential dilution pre-IPO and what position the senior manager will hold.

The industry where a company operates plays a large role in the expectations and size of a pre-IPO equity grant. Generally speaking, a service-based company will offer less equity than a company operating in a high-technology market.

FIGURE 19-1

Comparison of Potential IPO Scenarios

	Options Granted	Exercise Price	IPO Price	Option Gain at IPO
Current Offer	25,000	$2	$15	$325,000
Competing Offer	100,000	$13	$15	$200,000

Consumer service companies were found to have median total overhang (options outstanding plus options available as a percent of total shares outstanding) at IPO of slightly more than 14 percent, whereas technology companies had median overhang levels of more than 20 percent. Companies in the technology field tend to be younger and riskier propositions given the highly competitive and fast-moving marketplace. (See Figure 19-2 for a comparison of overhang in various industries.) Consequently, equity grants to technology senior managers generally are larger than those in the overall marketplace as companies attempt to mitigate the risk factor with an increase in the upside should there be an IPO.

Another key factor to consider is the importance of the company's structure in sizing executive equity grants. The size of the company, as measured in number of employees, annual revenue and/or market capitalization at IPO all correlate with the equity position at IPO — the smaller the company, the larger the equity position awarded. Using annual revenue as the company measure, Hay Group found (as shown in Figure 19-3) that companies with revenue of less than $25 million had median overhang of more than 19 percent at IPO, whereas companies with annual revenue of more than $150 million

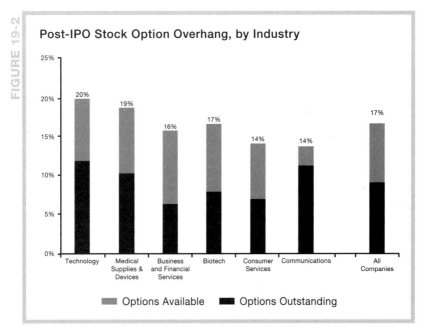

FIGURE 19-2

Post-IPO Stock Option Overhang, by Industry

Options Available ▪ Options Outstanding

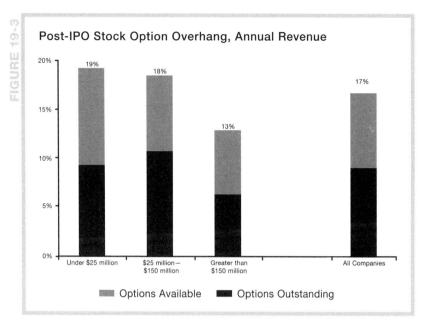

had median overhang of 13 percent. A company with higher revenue, market capitalization or a larger employee base generally will have greater overall value and, consequently, the company can give away less equity to the senior managers and still deliver competitive equity grants.

As mentioned, the expected dilution and the effect on individual grants is an important factor to consider when determining executive equity grants. A grant made to a senior manager hired in the period just preceding the offering will only be diluted by the IPO itself. Conversely, a grant made to a senior manager just after company formation could potentially be diluted by the IPO plus any additional rounds of financing that precede the IPO. The senior manager who comes on board just following formation is taking on a larger risk of individual dilution and the equity grant should likely reflect this inherent risk. Additionally, the earlier an executive joins an organization, the lower the probability the company will actually experience an IPO. The later a senior manager comes on board, the higher the probability the equity grant will have value in the marketplace. Consistent with equity investment, the greater the risk, the greater the potential reward.

Role and Responsibility

Finally, the company must consider the role and responsibilities of the individual senior manager being offered the equity grant. Will the senior manager have direct line of sight to the performance of the equity or does the position influence something that is measured less by company equity and more by a different company measure? An example of the position's importance in determining equity holdings can be found when looking at two senior management positions in the technology industry: chief technology officer and top sales and marketing executive.

Hay Group research suggests both positions had similar annual total cash compensation levels but the equity held at IPO (shares owned plus shares subject to options as a percent of total shares outstanding) was markedly different. A chief technology officer had median equity of more than 2.5 percent of the company at IPO while the top sales and marketing executive held less than 1 percent. Sales positions tend to have compensation geared toward annual performance while a top technology position is going to play an important role in developing company assets critical to the creation of long-term company value.

Looking Ahead

It is important to realize that there is no magic bullet in determining appropriate equity grants in pre-IPO companies, but there are critical questions that can be asked to narrow the focus and allow the company to make an informed decision while ensuring the participant is fairly compensated. The wild days of the late 1990s, where millionaire receptionists roamed Porsche dealerships, may be in the past, but there are still rewards for those willing to take the risk of working in a pre-IPO environment.

Preparing Compensation Programs for Public Company Life

When private companies seek to go public, they become interested in what is needed to prepare the compensation programs of a private company for the public eye. Going public through an IPO is not the end of the road; it marks the transition from operating as a private company to operating as a public company. Life as a public company means the company's stock is readily available for sale or purchase on a stock exchange. Public companies have easier access to capital and have liquid markets for their shares through such stock exchange listings.

The flip side is that a public company must comply with rules established by the SEC and the listing standards of the relevant stock exchange. As a consequence, a public company is required to disclose detailed information about business operations to investors and the general public. This mandated disclosure (see Chapter 14) contributes to significant differences in how privately owned companies can operate and in how publicly traded companies must operate, which can materially affect compensation program design and administration.

Required disclosure broadly falls into two categories: financial and compensation. In quarterly and annual reports, a public company must publish its income statements, balance sheets and cash flows, and management must explain these results. In the annual proxy statement (in which a company solicits the proxies, or votes, of shareholders), a company must disclose, discuss and analyze detailed information on the compensation of the CEO, the CFO and the other three highest paid executives (collectively, the named executive officers, or NEOs). In addition to detailed disclosure of NEO compensation, a public company must provide information on compensation paid to all members of the board of directors. Details on the beneficial ownership of company stock of each director and NEO also must be disclosed.

Because much of a public company's compensation levels and practices are publicly disclosed, it is important that they can stand up to scrutiny and are defensible, both to shareholders and other stakeholders. Well-designed compensation plans provide competitive pay opportunities, truly link pay to individual and company performance, and communicate the behaviors and outcomes that drive shareholder returns. Before going public, a privately held company should be sure its compensation programs are consistent with public company standards.

Annual Incentives

Private companies often have informal, discretionary bonus plans that lack clear performance criteria, funding mechanisms or targeted levels of awards. Well-designed annual incentive plans link an executive's pay to the successful achievement of goals important to company success. They also incorporate targeted incentives with base salaries so that pay mix and total cash compensation levels can be assessed.

An annual incentive plan used by a private employer (including a subsidiary of a public entity) may not necessarily be appropriate for a public company, potentially resulting in a review and modification of the plan post-IPO. For example, a startup company may maintain a plan that emphasizes revenue growth as it positions for an IPO. Once public, expense control and return metrics would be more appropriate than a top-line approach to incentives, although some newly public companies that seek to support aggressive growth goals may focus on top-line measures like revenue.

Consider another example in which a subsidiary's plan measures the unit's profit performance against a budget developed by the parent corporation. The subsidiary has no control over corporate cost allocations or the parent company's financial structuring decisions. If that subsidiary is carved out in an IPO, the new entity will have cost allocation and financial decision capability, and plan measures should be reconsidered.

Equity Compensation

Executives who join early stage startup and high-growth private companies can benefit by receiving equity compensation at then current-low valuations. Companies that successfully go public can expect significant increases in their valuations, and equity compensation allows employees to share in this value creation. Of course, there are downside risks as well. Many startup companies do not succeed and even successful companies may be unable to go public when equity markets dry up.

Private companies that plan to go public commonly use stock as an important component of their compensation programs, not just for executives but often for a broad group of (even all) employees. This helps conserve scarce cash and links employees' interests with those of stockholders, but dilutes the stakes of current shareholders. Potential investors in IPOs typically want to see that key employees have an ownership stake in the company so that they are motivated to increase its value. Likewise, it is important for key employees to have some unvested equity stakes so that they must stay with the company for at least a year or two post-IPO to capture gains from post-IPO appreciation; they should not be able to just "take the money and run." This reinforces the idea that an IPO is not about going public, it's about being public.

For many years, stock options were the currency of choice, but increasingly full-value shares (e.g., restricted stock, performance shares) are being used. Regardless of the available award vehicles, companies need to consider several issues when evaluating equity compensation plans. A crucial issue for investors, whether in private or public companies, is the dilution of their ownership stakes as a result of equity grants. The challenge is to balance shareholder concerns about dilution with the need to incentivize and retain the requisite talent.

Companies need to assess dilution from both outstanding grants and the number of shares authorized and available for future grant. (See Table 19-1.) Prior to going public, a company should obtain

TABLE 19-1

Effect of Stock Option Usage on Overhang

	Pre-IPO	At IPO	Post-IPO Year 1	Post-IPO Year 2
			Projections of Option Use	
Current Shares Outstanding	20,000,000	20,000,000	25,000,000	25,000,000
+ Shares Added through Financing	—	5,000,000	—	—
Total Common Shares Outstanding:	20,000,000	25,000,000	25,000,000	25,000,000
Options Outstanding (Beginning of Period):	500,000	1,200,000	1,900,000	2,700,000
Percent of Total Shares Outstanding	2.5%	4.8%	7.6%	10.8%
Options Available: Shares	3,000,000	2,300,000	1,600,000	800,000
Percent of Total Shares Outstanding	15%	9.2%	6.4%	3.2%
Options Granted:	700,000	700,000	800,000	750,000
Percent of Total Shares Outstanding	3.5%	2.8%	3.2%	3.0%
Options Available (End of Period):	2,300,000	1,600,000	800,000	50,000
Percent of Total Shares Outstanding	11.5%	6.4%	3.2%	0.2%
Total Overhang	17.5%	14.0%	14.0%	14.0%

This example shows a company that authorized additional options prior to an IPO. This allows the company to have equity available for compensation programs in place while maintaining stable overhang and run rates.

authorization for enough shares to cover projected grants for the next two or three years post-IPO (assuming dilution levels are not excessive). Acceptable dilution levels vary by industry, with high-technology and bio-technology companies generally higher than others. As a rule, potential dilution from shares granted plus those remaining for grant (also called overhang) between 10 percent and 20 percent of outstanding shares is within competitive market practice.

At private companies, entity valuations and stock prices generally are low relative to similar publicly traded companies. This minimizes the charges to earnings from equity compensation, whether stock options or full-value shares are used. Once public, valuations typically are materially higher and stock prices are much more volatile. Charges to earnings will be greater, which means companies often need to be more selective regarding participation in equity compensation programs and the size and value of individual grants.

Other Issues

Prior to a public offering, a company needs to establish an independent compensation committee (i.e., no insiders such as executives on the committee). The committee should establish a charter stating its duties and responsibilities and develop a compensation philosophy that will shape its compensation decisions. Both of these will need to be publicly disclosed, and should be crafted with transparency in mind. While not required, compensation committees generally directly engage an independent consulting firm for assistance with competitive market assessment and program design.

After a transition period (which needs to be carefully examined for its application to various types of awards), public companies are subject to Internal Revenue Code (IRC) section 162(m), which limits the deductibility of non-performance-based compensation to $1 million per year for each of the CEO and the next three highest-paid executives (excluding the CFO). Non-performance-based compensation includes base salaries, discretionary bonuses and restricted stock. Formula-driven annual incentive plans and stock options normally qualify as performance-based compensation but still need shareholder approval.

Key Processes for a Newly Public Company
Compensation Philosophy
A company's compensation philosophy establishes the framework for executive compensation programs and provides a link to the underlying business strategy. A newly public company should not necessarily rely on the compensation philosophy used while it was a private entity; rather it should develop a plan in accordance with its new status. As part of this process, the company should define the desired role of each compensation element and its respective sensitivity to the performance of the company, business unit or individual.

Competitive Review of Compensation
Along with a change in the ownership structure (i.e., public investment), an IPO results in changes in the responsibilities of many executives. To account for these different roles, a company may examine the competitiveness of its pay levels by identifying benchmark positions and developing competitive pay data through a mix of published and private survey sources.

When reviewing compensation levels, companies generally examine each pay element on an individual basis, as well as through a holistic, total compensation approach. While it is important that individual elements of pay be competitive and consistent with the company's compensation philosophy, a company typically would focus on target total compensation levels (total cash compensation and total direct compensation) more than on the individual pay components.

For example, a company may pay slightly below the competitive market for base salary, but provide above-market levels of target bonus opportunity and equity, thereby providing a competitive overall pay package.

Employment Agreements and Security Arrangements
The formation of a new public company may require employment or security arrangements for key personnel. Existing agreements should be examined and the need for new or updated arrangements considered. An employer is at a heightened risk of losing key employees during organizational change, especially an IPO,

and the retention of key executives often is critical to the ultimate success post-equity event. A company should take into account any additional risks assumed by executives during the transition and adjust compensation and severance protections accordingly.

Transaction-Specific Issues

Before developing or implementing any programs, a pre-IPO or newly public company should examine the practices of comparable organizations to establish competitive norms. When devising an appropriate comparator group, a company should consider factors such as industry, size, scope, business model and strategic objectives.

The determination of competitive compensation practices for a specific transaction is more complicated than the determination for ongoing compensation elements. Developing an understanding of why a similar company implemented a compensation program is as important as discovering what it did. An employer needs to consider the nature of the transaction, the historical compensation practices at the company examined, and any information on future pay arrangements.

Points to Remember

Compensation planning during the pre-IPO stage can be difficult. However, the development of an executive compensation program that is cost-efficient, competitive, performance-based and aligned with shareholder expectations is critical to the ultimate success of an IPO. Four key points to remember are:

- Keep concepts and plans simple.
- View compensation plans as a management tool to support business strategy.
- Recognize that plans must change with company strategy and maturity.
- Designate an individual or group as accountable for administration and communication of policies approved by the compensation committee.

20
Executive Compensation in Tax-Exempt Organizations

By James M. Otto and Ronald Seifert

Although their funding comes from private or public donors, membership fees, tuition, grants and services provided, tax-exempt organizations mimic compensation practices of their for-profit competitors. In the field of health care, for example, tax-exempt organizations are important players whose major competitors can include large publicly-held health-care companies and a variety of life-science organizations. Like the for-profit companies with whom they often compete for board and executive talent, tax-exempt organizations must attract and retain talented management and provide sufficiently competitive levels of pay and benefits.

Tax-exempt organizations are the focus of considerable external scrutiny, especially regarding governance issues relating to executive compensation. Much like the heightened sensitivities within audit committees that increased their workload, tax-exempt boards must now devote considerably more time justifying their executive compensation decisions than they did in the past. The tax law's requirement to pay no more than reasonable compensation (now enforced by the "intermediate sanctions" standards) and governance reforms and changes in the private sector have prompted many tax-exempt boards to go beyond mere compliance and adopt best practice models of governance found in successful private and public companies. Today, the issues and concerns surrounding executive pay and benefits in many tax-exempt organizations are largely the same as those in for-profit enterprises.

This chapter:

- Discusses how the current climate of accountability and transparency in the private sector has challenged tax-exempt organizations to develop governance practices beyond the mandated disclosure requirements.

- Reviews the intermediate sanctions provisions of the Internal Revenue Code (IRC) and outlines the key elements of good governance practice and related issues such as the need for a precisely articulated compensation philosophy. A total remuneration ("Total R") approach that unites all pay elements in one coherent philosophy and compensation program is presented.

- Describes the use and design of long-term incentives (LTIs) and supplemental executive retirement plans (SERPs) in tax-exempt organizations as part of a comprehensive approach to compensation.

- Answers the question, "Should we pay our board?" The factors that go into determining board pay as well as how and what to pay directors are discussed.

Today's Environment and Its Influence on Executive Compensation in the Tax-Exempt Sector

From small associations operating in local communities to well-recognized international charities, educational institutions, private foundations, museums and health-care organizations, tax-exempt organizations span a broad organizational spectrum. Guided in all of their operations by their missions and values, these organizations have been established and are operated to satisfy the rules that exempt them from federal and state income taxes. Keeping this status is a vital concern, and oversight of executive compensation plays a crucial role in maintaining this status.

While the rules that affect this oversight responsibility have been in place for a number of years, the importance of paying executives based on the outcomes of good governance practice has never been more important. The influence of stakeholders of tax-exempt organizations has increased significantly and shapes how board members and senior leaders conduct the affairs of the organization. These groups include donors, employees, bond holders, local communities, service recipients, labor unions, state legislatures, the media and the Internal Revenue Service, each of which finds the incendiary aspect of executive compensation an avenue for them to exert influence in one way or another.

The call for increased accountability and transparency that pervades all aspects of corporate governance today in public companies is being felt in tax-exempt organizations. This phenomenon was first apparent with the passage of the Sarbanes-Oxley Act of 2002, and the specific provisions of the act that affected executive compensation at publicly traded companies (e.g., the ban on loans from corporations to officers). Tax-exempt organizations, many of which include prominent for-profit executives on their boards, were encouraged to adopt some or all of the governance and accountability standards imposed by this act and the governance and disclosure practices utilized within their own companies. (See "More Influences from Sarbanes-Oxley.")

This influence continues with the passage of the Dodd-Frank Wall Street Reform and Consumer Protection Act of 2010. There are a number of provisions that affect executive compensation at publicly traded companies (e.g., independence of compensation committee members and recoupment of incentive payments in certain instances) that will be considered and adapted by tax-exempt organizations to augment and improve the oversight of executive compensation.

More Influences from Sarbanes-Oxley

Loans to Executives
One of the most publicized aspects of Sarbanes-Oxley is its prohibition of most personal loans by a covered company to a director or an executive officer. In the past, tax-exempt organizations occasionally made loans to executive officers, often to enable them to purchase a house upon hire or transfer into a more expensive real estate market. Although such loans still are possible in tax-exempts that have not instituted a policy barring their use, current best practices would require an especially strong reason for using this much-criticized practice.

Codes of Ethics
Under Sarbanes-Oxley a public company must disclose whether it has adopted a code of ethics for its senior financial officers. In the event there is no such code, reasons for this failure also must be disclosed. The basic concept of a code of ethics is readily transferable to tax-exempts, as is the developing view that such codes should also be extended to other officers and board members.

Not only has legislation affected how tax-exempt organizations oversee executive compensation, but the regulations that have been developed by both the IRS (discussed later in the chapter) and the rules issued by the U.S. Securities and Exchange Commission (SEC) that operationalize relevant laws have been a major influence. For example, committees that oversee executive compensation in tax-exempt organizations are much more aware of the need to answer the "how" and "why" questions about the levels of compensation provided and the modes used to deliver it. These questions reflect the intent of the Compensation Discussion and Analysis (CD&A), which is a part of the proxy statement for most publicly-traded companies. In essence, the CD&A must describe the actions of compensation committees and the reasoning behind their decisions.

Finally, the IRS' overhaul of Form 990, which includes much more detailed disclosure of compensation for senior executives and detailed description of how executive compensation is determined, also has influenced the oversight of executive compensation in tax-exempt organizations.

At the same time that environmental factors are increasing the focus on, and affecting the oversight of, executive compensation, tax-exempts must attract and retain talented management and provide compensation programs that enable them to deliver upon their core mission. This often requires competing for talent with for-profit entities. For example, in the field of health care, most major providers are not-for-profit organizations whose talent pool can include large publicly held health-care companies, managed-care organizations and life-science companies.

These two dynamics — increased scrutiny of executive compensation and the need to attract and keep management teams — provide challenges to any organization (tax-exempt or for-profit). A well-considered oversight process is the bridge to addressing both of these and maximizing the benefits for the organization at the same time.

Good Governance Practice

The requirement that tax-exempt organizations oversee executive compensation and pay "reasonable" compensation to its key executives has been in place for decades in the IRC. However, the relatively recent enactment of the "intermediate sanctions" provision in the code provided these organizations with guidance on how to oversee executive compensation in a manner that is intended to support the results of any decisions on executive compensation. (See "Intermediate Sanctions.")

Although contained in the intermediate sanctions regulations, the requirements that support the presumption that compensation is reasonable are now considered to be part of a good governance practice. These requirements, coupled with the increased scrutiny of executive compensation and the fact that boards can be held accountable for unreasonable compensation, have encouraged organizations to establish good governance practice to oversee executive compensation, regardless of whether the organization seeks to establish the presumption of reasonableness of compensation.

Key Elements of a Good Governance Practice
'Independence' of Board or Committee Members Overseeing
Executive Compensation
The intermediate sanctions regulations describe independence in a way that is fairly narrow in scope: Is each member of the board or committee free of any conflict of interest when deciding on compensation for a particular executive? An example of a conflict is when a physician is on the board that determines the compensation of a CEO of Healthcare System, and that CEO is involved in negotiating the compensation of that physician, who is an employee of Healthcare System. Tax-exempt organizations are taking into consideration a more expansive definition in determining whether a committee member is independent, which typically includes referencing the "independent" definitions that exist in the national exchange rules. The objective is to ensure that the organization can take the position that the committee overseeing executive compensation is independent of the organization in making these decisions (and not just free of conflict with respect to a particular compensation arrangement).

Intermediate Sanctions

To maintain their tax-exempt status, organizations have been required for decades to pay reasonable compensation to executives and avoid private inurement (net earnings of the organization cannot "inure" to individuals or shareholders) and private benefit (activities must serve public rather than private-benefit interests) when determining the level and method of compensating executives and other identified employees.

IRC section 4958, more popularly known as "intermediate sanctions," is a recent provision that affects executive compensation at tax-exempt organizations. Statutory language is supplemented by extensive regulations that give the IRS the ability to assess financial penalties on both executives and board members of section 501(c)(3) and 501(c)(4) organizations for any "excess benefit transaction" involving a "disqualified person." (Prior to intermediate sanctions, the IRS could either revoke the organization's tax exemption or overlook the violation when it determined that an executive was paid an unreasonable amount.) Although the intermediate sanctions legislation was enacted in 1996, it was not until the regulations were finalized in early 2002 that active enforcement began.

Paying unreasonable compensation to a disqualified person is an excess benefit transaction. A disqualified person is a person in a position that currently can exert substantial influence over the affairs of a tax-exempt organization or could do so during a five-year "look back" period. Top executive officers and board members generally are disqualified persons. The value of all consideration and benefits received by a disqualified person in a year is examined in determining whether there has been an excess benefit transaction for that year. Both the individual receiving the unreasonable compensation and the board members who authorized payment of the unreasonable compensation may be subject to the financial penalties under IRC section 4958.

Why Are We Making the Decision That We Are?

The use of comparability data provides the committee with context in which to make its decisions that are specific to and support the needs of the organization. In the past, committees and boards were prone to following the market (i.e., doing what the market says other organizations are doing because other organizations are doing it). Committees and boards are now being asked, and are demanding of themselves, to articulate why they are making any decision that affects any executive's compensation arrangement. For example, "Why should the organization adopt a supplemental executive retirement plan?" By asking and answering this type of question, committees are articulating the business rationale for the decision and how their decision makes sense for the organization. Committees also are requiring greater insight from their consultants and HR departments, particularly with respect to

To avoid concerns with intermediate sanctions, tax-exempt organizations must be able to demonstrate that a covered executive's total executive compensation is reasonable. The regulations provide three requirements that, if met, establish a "rebuttable presumption" that compensation is reasonable, which shifts the burden of proof to the IRS to show that the compensation is unreasonable. The three requirements are:

• Executive compensation arrangements should be approved by an independent body with no conflict of interest.

• An independent comparability study that considers all elements of compensation should be conducted and the results used to assist the independent body in determining compensation levels. This data may be obtained through compensation surveys, an examination of compensation of similar individuals in similar organizations and/or an expert compensation study.

• Approval of executive compensation arrangements should be documented before the later of the next meeting or 60 days after the final actions of the decision-making body; this documentation should include:

  - The specific terms and conditions of the approved transaction and the date approved

  - The members of the decision-making body who were present during debate on the transaction that was approved and their votes

  - The comparability data that was relied on by the decision-making body and how the data was obtained.

the relevance of a comparator group and data that is developed based on that group.

Process and Roles

The intermediate sanctions regulations imply a process that culminates in documenting the decisions made. Organizations are expanding this documentation requirement to codify the process by which executive compensation is reviewed and modified. This codification can take the form of items such as:

• Compensation philosophy

• Compensation program documents (e.g., annual incentive plan, LTI plan, severance policy)

• Committee charter (number of members, "independence" definition, scope of authority, reporting responsibility, succession)

• Committee calendar (number of meetings, typical agenda items)

- Role of compensation adviser, legal counsel and staff support
- Maintenance of meeting minutes
- Attendance at each meeting by outside counsel.

This level of detail provides the foundation on which organizations can complete the information required on Form 990 and develop the manner in which the organization wants to respond to any stakeholder inquiry on executive compensation.

To evaluate the degree to which the board is driving the process and the decisions, the IRS can access the board's documentation to understand how decisions are made, including compensation committee and board minutes, documentation of decision-making, rationale for the market positioning of specific executives and the board's executive compensation philosophy.

Compensation Philosophy and Components of the Compensation Program: Critical Sub-Elements

A compensation philosophy is the touch point when making compensation decisions. A philosophy can furnish critical guidance for the board, the compensation committee and executive leadership in making consistent pay decisions, and is a key document for the IRS to review in an audit. A philosophy articulates:

- **The "market."** Which organizations are to be compared with the organization? From where does the organization recruit executive talent and to where does the organization lose executive talent?
- **Job match.** How should the organization's jobs be compared to jobs at these comparable organizations?
- **Compensation elements.** What are the components of the compensation program (e.g., base salary, annual incentive, long-term incentive, benefits [including executive-level only])? Why are they being used? How does the component play a role in facilitating performance, retention or recruitment?
- **Compensation mix.** How do the components interrelate? For example, how much of cash compensation should be based on performance (incentives) and how much is to be based on service or the job (base salary)? How should benefits be taken into account, in particular any executive-level benefits?

- **Compensation positioning relative to the market.** What is the target market level for the various components of pay and the various combinations of pay? What is the desired pay positioning with the competitive market for talent and the rationale of that positioning?
- **Pay administration.** How are the CEO and committee to interact when determining pay levels? For example, does the committee approve all pay changes based on CEO recommendations?

The discussion involved in developing an organization's compensation philosophy provides a timely opportunity for the compensation committee and management to agree on how compensation is linked to the organization's mission, and what messages the organization wants to send to its external and internal constituents. The philosophy needs to be approved by the committee or board and referenced as a check when executive compensation is established and annually assessed. (See "Total R.")

The Internal Revenue Service has made clear that a compensation philosophy is the foundation on which compensation decisions should be made and is an indicator of good governance practice; the IRS believes that organizations are less likely to pay unreasonable compensation if good governance practices are followed.

A compensation "program" captures the compensatory components identified in the compensation philosophy and the documents related to these components. Therefore, the program includes such items as base salary, incentives, specific benefits and the manner in which each of these is documented (e.g., for an incentive component, through the combination of a plan document and specific actions taken by the committee that are memorialized in committee minutes). The continuous review of the philosophy and the resulting compensation program are a key part of the ongoing oversight of executive compensation.

SERPs and LTIs: Components of the Compensation Program and Design Issues to Consider

One element that committees consider adding to the philosophy and the program is a SERP, a plan that long has been and continues to be a key component in compensation programs at tax-exempt

---

Total R

Link Total R to Performance

Total Remuneration, or "Total R," is the resulting combination of all of the compensatory components of the compensation program. Total R should reinforce priorities and focus employees on the desired behaviors and outcomes for the organization. Hay Group research with *Fortune* magazine's "Most Admired" companies shows that these organizations differentiate rewards based on performance. Top performers are rewarded highly, while pay is limited for poor performance. In our experience, tax-exempt organizations that successfully link Total R to performance:

- Take the time to discuss what performance is and what success looks like. For many organizations, what constitutes real performance is often not obvious.

- Look at relative performance, understanding how the organization compares with similar ones.

- Examine and negotiate performance measures rigorously.

- May not always pay out incentives. Boards can now look back over some prior period and see how performance compared with payout. What was the payout each year? Was there variability? Did the payouts align with the perception of success?

- Reinforce the importance of the top team by linking a substantial amount of pay to achieving organizational goals.

Broaden Total R to Promote Succession

Organizations that recognize the need to develop and retain experienced, innovative executives are establishing succession strategies based on intrinsic Total R components as well as extrinsic components (base salary, incentives, benefits and perquisites). Executives identify quality of work, development opportunities, work-life balance, satisfying work environments, reputation and values, and

---

organizations. Boards and compensation committees at tax-exempt organizations continue to use this type of plan in a variety of situations, in large part because of the design flexibility afforded.

Organizations must take into account the specific income tax rules that apply to these plans when sponsored by tax-exempt organizations. SERP benefits are taxable when no longer subject to a "substantial risk of forfeiture," which essentially means upon vesting. An executive no longer risks forfeiture that is substantial when he/she does not have to provide any future "substantial services" to the employer to receive the benefit. (In general, this is not the same way that the IRC addresses SERP benefits sponsored by taxable

leadership effectiveness as the top factors that influence their desire to stay with an organization and assume bigger positions. Organizations that focus on those variables show measurable results in attracting and retaining talented executives and achieving business objectives.

Communicate Total R to Participants

Communication translates leadership decisions about Total R into clear messages for executives. Organizations that are most successful in communicating Total R emphasize the integration with mission, strategy, performance and desire to raise employee satisfaction. One approach provides executives with online access to the value of their individual total remuneration arrangement. This approach helps executives understand the true value and employer cost associated with each pay component.

Assess and Update Total R Annually

This process can be conducted internally or through the use of independent advisers. Most organizations prefer outside advisers for their expertise, objectivity and access to benchmarks. The process must involve compensation committee deliberation and use relevant market data as a basis for setting executive pay.

Engage a Third Party to Confirm Reasonableness of Compensation

An independent third party that is qualified to professionally assess compensation can help demonstrate the reasonableness of compensation. A third party can conduct an analysis of total remuneration levels and assist in determining that compensation levels are within a reasonable range The third party also can issue an opinion letter to confirm the use of comparable data as part of the effort to establish a rebuttable presumption of reasonableness (and shift the burden onto the IRS to overcome this showing) and minimize the risk to the committee members that they would be subject to financial penalties under the intermediate sanctions provision if the IRS were to determine that compensation was unreasonable.

organizations — those plans can be structured so that benefits vest and are taxed later, when they are paid).

The IRS has allowed exceptions to this vesting/tax timing rule, so that a SERP benefit could vest and be taxed earlier than the vesting schedule provides if the executive dies, becomes disabled or is involuntarily terminated without cause before he/she is vested according to the vesting schedule. These exceptions are typically made part of the SERP; however, the normal vesting schedule is a key design issue because of the unique tax rule that applies. Committees have flexibility in designing this schedule within a plan; for example, the same vesting schedule does not have to apply to all participants in the plan, so the vesting schedule for a mid-career hire who becomes a participant in the plan at age 55 may be different from a newly-promoted 40-year-old executive who has always worked at the organization.

In contrast, LTI arrangements are an increasingly common compensatory element in compensation programs at tax-exempt organizations. These plans typically are designed to complement the goals of the annual incentive plan and focus a select group of executives on achieving specific, multi-year, organization-wide goals based on the organization's strategy. The plan allows the organization to identify, pursue and measure progress toward performance objectives that further the mission and strategic goals over a sustained period of time and help balance each participating executive's focus between and annual and long-term objectives.

In constructing an LTI arrangement, the committee and senior management must address issues similar to those in an annual incentive arrangement:

- Purpose
- Eligibility and participation
- Administration
- Performance period
- Plan circuit breaker (i.e., below what performance level will the plan shut down?)
- Incentive opportunity
- Performance measures, goals and weighting
- Funding and distribution.

Note, however, that these plans are almost always paid in cash because the use of equity and the transfer of tax-exempt assets are governed by strict state and federal laws; there is no available equity that can be awarded. Of course, with any compensation element, how an LTI is to "fit" with the other compensation elements is part of the design process.

Considerations for Board Pay

As the accountabilities and liabilities of board members have increased, a director's job has become considerably more difficult and time-consuming. This has made the recruitment and retention of directors a much more important and challenging task, often resulting in greater compensation of these directors. Increased board responsibilities, however, are not unique to directors of public companies. Tax-exempt board members also are finding themselves with significantly more responsibility.

While many tax-exempt organizations historically have not paid their directors, more are asking whether board pay is not only appropriate but necessary. In the increasingly stringent environment of tax-exempt board governance, director roles are getting harder and carrying more weight.

In consulting with numerous tax-exempt organizations, three related issues affecting the compensation of tax-exempt board members have been examined: whether to pay, how to pay and what to pay.

A Changing Environment

In recent years, tax-exempt board membership has shifted from risk-free public service to time-consuming stakeholder accountability. These directors now have much greater responsibilities that include the same types of tasks that publicly traded directors face, including those related to audit, fiduciary matters and executive compensation. Clearly, tax-exempt board governance has changed.

As responsibilities and accountabilities have grown, a debate has emerged whether it is appropriate to pay tax-exempt directors for their services.

There often is a perception that paying tax-exempt directors is inappropriate and that the practice runs counter to the missions of such organizations. In fact, the U.S. Senate Finance Committee commissioned an independent-sector report formally discouraging any compensation for tax-exempt board members unless the complexity, time commitment or skill requirements of the board so warrant. In practice, board pay has been infrequent across the tax-exempt universe.

There is a growing sense that as the role of the tax-exempt board evolves, board pay may not only be appropriate but also necessary to attract and retain the high-caliber directors needed. In general, board compensation is permissible as long as the organization's bylaws allow it and the payment does not result in private inurement or private benefit, and is considered reasonable for the services rendered. Essentially, this requires that pay not exceed the amount that ordinarily would be paid for like services by like enterprises under like circumstances. Also, many tax-exempt directors have opportunities to serve on for-profit boards that pay significant director fees. If particular tax-exempt organizations are competing with their for-profit brethren for top talent, paying directors may be a necessity.

There can be a rationale for compensating tax-exempt directors, and payment can be appropriate when the specific situation of the organization warrants.

Whether to Pay: Five Factors to Consider

The decisions on whether to pay and what to pay tax-exempt directors should be considered very carefully and driven by a number of factors unique to each organization. Based on review of existing research and consulting expertise, the decision to pay the board should be guided primarily by five considerations:

- **Complexity of the organization.** Does the organization have various moving parts or particularly difficult issues, whether strategic, regulatory or optical? If so, the added complexity may furnish support for paying directors.
- **Time commitment required.** Are directors spending significant amounts of time either in the boardroom or otherwise performing board duties and responsibilities? If so, it may be appropriate for directors to be paid for their time.
- **Level of direct operational involvement and special skills required.** Do directors have any direct operational involvement in the organization? Is the organization involved in a situation that requires a specialized skill set? If so, then this is an indication that the director talent may have a substantial effect on the organization's success, and there may be greater justification for paying them.
- **Competitive market for director talent.** With what types of organizations does the board compete for director talent? Are these

organizations compensating their directors? If so, these organizations may provide a reasonable benchmark for pay practices. In particular, tax-exempts that directly compete with for-profit companies may determine they need to compensate their directors or lose out on certain candidates.

- **Affordability.** Can the organization afford to pay its directors? Would director pay limit programmatic offerings of the organization in any way? Simply put, directors should only be paid if the organization can afford to do so.

Two types of organizations that tend to meet these criteria are health-care providers and large foundations. These employers typically are complex tax-exempt organizations; they are highly regulated, publicly and legally accountable, and require specific skill sets. Also, in the case of health-care providers, tax-exempt providers may compete with large for-profit health-care systems for board talent. As a result, many such organizations may be strong candidates for director pay. Conversely, organizations that do not meet the bulk of these criteria generally would not appear to be suitable for director pay.

How to Pay: The Components of Director Pay Packages

If an organization, after evaluating itself against these factors, decides to pay its directors, it has various alternatives for delivering that pay. The typical components of director pay include:

- **Annual retainers.** Similar to base pay, a retainer normally is a guaranteed cash amount.
- **Meeting fees.** These are fees for every board and/or committee meeting attended. Some committees, like audit, pay a premium relative to other committees to acknowledge increased importance and accountability.
- **Chairperson fees.** A member who chairs a committee may receive a special retainer for his/her services in the form of an additional retainer or additional meeting fees.
- **Committee membership fees.** Those who serve on a committee may receive an additional retainer for membership.

While these forms of director compensation are typical in the for-profit world, not all may be appropriate for a tax-exempt setting.

Given the optics of compensating tax-exempt board members, the structure of pay packages and the vehicles used should be considered very carefully.

In keeping with the pay-for-performance philosophy that organizations increasingly are adopting in their executive compensation philosophies, tax-exempt organizations may decide to structure their pay packages heavily toward a time-commitment orientation. While it is common in general industry to maintain a significant portion of the overall pay package in the form of a guaranteed retainer, at some tax-exempts it may be more appropriate to limit the guaranteed component in favor of meeting fees, which only pay members for the time they spend in the boardroom.

What to Pay: Benchmarking Against Comparable Organizations

Evaluating what target level of compensation is appropriate for a board can be a tricky. As discussed, tax-exempt board pay has not been a prevalent practice and, as a result, there are few survey sources available that collect this information.

Given these constraints, an organization should customize its data collection to the specific director talent market of that organization through the development of two "peer groups" — one tax-exempt and one publicly traded — that the organization may compete with for board members. These groups could include organizations that are involved in comparable activities, are similar in size and scope, and/or that share a geographic area. Some tax-exempt organizations recruit directors locally and may be competing for directors with the publicly traded company across the street, regardless of the business focus of that company. A good peer group may be a blend of each of these three factors, but at the end of the day, it should fairly represent the competitive market for director talent.

Tax-Exempt Peer Groups

Within the tax-exempt peer group, data can be collected from public Form 990 filings, which have board compensation information. While improvements recently were made to this form, information can be spotty and incomplete, and may not be publicly available for two years. This time lag may present data that does not capture recent increases in tax-exempt board compensation. For this reason, a custom survey of similar tax-exempt organizations can be quite helpful when there is adequate time and budget to undertake this approach.

Public Company Comparisons

Use of a for-profit peer group can provide another appropriate benchmark, although it should not be the sole source of comparison. Within a for-profit peer group, data can be collected from public proxy filings, which provide more complete and up-to-date information on all forms of compensation provided to their directors than Form 990 provides. However, in most circumstances, tax-exempt organizations should not look to fully replicate for-profit director pay packages. On average, the job of a director at a publicly traded organization is subject to greater scrutiny and has more accountability and liability than that of a tax-exempt director. This means that the pay data provided by these for-profit companies generally should be discounted when being used as context for developing board compensation in tax-exempt organizations.

One way to provide an appropriate discount is to eliminate from consideration any equity or LTI grants. In other instances, referencing only the 25th percentile of pay practices in the peer group may be appropriate. The right target-market positioning will depend on the organization itself and the degree to which it competes with these for-profit organizations.

Preparing for Scrutiny

In the end, any tax-exempt organization that chooses to compensate its directors should be prepared for scrutiny of the practice. While we believe tax-exempt board pay will continue to increase in prevalence as board accountabilities grow, some constituencies will continue to see board service as a public service and will understandably be opposed to the practice.

Consistent with the documentation on executive compensation decisions, tax-exempt organizations should maintain transparency of the process for and full documentation of all pay decisions related to an organization's directors. In particular, the written rationale — either in the form of a policy or a formal philosophy — regarding the decision on payment of directors (taking into account the factors stressed in this chapter) is a key part of this documentation.

21
International Compensation

By Carl Sjostrum (Europe); Christopher Chen (Canada); Allan Berry and Karyn Johnson (Australia); Peter Boreham (United Kingdom); Christine Abel, Ph.D. and William Eggers (Germany); Enor Signorotto (Italy); and Malcolm Liu (China)

Companies cross borders and talented individuals cross borders, making the understanding of international practices essential for anyone who wants to grasp the subject of executive compensation. Pay practices differ from country to country, driven by economics, culture, legislation and innovation. But equally, practices cross-pollinate where markets for the people that can truly affect the fortunes of an organization sweep through borders without regard for barriers and traditions. And it is not only where people are based that matters but also the context of the industry, the company and the company's stakeholders. This chapter seeks to give some of these flavors to the diversity of executive compensation practices, looking at such different corners of the world as Australia, Europe, China, Brazil and Canada; as well as the settings of family-owned businesses, non-capitalist countries and corporate governance debates.

When one looks at differences between geographies one can often generalize, for example:

*   CEO packages tend to be the highest in the United States for total compensation, in particular the long-term incentive (LTI) portion.
*   Companies in North and South American countries tend broadly to follow U.S. approaches, though with somewhat lower levels and with local variations.
*   European companies tend to have more significant pension benefits.
*   Executive pay tends to be significantly lower in Japan and in Northern European countries than in most other highly developed economies with more fixed than variable compensation.

• In most companies in Europe, the pay differential between the CEO, the CEO's direct reports and other top executives in the same company is much less than is typical in the United States. However, comparing the compensation packages of executives in different countries is fraught with difficulty. Compensation levels vary greatly and the differences are rarely explainable by differences in taxation or living standards — some of the developed countries with the lowest levels of executive pay, such as in Northern Europe, have high living costs and tax rates. These quirks are evidence of the importance of understanding the cultural differences within which executive compensation exists. A Dutch executive accepts lower compensation and a higher tax rate than a Swiss executive, at least partly because of the cultural difficulty of paying Swiss levels in the Netherlands. That does not mean that the same executive would accept lower compensation in Switzerland.

There also are large differences between countries in the provision of retirement benefits for executives. A Swedish executive, for example, may agree to a lower salary than a British executive but expect twice as high a pension contribution. An Asian executive may not have a pension provision at all in the traditional sense, while the retirement benefit provisions of Australian or European executives could form one of a company's largest liabilities.

Faced with significant differences in compensation practices from country to country, and in many cases within countries, most international corporations base the compensation for top executives primarily on practices and levels in the market where the executive is based. However, it is not unusual to see exceptions to this in short- and long-term incentive plans as a result of corporate innovation in combination with home country legislation driving more global practices. Such innovation and legislation often are a result of the corporate governance debate of the country where an organization has its headquarters.

The topics of executive compensation in corporate governance have evolved swiftly together throughout the world and are now on the agenda of most large company boards as well as those of most investors and legislators. There are several factors that have driven this increased attention. The first, and perhaps most significant, factor has been the increasing institutionalization of ownership creating sharp contrasts between, for example, the practices of quoted companies and those of family-owned businesses.

Most companies begin their days under the ownership of a single individual, family or organization. Increasingly, however, with the search for economies of scale and other synergies, companies around the world have gone in search of capital. At the same time, individuals have sought cost and return economies on their savings by using institutional investments (e.g., insurance, pensions) that seek to reduce risk and increase returns through a diversified portfolio of investments. One consequence has been the emergence of a small number of institutional investors that hold hundreds of investments in every fund. A second consequence is that, in effect, all the individual investors have subcontracted to institutional investment managers not only investment decisions, but also corporate governance decisions.

The investment managers have in turn realized that they cannot consider each and every ownership issue that arises at every investment so have had to find cost effective ways of casting votes and influencing investments, if doing so at all. Thus the "corporate governance industry" has evolved and through it a set of "truths" and practices that come more out of need for institutional investors to expedite the decisions on thousands of requests for votes every annual meeting season. These institutional views have led to the widespread development by investors and their umbrella organizations and proxy advisers of guidelines on corporate governance. And the most prominent place among all the guidance has been given to the subject of executive compensation.

The UK was in most aspects the first out in the 1990s and has now had a string of codes of corporate governance that have been copied and tailored by country after country across Europe and the rest of the world. Questionable incentive design practices, such as the retesting of performance conditions, have come under close scrutiny and many have been effectively eradicated. Other practices have been noted as undesirable, but to accommodate the understanding that there will be different needs for different situations, many codes ask companies to either comply with the guidance or explain the reasons for deviation.

Where concerns of investors spill into the more public debate (e.g., where votes are cast without one party having understood the arguments of another), the media, the wider public and, eventually, the legislators can begin to lose trust in the quality of corporate governance. This second factor of political interference in executive compensation has two further drivers — scandals and emotions.

Since the beginning of time, mankind has been hit by scandal on a regular basis, in particular where money and power are featured. With plenty of examples in recent times of misman-agement of shareholders' and, in some cases, public resources, politicians throughout the world have pointed to executive pay as a driving force behind poor judgment and occasional criminality. Many commentators thus see the way a company pays its senior executives as not only information needed to assess these often significant costs but, more importantly, as an indicator of the moral compass and effectiveness of the board's decision-making process.

Thus, legislators have introduced increased reporting and conduct codes and regulations affecting compensation decisions in the wake of the financial turbulence of the past decade. The financial services sector has been the hardest hit, but most large quoted companies have been affected in one way or another. For some societies where the interests of other stakeholders besides shareholders play a large part in the determination of strategy and operations, this has been less traumatic than for more pure-capitalist environments.

The key message is that companies can no longer expect to create compensation arrangements for their senior executives according to commercial logic alone, but the views of other stakeholders play an ever-increasing role throughout the world. This in turn has several consequences:

- There is a risk that a single focus on compliance with rules and regulations leads to a failure to create the right compensation structure for the organization. Decisions are made first and foremost to align with processes and tests rather than with strategy and culture.

- A fear of not complying tends to lead to a pursuit of being in the middle of the pack and a subsequent over-reliance on benchmarking rather than the business case of rewards. This often results in the upward ratcheting of pay even when performance may not justify it; competitors chase a median point that automatically moves up as there are only increases with no matching decreases in the market.

- Finally, much of the regulatory interference is focused around risk associated with levels of pay and performance conditions; however, companies often forget to take the risk built into the design of compensation elements into account. One incentive or benefit may deliver the same target value as another but the range of possible outcomes may vary dramatically, hence the "how" matters more than the "how much."

Key Executive Pay Topics Outside of the United States

The balance of this chapter provides overviews of executive compensation in seven diverse international settings, Canada, Australia, the United Kingdom, Germany, Italy, China and Brazil. The sections describe not just pay practices but important aspects of compensation in these geographies.

- The first section, "Linking Total Shareholder Return with Executive Rewards in Canada," focuses on the use of relative total shareholder return (TSR) in publicly traded companies as a performance measure in incentive plans. Criteria for selecting, testing and weighting a peer group are provided and, when necessary, how to incorporate non-Canadian companies into the peer selection process. Instances when using relative TSR may not be appropriate are also outlined.

- The second section, "Executive Compensation Design in Australia," describes the fixed-reward approach whereby employees choose between a variety of benefits, particularly cars and retirement savings, with the balance provided as base salary. The section also discusses short- and long-term incentives, performance measures and governance issues that distinguish executive pay in Australia.

• The United Kingdom provides a look at how non-binding, advisory votes by shareholders on executive pay have worked there in the section "Say on Pay: Lessons from the United Kingdom." After contrasting say on pay in the United Kingdom and the United States, we focus on the United Kingdom and discuss both the positive and negative outcomes resulting from shareholder votes on pay in UK companies. We provide guidance on how to avoid a negative vote and end with a case study of a company that lost a vote on say on pay.

• The next section, "Germany: New Rules on Executive Compensation" reviews the Act on Appropriateness of Executive Compensation (VorstAG), which affects both private and publicly listed companies in Germany. VorstAG redefines the role of the board of directors and compensation committee in setting base pay and incentives and includes regulations on such issues as say on pay, board and executive liability and pay disclosure. Its effect on the pay-decision process, the mix of pay elements, use of peer groups and external benchmarking is far-reaching.

• In "Executive Compensation in Family-Owned Businesses," we examine executive pay in two types of corporate structure commonly found in Italy and other European countries: private companies in which the family is the sole owner and publicly traded companies in which the family owns the controlling share. We contrast how they set base pay and incentive levels, how risk-taking affects their reward systems, the role of the chief executive, and the increasing use of the compensation committees.

• Next, we look at two interesting topics affecting executive pay in China. "Executive Pay Practice of A-share Listed Companies in China" describes the pay programs found in privately owned (i.e., not state owned) companies. While many pay concepts and practices are similar to those used in the West — benchmarking, a pay-for-performance philosophy, annual and long-term incentives — public opinion and the press can materially affect amounts paid to executives.

- "Executive Pay in China: The 'Red CEO'" focuses on the compensation arrangements of CEOs of large state-owned companies. Appointed by the Communist Party of China rather than recruited from the private sector, these so-called "Red CEOs" have unique compensation arrangements that link them more to the political than the industrial establishment.

- Finally, in "Executive Compensation in Brazil" we discuss the use of short- and long-term incentive pay in Brazil's fast-growing economic environment. We outline how union clout, high taxes on base salaries and memories of hyperinflation have influenced incentive pay in both foreign multinational and local company pay programs. We also discuss recent efforts to regulate equity compensation, the need to provide for senior executive safety, and the current state of executive pay disclosure.

Linking Total Shareholder Return with Executive Rewards in Canada

Many Canadian publicly-traded companies use TSR as a performance measure for a part of their executive rewards. TSR is generally defined as share price appreciation plus dividends paid. One aspect of the principle of pay for performance reflects that executives are appropriately rewarded when shareholders gain wealth. If a company chooses to use TSR as a performance measure, does it make sense to use an absolute TSR or a relative TSR measure?

Use of Relative TSR

The great majority of S&P/TSX 60 performance share unit plans adopt a relative TSR approach by comparing their return achievements to a performance peer group. For example, TSR often plays a significant part in the rewards plans for mature and/or cyclical companies in the mining, energy and financial sectors.

S&P/TSX 60 and cyclical companies are often affected by macro external factors within the domestic and global environments. Relative TSR is a reasonable method for these organizations to distinguish the achievements of management from the overall movement of the markets.

When using relative TSR, the selection of an appropriate performance peer group is critical because the choice of peers can have a significant effect on plan outcomes. Some common "malpractices" in peer group construction are:

- Organizations reluctantly adopt a peer group on the grounds that their majority investors require it.
- Organizations spend too little effort on choosing a peer group.
- Organizations focus primarily on the domestic market without any articulation of the global market.

Developing a Performance Peer Group

When relative TSR first became a common measure in the late 1990s, the usual approach was to base the peer group on the most obvious alternative investments for a shareholder. This reflected the origins of relative TSR in the performance-driven relative bonus plans operated for fund managers themselves. It often meant using the broader market composite or comparators.

Hindsight and experience have exposed this type of thinking. Such broad comparator groups include a high degree of randomness due to the very dissimilar degrees of volatility and cyclical exposure faced by different sectors and businesses. It becomes necessary to think about relative TSR in an alternative way.

In essence, this means considering businesses that face broadly similar economic, market, regulatory and operational challenges. This generally includes direct business competitors and/or businesses with a similar profile in terms of products, sectors and locations. Given the smaller size of the Canadian market relative to that of the United States, finding a peer group that is comparable across all of these metrics often can be a more significant challenge, contributing to the complexity of the selection process. Company size also can be a factor, but wider company size variations can be accepted for TSR than would be appropriate when selecting a peer group for compensation market benchmarking purposes. This also may contribute to the popularity of TSR use in the Canadian market, particularly in cases in which foreign competitors are larger in size and other measures, such as revenue or earnings before interest and taxes (EBIT), are directly affected as a result. The following are some common considerations when selecting a group:

- **Correlation.** How well does the historical TSR of the overall market correlate to your company and sector?
- **Volatility.** How does the historical share price volatility of the overall market compare to your company and sector?

Testing the Performance Peer Group

Having developed a potential performance peer group, it is important to model and test this group. This means tracking TSR for the potential comparators over several overlapping historical performance periods and computing what the plan would have paid in these scenarios. This modeling allows the following key questions to be addressed:

- Do the performance outcomes fit with what you believe about the historical performance of your business?
- In a small group, are any comparators miscorrelated?
- In a larger group, are any sectors miscorrelated to you and your main competitors?
- In a global group, are any countries miscorrelated?

However, it is possible that the modeling will produce a set of notional historical payments that seem to be driven by random factors rather than the performance of the business. In that case, either the proposed comparator group needs to be significantly revised or the use of relative TSR as a measure needs to be re-thought.

Compensation committees often are nervous about moving away from the current performance measurement method due to the preferences of investors. In such cases, an empirical approach perhaps is more effective in developing the decision.

Weighting the Performance Peer Group

Some companies may have a small number of highly relevant comparators and a larger number of companies with whom they have some similarities. Some companies may have the opposite characteristics.

In either case, the aim is to make sure the performance peer group is large enough to be robust without it being dominated by the less relevant comparators. The answer here is to weight the peer group such that the most relevant companies have a bigger impact on the result.

Performance Measurement and Payment

There are three basic ways to assess performance against a peer group. Currently, the simple ranking method is widely adopted among S&P/TSX 60 companies:

- **Simple ranking.** This is the simplest and most common approach. Incentive payments are sensitive to the clustering of comparator performance (e.g. 50th percentile to 75th percentile). Therefore incremental improvements to TSR may have very large or very small effect on the vested amount, depending on how wide each performance cluster is defined.
- **Percentage outperformance.** Vesting is determined by a company's TSR above a TSR percentile value (e.g. P40 or P50) or above the TSR of an index. To further calibrate the baseline requirement, some companies add a premium spread on top. The outperformance gap over the premium requirement determines the size of the incentive payment, which often is calculated using interpolation.
- **Smooth ranking.** This is a compromise option between the two approaches described above. For example, your payment size is calculated based on interpolation between the median TSR value and maximum TSR value of the peer group.

Simple ranking works best for very large comparator groups. Otherwise the other methods are preferable. If the peer group is very small, the percentage outperformance approach is generally more appropriate.

Treatment of International Peers

Deciding how to best treat international comparators is an especially pertinent consideration for S&P/TSX 60 firms, as many use U.S. peer groups of comparable size in cases where companies with many parallels are sparse in the Canadian market. Many believe that international peers should not create any issues in TSR comparison — TSR is expressed as a percentage term, therefore, an international peer group should not be affected by currency exchange as long as the raw TSR calculation of each peer company is kept on the same currency basis.

Hay Group, however, has a slightly different opinion when the issue is examined more in depth. Consider converting all returns to a consistent currency for the following reasons:

- Using a consistent currency will provide an accurate reflection of the relative returns that would have been achieved by an investor who bears the exchange risk.
- The local currency approach is technically flawed because high inflation in that country could inflate nominal rates of return — so could currency devaluation for a company with substantial foreign earnings. A high nominal return in such circumstances may not be an indicator of good management performance.
- For multinational companies, measuring TSR in a consistent currency is similar to financial reporting. When a single currency is consistently adopted among the peer companies, we can fully appreciate the correlation between other performance metrics (e.g. EPS) with TSR.

When Not to Use Relative TSR

As stated, relative TSR is most relevant for mature, cyclical businesses. Conversely, relative TSR is of limited validity for the following types of companies:

- Businesses targeting substantial growth
- Businesses in a turnaround situation
- Businesses that are not competing with other businesses for direct customers to any meaningful extent (e.g., biotech)
- "Infant" businesses (e.g. startups, upstream oil exploration, mining exploration, biotech).

For these companies, what matters is their absolute performance. A stable peer group is difficult to identify while the comparison results are often too volatile to manage in the context of incentives.

What Is Next?

Should TSR be tied to incentives for lower-level executives or managers? In general, the idea in the past was to ensure that "we were all in this together." However, this perspective undermined the value of LTIs for many executives below the top-team level. Today, current thinking is to consider the extent to which LTI plan design can and should vary within the executive population. This variation allows a more tailored approach to designing incentive plans under a consistent compensation philosophy, but is balanced with line of sight.

Executive Compensation Design in Australia

Although geographically positioned at the southern end of Asia, Australia is culturally more closely aligned to Western economies. The government, legal and social frameworks were derived primarily from the United States and United Kingdom, so executive rewards in Australia have many similarities to the models used in those countries.

The geographic separation from Northern Hemisphere ancestors has, however, led to the emergence of some features that are quite different. While these variations are not as extreme as those seen in some of the country's unique animal species (e.g., kangaroo, wombat, platypus), they do have some endearing aspects that sit well within the Australian business environment.

After explaining the general picture of executive pay in Australia, specific areas that are different from a typical U.S. practice are addressed.

Fixed-Reward Approach

In the 1970s, Australian tax regulations allowed a number of noncash benefits to be taken with little or no tax payable. This encouraged companies to provide significant levels of perquisites to middle and senior management. The most common perquisite was a company-provided (and fully maintained) car. Other common items included travel, club fees, entertainment expenses and housing or low-interest housing loans. The use of perquisites became a gray area; the "tax-free" position of many was based on assertions that the activity (e.g., travel or entertainment) was for business purposes.

Fringe Benefits Tax

In 1986, the Australian federal government introduced a fringe benefits tax (FBT) that was levied on employers for any benefits provided to employees. The FBT was designed so that the cost to the company of providing $100 in after-tax cash to the employee was the same as the cost of providing $100 in benefits. While this legitimized the provision of benefits by companies provided the FBT was paid, it also removed the financial incentive to use perquisites instead of cash. A few benefits, such as employer-provided cars, received discounted FBT costing, and "superannuation" (pension plan) contributions were fully exempted from FBT to encourage saving for retirement.

Employee Choice

The compensation response to the FBT was for companies to define the value of fixed reward they were prepared to pay for each individual. This fixed package or fixed annual reward could be taken by the employee in whatever form he/she chose. Each benefits item is valued at the cost to the company, and the balance is provided as cash salary. Some executives elect to take most or all of the package as cash, while others take a substantial portion in benefits.

Initially, companies provided a fairly wide selection of benefits for executives to choose from; over time the range usually has been reduced as employers sought to eliminate the administrative costs of furnishing benefits that offered no financial advantage. The most common remaining forms of benefits are cars, car parking and superannuation contributions. Companies generally communicate to staff and advertise positions using fixed reward figures.

Effect on Reward Comparisons

A consequence of the employee choice approach is that virtually no Australian companies make external reward comparisons based on base salary. Because individual executives choose the components they want within the total package amount, base salary is a balancing item that reflects not only what companies are paying executives, but also the choices individual executives have made on how to take their fixed pay.

Increasingly, organizations are not tracking the salary component at all and providing fixed-pay figures as the base salary for Australian pay surveys. For market comparison purposes, the total fixed-pay figure should be used as the reference point, as base salary survey data is not as robust or relevant in setting market targets.

Some companies with overseas parents still use a defined salary and specified benefits because they may have trouble explaining the Australian approach to the parent organization. Given concerns about the validity of the base salary survey figures, consider using the fixed-pay figures less the value of the standard benefits provided by the employer. This gives the salary figure the company will need to provide to ensure the fixed-pay figure is on target with the market.

Superannuation

At roughly the same time that the government introduced the FBT, it also supported a move to require employers to contribute to retirement savings. The government was concerned that the aging Baby Boomer population was approaching retirement with insufficient resources and would expect the social security system to fill the gap. The government decided to shift the focus of responsibility to employers and employees. The initial requirement was for 6 percent of pay, and this has been progressively increased to 9 percent, offset partly by union-agreed reduced salary increases. The contributions are fully vested and must remain in approved funds until retirement even if the employee leaves the employer.

At around the same time, Australia saw a major movement from defined benefit (DB) funds to defined contribution (DC) plans. This shift in preferred plan design was prompted by several factors:

- There was social and regulatory pressure to provide portability between employers, which is more easily managed with DC plans.
- Many existing DB plans were in surplus due to high investment returns.
- The overfunding made it possible to offer attractive transfer values to encourage employees in switching to a DC fund.
- Some companies were able to "reclaim the excess" when members transferred.

- DC plans work more easily with flexible fixed-pay packages.
- Most companies now allow executives to elect how much they want to contribute to superannuation provided they choose the regulatory minimum (9 percent of normal pay up to a maximum required contribution of $13,129 per annum). Contributions are very tax efficient up to $25,000 annually ($50,000 for some executives), at which point they become tax inefficient.

Cars

Before fixed-reward packaging, company-provided cars were not only a tax-effective form of reward, but also were a major status symbol. HR managers were under constant pressure to increase the level of cars provided. Hours were spent arguing about lifting the price limit so the executive could get a better car or a better sound system or a tow bar.

Once fixed packaging was introduced, the arguments ended. An executive can have whatever car desired, with unlimited options; he/she just has to pay the price. Instead of pushing for better cars, executives often downgraded or elected not to take a car at all, once they appreciated the cost and the cash alternative.

The most common mechanism for providing cars is now through a fully maintained lease. The leasing company handles all the administration and maintenance costs, with fixed monthly costs deducted from the fixed-reward package. A common variation is known as a novated lease, which keeps the primary lease between the lease company and the executive. It allows the company to pay the monthly costs while the executive is employed, but the lease obligations stay with the executive on cessation of employment.

Other Benefits

While there are other benefits that may be provided by a few companies, the value is usually small in relation to the executive package. Insurance has never been a significant element of Australian reward. Life insurance is provided as a component of superannuation and there often is an option for the executive to increase the standard level of coverage. A few companies, often with North American connections, provide salary continuance insurance.

Medical insurance is highly regulated in Australia and companies cannot provide their own coverage for employees. While contributions to approved insurers can be paid by the company, there is no financial benefit and it limits the employee's choice of insurer, so few companies make such payments.

Short-Term Incentives

The use of executive short-term incentives (with a performance test and payment period of up to 12 months) is common in Australia.

Over time, the size of the short-term incentive (STI) opportunity has increased from a small component of fixed annual reward to a significant percentage. The STI proportion varies with the size of the job and the industry. Amounts for senior executives range from 30 percent of fixed annual reward to 100 percent or more in sectors such as financial services and resources.

Historically, there was some variation in the type of STI, whether the plan was a target-based incentive with a defined opportunity size or a bonus paid retrospectively. Hay Group now estimates that approximately 75 percent of companies use a target-based STI plan. The amount of the incentive payment varies from year to year based on the achievement of specific targets set at a corporate, business-unit and/or individual level. Targets are determined and agreed upon in advance, as are the rewards for achieving and exceeding those targets.

The most frequent performance measure used in target-based STI plans is profit, with a significant majority of companies using this measure. Other performance measures used (not always exclusively), in decreasing order of prevalence, are key management behaviors, return on capital employed, cost control and cash flow.

Recent Trends

Years of economic growth and the positive effect of strong commodity prices on many companies in Australia have resulted in a war for talent and strong corporate performance for many companies, notwithstanding the global financial problems of the last few years. These aspects have been affecting STIs for executives as follows:

- While STI opportunities usually are presented as a percentage of fixed reward, many plans provide for extra payments if stretch performance targets are achieved. Much of the increase in STI payments appears to be attributable to the provision of these additional upside opportunities.
- There is a small but growing trend of deferring the payout of executive STIs. This is designed to support the retention of critical executives in the tight talent market. Some companies use a timing deferral — paying the cash over longer periods — and others pay the incentives in restricted shares.

Long-Term Incentives

LTIs in the Australian market have been characterized by the use of time and performance hurdles. Shareholder groups have made rigorous performance hurdles virtually compulsory with the intent of increasing the alignment between executives and shareholders.

The typical plan design has a performance period of three years, with a few companies using five years. The combination of the performance and time hurdles means that approximately 50 percent of all allocations do not vest.

The design of LTIs for Australian residents needs to be carefully considered to structure them appropriately for Australian corporate accounting, corporate taxation and individual taxation regulations. Inappropriate design can result in LTIs being taxable before they vest. This can affect the suitability of overseas-based equity schemes to Australian residents.

Performance Measures

The majority of plans use a relative TSR measure — the combination of share price growth and dividends paid compared to a comparator group of companies. While there has been a gradual movement away from using relative TSR as the key performance measure to the use of other measures (sometimes in combination with relative TSR), TSR remains the overwhelming choice.

The big change in executive LTI approach in recent years has been the shift from share-option plans to performance-share plans.

The change is striking: stock options declined from a substantial majority of senior executive awards to a significant minority, while the results were the reverse for performance shares, which now account for a significant majority of these awards.

Governance Issues

Australian governance requirements are fairly similar to those in the United States and the United Kingdom. There is an obligation for listed companies to include a Remuneration Report as part of the annual report. This must disclose all director compensation for the past year plus detailed pay information for key management personnel; companies generally disclose five or more executives. The report also must furnish details of the company's reward philosophy and policies including incentive plans and performance criteria. Share-based equity must be disclosed in line with the international accounting standards, and details of past awards not yet exercised must be shown.

There is a requirement for a nonbinding shareholder vote on acceptance of the Remuneration Report at each annual general meeting. Most boards have been very reluctant to proceed with remuneration items that are likely to receive a significant number of negative votes.

From July 2011 there has been a legal obligation for companies that receive a negative vote of 25 percent or more on the Remuneration Report at two consecutive annual general meetings to have an immediate vote to spill all board positions and have a new election within three months. This is expected to ensure boards take action to avoid negative votes on the Remuneration Report.

There is a prohibition on listed companies making any termination payments that are linked to change in control, preventing change-in-control payments from being used by existing management and directors as a poison pill to discourage takeovers. Payments can be made following a change in control, but only if triggered by factors that would apply in other situations (e.g., the termination of the executive).

Legislation limits the maximum termination payment for executives, under any circumstances, to 12 months base salary unless there is specific shareholder approval for the greater payment.

It is not expected that boards will approve payments that require special shareholder approval.

Key Differences

While strong similarities exist between the approaches to executive reward in Australia and the United States, there are a number of important differences:

- The different structure of fixed-pay practice makes the use of base salary and total cash for market comparisons in Australia potentially misleading.
- The Australian regulations on company contributions for retirement income savings make it a very tax-effective form of income.
- There is generally a somewhat smaller proportion of overall pay provided as STI and LTI in Australia.
- The Australian shareholder requirements for strong performance hurdles that result in a high risk of LTIs not vesting may not be necessary for subsidiaries of U.S. companies.
- Australian LTI tax provisions can result in equity LTIs being taxable before vesting, so care should be taken with the design.
- Basic reward philosophies of U.S. organizations can be applied in Australia, but some adjustments to the mechanics of pay structures and comparisons may be needed to ensure desired market competitiveness.

Say on Pay: Lessons from the United Kingdom

Since 2003, UK companies have been subject to shareholder oversight on executive compensation through a mandatory, nonbinding shareholder vote (say on pay) on their compensation report, held on an annual basis. The vote covers both forward-looking policy and the prior year's compensation. Though advisory in nature, the adverse reputational effects and the effect on shareholder relations of a significant negative vote cause companies to take steps to avoid such an eventuality.

Following the UK experience, in 2004 Dutch shareholders also secured the right to cast a vote on executive compensation. A crucial difference with the UK regulations is that the vote cast by shareholders in the Netherlands is only forward-looking and each company is bound to comply with the outcome of the vote. Moreover, the vote in the Netherlands is not necessarily annual — if a company does not make significant changes to executive compensation policy, then it is not obliged to put its policy to the vote.

During the years since the early emergence of say on pay in Europe, many more countries have adopted the practice, with a mandated vote now also in place for public companies in France, Spain, Sweden, Norway, Denmark, Australia and most recently the United States. It is likely that say on pay will spread further in the next few years.

In addition, Germany has taken the approach of empowering shareholders to cast a vote on executive compensation should they so wish; however, a company is not obliged to put the vote on the meeting agenda unless it is requested to do so by shareholders.

We examine here key issues around say on pay, drawing on the experience of the United Kingdom, as it is the country with the longest history in shareholder voting on executive pay issues. We also compare UK practices and experiences to say on pay voting in the United States under the Dodd-Frank Wall Street Reform and Consumer Protection Act of 2010 and discuss the issues of relevance to companies (both in the United States and elsewhere) that are or will become subject to a shareholder vote on their compensation practices.

Background and Comparisons with the United States

Shareholder voting on executive compensation in publicly listed companies became mandatory in the United Kingdom following the Director Remuneration Report (DRR) Regulations of 2002. The regulations followed a long period of increased concern by shareholders and legislators alike around rapid growth in the levels of executive pay, lack of transparency and stories around "fat-cat pay" and "rewards for failure."

Prior to the introduction of the regulations, the Combined Code (then the "comply or explain" UK code of corporate governance) recommended that companies voluntarily put their DRR to a shareholder vote. However, only a minority of companies held a vote prior to it becoming mandatory.

The regulations provided for a required but nonbinding (i.e., advisory) vote on executive compensation issues, including both forward-looking policy as well as compensation realized by or awarded over the past year.

At the same time, the regulations introduced disclosure requirements that, in broad terms, required listed companies to prepare a compensation committee report to be included in the annual report and accounts. The regulations divide the disclosures into:

- Those that must be audited, which primarily comprise numerical information regarding the amounts paid to both executive directors and nonexecutive (outside) directors
- Information not requiring audit, generally relating to executive compensation policy (overall and for each element of compensation) both for the year under review and going forward, including the use of external advisers.

Say on pay in the United Kingdom is reasonably similar to its development in the United States. The main difference is that it is not mandatory for a U.S. firm to conduct its vote on an annual basis, although in practice most apparently will given the results of U.S. say-on-frequency (whether every one, two or three years) voting.

Another difference is that, as part of the Compensation Discussion and Analysis (CD&A), U.S. companies are to address the most recent vote and discuss its effect on compensation policies and decisions in the current year; UK companies are not subject to such a requirement. Although in practice high levels of voting dissent would normally lead to a review of executive compensation policies, there is no requirement to disclose the effect of voting on the compensation committee's activities and decisions.

An analysis of disclosures in the DRRs of the UK companies with the highest level of shareholder dissatisfaction since say on pay was mandated in 2002 (as expressed by voting dissent and identified by Manifest, a UK-based proxy voting agency) shows that subsequent reports contained only vague references about the effect (if any) that the vote had on decisions by the compensation committee.

How UK Say on Pay Works in Practice

The advisory nature of the vote means that any payments made are not subject to approval and do not have to be repaid in the event that the DRR is not approved by shareholders. However, the reputational risks (both personal and corporate) associated with a defeated resolution can be significant. For example, a number of compensation committee chairs have resigned from their posts not long after the relevant DRRs being defeated or receiving a large dissenting vote. In practice, therefore, most UK companies tend to respond promptly to negative votes (or the fear of a large negative vote) to avoid the real or perceived embarrassment associated with such a vote or the fear of "punishment" by the market.

It has also been argued that it is exactly this nonbinding nature of the say-on-pay vote that enables investors to express their discontent with executive compensation without severe consequences for the companies in which they invest. The legislative intention was to create ongoing dialogue between investors and companies; only as a last resort would investors vote against the DRR. The general consensus is that to a large extent this has been successful, as most UK companies are now in regular dialogue with their major shareholders and shareholder bodies regarding executive compensation. But there are still lessons to be learned and the main challenge is now for the quality of this dialogue to be improved.

An additional tool in the shareholder toolkit when investing in UK companies is the vote being actively "withheld." In the United Kingdom, only "for" and "against" votes are taken into account when deciding whether a resolution is carried or not. However, a vote actively withheld (also known as an abstention) allows shareholders to register their unease over a matter without resorting to a possibly confrontational negative vote. A withheld vote can serve either to allow for the recognition of mitigating factors in a situation in which a vote against might otherwise occur or as a warning shot. In this latter case, if the matter is not resolved to shareholders' satisfaction within the following year, it would reasonable to expect shareholders to vote against the compensation report in future years or even to vote against the re-election of directors who are compensation committee members.

In terms of actual voting outcomes, according to Manifest, the historical average dissent (defined as the sum of votes against and votes withheld/abstentions) since the introduction of voting on the DRR in the UK is 9.4 percent. This percentage has slightly fallen over time. However, it remains the case that shareholders are generally more likely to vote against the DRR and other pay-related resolutions compared to proposals not related to executive compensation. Despite those seemingly low (on average) levels of dissent, the introduction of say on pay in the United Kingdom and investor activism more generally has significantly influenced executive compensation practices.

Consequences of Introduction of Say on Pay

The UK executive compensation landscape has changed significantly in the years since the introduction of the 2002 regulations. Empowered with the say-on-pay vote, more UK investors have become activists and are credited with bringing about a number of changes to UK compensation practices that are generally considered positive. These include:

- A reduction in executive director contract lengths (and therefore the value of severance payments) from three years or more to one year (or less in some cases)
- The removal of "re-testing" provisions when performance conditions are missed
- The near-universal use of extremely stretching performance conditions on the vesting of share and share option plans
- The virtual elimination of "golden goodbyes" (i.e. large, discretionary payments to departing executives as compensation for loss of office, which was often viewed as "reward for failure" in the case of underperforming companies).

While there is some evidence that firms with the highest CEO pay attract greater voting dissent, there is little evidence to suggest that large negative votes themselves have led to lower pay at the affected firms. However, it should be remembered that the greatest effect of say on pay has been through companies responding to the explicit or expected threat of voting dissent. In practice, most changes to executive compensation policies take place in the run-up to the shareholder meeting, following consultation.

However, there are at least some individual examples in which say on pay has led to immediate changes in companies' compensation policies. For example, GlaxoSmithKline, the first company to "lose" its say-on-pay vote in the United Kingdom, attracted significant adverse publicity regarding the severance arrangements for the then-CEO Jean-Pierre Garnier. The arrangements were perceived by shareholders as being "excessive" and not in line with CEO pay at other UK companies. Ultimately, this resulted in changes in the executive compensation package that were seen as being more "shareholder-friendly."

Despite the aforementioned positive changes, the introduction of say on pay also had a number of unfortunate unintended consequences:

- The years following the 2002 regulations coincided with large increases in the overall level of executive pay, although, arguably, it was the introduction of public disclosures in the DRR (rather than the say-on-pay vote) that contributed to increases in executive compensation. It is possible that certain investor demands seen as "best practices" (e.g., the demand for tougher performance conditions on the vesting of LTIs and the reduction in the length of service contracts) directly or indirectly led to larger awards and/or overall higher total executive compensation.

- Investors have too many proposals to consider in a short period of time (i.e., the proxy season). This is part of the reason why they rely (often disproportionately) on the advice from proxy voting advisers, who in turn may apply one-size-fits-all policies leading to a focus on box-ticking.

- As a result, at least prior to the start of the financial crisis in 2008, we saw an unprecedented uniformity in executive compensation policy and practices. The majority of companies followed institutional shareholder guidelines fairly rigidly, without adapting them to their individual circumstances and unique business strategies. In this regard, UK boards have generally been averse to making controversial decisions that could spark (minority) votes against their DRR, even if these ended up being supported by a large majority of investors. The practice of some investors and shareholder bodies, who were in reality unwilling to give support to any proposal not meeting their policies or to even consider explanations provided by companies, led to a large extent to the cancelling in practice of the "comply or explain" approach described earlier. The picture is now changing in the United Kingdom with investors expecting a greater degree of tailoring to strategy and sector.

Avoiding a Negative Say on Pay Vote

During the first few years after the introduction of mandatory say-on-pay voting in the United Kingdom, it was relatively easy to foresee the issues that would lead to a large negative vote. These included executive contracts in excess of one year, re-testing of LTI performance conditions and large payments upon dismissal.

As executive compensation policies converged and those afore-mentioned practices almost extinguished, it became harder to predict how investors would vote as the range of issues considered widened and investors themselves became more sophisticated.

In general, having in place a well-thought compensation philosophy that is aligned to the business strategy and clearly communicated to shareholders in the annual report (or equivalent document) is a necessary first step in ensuring that the say-on-pay vote will not yield any surprises. In addition, it is worth considering the following:

• **Shareholders are increasingly concerned with the lack of alignment between pay and performance.** In the United States, Institutional Shareholder Services (ISS) analyzes total shareholder return over one- and three-year periods and, if companies fall in the bottom half of a relevant (industry) comparator group, ISS also expects a "material" reduction in executive pay. In the United Kingdom, investors and their representative bodies also have signaled that they expect the quantum of pay to track the performance of the company, but it is less clear how this is being defined or monitored by shareholders (other than by a simple reference to share price and profit movements over the financial year). Assuming a well-thought compensation policy is in place, it is important for companies and boards to communicate extensively with investors should the level of executive pay not move in the same direction as such simple/generic measures of performance.

- **Proxy voting agencies have a major influence over how share-holder votes are cast.** It is therefore important to understand the requirements of the different voting advisory services and for companies to understand how their shareholder base is likely to behave. For example, foreign investors may be more likely to follow automatically an "against" voting recommendation by ISS compared to a company with local investors. In the United States the CD&A is properly used as a proactive communication rather than a reactive disclosure tool. Anything out of the ordinary (in terms of amount, compliance with shareholder guidelines or previous practice within the company) should be clearly and meticulously explained.
- **Compensation committees should make the effort to talk directly to shareholders.** Such communication should take place well in advance of the shareholder meeting and, if possible, involve fund managers in addition to the corporate governance analysts.
- **Shareholders are more likely to use the say on pay vote to express their dissatisfaction if they perceive poor governance practices in general, even if these are not related with the area of compensation.** Similarly, anecdotal UK experience suggests that companies whose financial performance disappoints the markets may be subject to tougher scrutiny around remuneration. It is important for boards to understand this and the amount of goodwill they have with investors overall.

Case Study: Bellway, a UK Company that Lost Say on Pay Vote in 2009

Partway through the 2007/2008 financial year, Bellway (a real-estate developer) moved away from a traditional, formulaic and profit-driven bonus plan to a plan under which "the financial performance should be assessed at the end of the year, and the basis for the bonus should be determined at that time." Actual payments for the two executive directors for 2007/2008 performance were 55 percent of salary compared to a normal bonus maximum of 120 percent.

The justification for the bonus payments was set out in a footnote to the table of directors' emoluments. The bonus payments were badly received by investors who had seen significant falls in both profit (EPS down by 80 percent) and the share price. As a result, around 58 percent of investors voted against accepting the DRR at the company's 2009 shareholder meeting.

There are four key lessons from this case for compensation committees, both in the United Kingdom and elsewhere:

Don't Move the Goalposts

The DRR regulations require disclosure of forward-looking executive compensation policy. Although there may be (rare) circumstances where fundamental changes are required mid-year, in general investors are uncomfortable with such changes, particularly when they work in the favor of executives. In the case of Bellway, the 2006/2007 Annual Report stated that the 2007/2008 bonus plan would be based on a "challenging" budget for operating profit; however, payments made for 2007/2008 were based on Bellway's performance in a bad market compared to its peer companies.

Remember the Context

Many investors, governance bodies and proxy advisers will take at least some account of the remuneration context — specifically the rest of the package and historical payment levels. In the case of Bellway, the bonus plan had paid out at maximum for the previous last five years and this perhaps contributed to the adverse shareholder reaction.

Discretionary Plans Need to Be Sold Carefully

Investors often become concerned if they perceive that a high component of pay depends on subjective assessments of performance.

Qualitative assessments of performance do have a legitimate role, provided the criteria to be considered are determined in advance and clearly communicated to investors. In the case of Bellway, not only were bonuses assessed on a discretionary basis, but the basis for making this assessment seems also to have been determined at the end of the year.

Communicate, Communicate, Communicate

Any potentially controversial bonus or other payments should be explained clearly in the main body of the DRR/CD&A, while a material change in plan philosophy should additionally be explained to major shareholders and proxy voting advisers directly.

Germany: New Rules on Executive Board Compensation

The new Act on Appropriateness of Executive Compensation (VorstAG) became effective in August 2009. VorstAG is applicable to listed and nonlisted legal entities of types AG, SE and KGaA. VorstAG has a considerable effect on the practice of executive directors' compensation as well as its determination by the supervisory board. Among other effects, VorstAG substantiates the appropriateness of executive directors' compensation. In addition, listed stock corporations must implement compensation that is sustainable and aligns with long-term company development. VorstAG also is applicable, in part, to foreign-owned companies in Germany. In addition, there is an increasing influence from the European Union and the financial services industry on corporate governance related items.

Overview: VorstAG

VorstAG sets new rules for determining the compensation of management board/executive directors. There are additional regulations for listed stock corporations that focus on incentives for sustainable (value) management. The new law intends to correct undesirable developments. Besides, board management compensation should be internally consistent and internally appropriate. At the same time, the responsibility of the supervisory board (nonexecutive directors) of the management board's compensation shall be emphasized and transparency improved for shareholders and the public.

In July 2009, the government commission of the German Corporate Governance Code (GCGC) updated its code by the amendments made by the VorstAG. Thus, mandatory legal provisions were included in the GCGC and further regulations were included as recommendations or suggestions.

- **Competence for determining management board compensation:** Whereas previously a subcommittee of the supervisory board could determine the management board's compensation, now, under VorstAG, the supervisory board as a whole must decide on the management board's compensation. In detail, the supervisory board has to decide on the base salary, any component of variable pay, allowances, pensions, insurance premiums and so on — for each member of the management board.

  This entails a major change to the previous practice, in which the entire supervisory board decided only on the management board compensation policy and not on its details. Now, VorstAG assigns only a preparatory function to the compensation committee. The mandatory competence of the full supervisory board also applies to a possible reduction of the compensation (section 87 [2] of the German Stock Corporation Act, AktG). In addition, the supervisory board members are personally liable for any kind of inappropriate pay.

- **Appropriateness of management board compensation:** Not only must the supervisory board ensure that compensation is appropriate in relation to the performance of the respective management board member and the situation of the company, it must also make sure that "customary/common" compensation is not exceeded without a particular reason. The exception for one of these particular reasons has been introduced for flexibility reasons to react to special circumstances such as international board members or unique industries.

  According to the legislative material, the supervisory board has to consider the industry, size and number of countries to determine what compensation would be customary/common (so-called "horizontal comparability"). In any case, the focus of the law is the German "market" that needs to be benchmarked against according to the prevailing legal opinion. International peer groups also can be selected. Furthermore, the compensation paid within the company must be considered (a so-called "vertical comparison"). Under this concept, the supervisory board has to make sure that the compensation of the management board members remains in proportion to the compensation system within the company. This approach supports internal consistency and replaced the preliminary intention of the government to introduce a general cap or multiple for the compensation of the board relative to the other employees of the company. The vertical comparison takes into account the diversity of company size, industries and organizational structures of the German economy that cannot be reflected by general caps nor by multiples.

• **Alignment of incentives with sustainable company development (for listed companies only):** The supervisory board is obliged to implement a compensation structure that supports sustainable company development. This is a reaction to the fact that listed German companies focus their pay mix on the annual performance and less on longer term performance. Listed German companies used to pay the biggest bonuses in Europe.

However, the law does not define the exact meaning of sustainability. The long-term effects of variable pay must be kept in mind.

– According to controlling legal opinion, annual bonus payments are still acceptable as long as the long-term components have a heavier weight regarding all variable components (annual and long-term).

– Variable components are to be based on multiple year performance (multi-year perspective).

– According to the law, stock options must have a vesting period of at least four years. VorstAG as well as the GCGC leave room for other long-term plan types. General legal opinion views vesting and performance periods of two years are seen as compliant with VorstAG; however, performance periods of three years are recommended for long-term cash plans and

three to four years are preferred for equity-based plans other
than stock options.

– The GGCG also recommends that compensation may not incentivize management board members to take inappropriate risks.
For variable pay plans, the supervisory board shall include a cap
to limit payout possibilities due to extraordinary developments.

* **Reduction of management board compensation during a crisis:**
If a company's situation deteriorates, the supervisory board shall
reduce the executive's board compensation to an appropriate
amount. This is a soft regulation, as it encourages but does not
contain enforcement mechanics. It even includes pensions, but
a reduction is possible only within the first three years after the
management board member has retired.

* **Liability of the supervisory board:** Before VorstAG, the members of
the supervisory board were already personally liable for negligent
determination of inappropriately high compensation. Now, this
liability has been emphasized.

* **D&O (directors and officers) liability insurance deductible:** If
a company provides for insurance to protect a member of the
management board against risks arising from his/her professional
activities, the insurance policy must provide for an individual
deductible of at least 10 percent up to a minimum of 150 percent
of the fixed annual compensation of the respective executive
board member. Management board members may cover the
cost of the deductible with additional insurance, as long as the
company does not reimburse for the premium. In addition, the
GCGC recommends using the same deductible for supervisory
board members in the D&O insurance.

* **Say on pay — advisory vote on the compensation system at
the annual shareholders' meeting:** In listed companies, the
shareholders' meeting may vote on the approval of the compensation system for the management board. However, the vote is
non-binding.

* **Extended disclosure rules:** The existing disclosure rules regarding
management board members' compensation (policy and individual disclosure) in the annual financial statements and group

accounts are amplified by VorstAG, especially for benefits that accrue after the termination of employment such as pensions and severance payments.

Major Effect on Current Practices

Concerning management board compensation, there are four clusters of major impact:

- **Process.** The general approval of the policy and of the individual compensation of the management board by the entire supervisory board is enforced by the personal liability of each supervisory board member. This raises their awareness on management board compensation. In fact, compensation-related items have come on many agenda meetings. The newly introduced say on pay for listed companies supports this too; a negative vote at the shareholders' meeting may harm company and personal reputation.
- **Change in variable pay mix.** In listed companies the variable mix is moving from an annual focus to long-term performance measurement. (See Figure 21-1.) As a trend, non-listed companies are adopting this procedure.

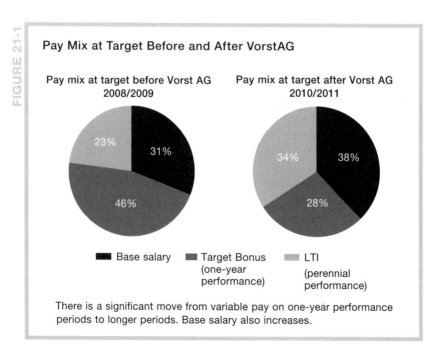

FIGURE 21-1

Pay Mix at Target Before and After VorstAG

Pay mix at target before Vorst AG
2008/2009

23%
31%
46%

Pay mix at target after Vorst AG
2010/2011

34%
38%
28%

■ Base salary   ■ Target Bonus (one-year performance)   ▦ LTI (perennial performance)

There is a significant move from variable pay on one-year performance periods to longer periods. Base salary also increases.

- Bonus/variable pay with one-year performance measurement. In the major listed companies (DAX30), only 85 percent of the companies pay variable incentives based on a one-year perspective. Sixty percent of these companies practice some kind of bonus deferral plans. The target percentage as well as the caps are decreasing.
- Long-term plans. The target volume is increasing and the number of plans per management board is moving from one to two plans. The performance periods are prolonging from to three to four years.
- **Benchmarking and external appropriateness.** There is an increasing pressure on job pricings and pay benchmarks by focusing on appropriate peer groups and reliable, robust methods. In particular, peer-group selection for global players is an even more challenging exercise. In the light of liability, documentation of ratios and assumptions to achieve the benchmarks become more important. Up to now, we have seen a trend to outsource benchmarking to external consultants. Currently, the awareness of the supervisory boards on robust and solid benchmarks is still limited; this especially applies to the effect of peer groups and values of variable pay. However, there is an increasing awareness of investors and shareholders on such questions.
- **Internal consistency and internal appropriateness.** This check is less popular and new to address. The employee representatives on the supervisory board have an eye on this check, as they use also it as an indicator for salary raises of the nonexempt and exempt, nonmanagerial jobs (See Figure 21-2). A pragmatic approach to check the internal appropriateness looks like:
  - Analysis of Pay Mix
    - Does the variable percentage (target and actual) increase by increasing job size?
    - Does the long-term variable part increase with increasing managerial effect on results and strategy?
    - In case of "breaks," are there good reasons?
  - Analysis of pay volume and the increase by job size
    - Our general experience shows that the base salaries for all employees including the board of management can be

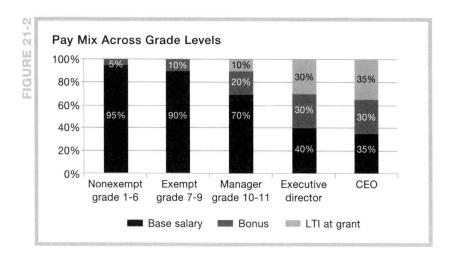

FIGURE 21-2

cross-checked by a line based on the company grading approach. (See Figure 21-3).

- Total cash (base salary plus bonus) usually are represented by a curve rather than a linear line.
- As for pensions, the service costs cannot always be presented by a continuous curve — especially when there are different pension plans for the management board. There is room for discussion on internal appropriateness.

Lessons Learned

- **Process:** The process has changed when we look at decision making on pay and reviews. There is also more transparency. However, reviews have become more time consuming.
- **Peer groups:** For any market benchmark a peer group needs to be defined. However, global players often are so large that it is difficult to find a sufficient number of peers in the same industry. This also applies to German and international peer groups (e.g., BASF, Munich Re, Siemens, ThyssenKrupp). We recommend focusing on similar industries to generate stable and larger peer groups.
- **Variable pay and link with performance:** As VorstAG calls for consistency with the company's situation, any variable pay has to be checked before payout even if the benchmark is in

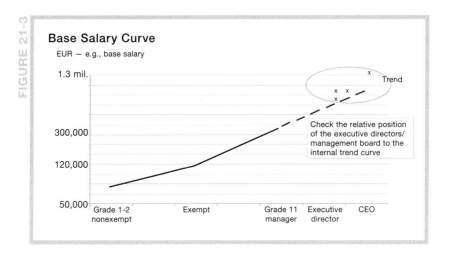

line with the peers. There is an increasing pressure on pay for performance and cross-checks of the variable payout versus key performance indicators and the major competitors. As a result, relative performance measurements have become more popular.

- **New forms of variable pay:** In listed companies, bonus deferrals have become very popular. Up to now, there have been no companies for which bonus deferrals have not been paid; this may be, in part, related to the fact that German companies recovered quite well and quickly from the global financial crisis.

- **Perennial variable pay increased:** Pushed by VorstAG, variable pay is more based on performance periods exceeding one year. To mitigate the risks of longer-term performance periods, there is a trend to introduce more than one LTI plan.

- **Increase in complexity, especially in the finance industry:** Due to new bonus deferrals, more complex performance hurdles, and more variable play plans, the compensation structures for management boards have become more complex both to under-stand and to administrate.

- **Say on pay:** Up to now, the majority of voting results exceeded 90 percent approval. However, we do see a negative effect of voting results around 50 percent that have occurred at a few companies.

- **Foreign-owned companies in Germany:** In general, these non-German companies are not listed and only have to apply some of the regulations of VorstAG. However, the (international) supervisory board members often have not been sufficiently informed about the changes and the effect. Thus, the check on external appropriateness leaves room for transparency and the quality of peer groups. Sometimes checks on internal appropriateness have not been conducted.

- **Foreign and international supervisory board members:** Due to the international growth of business and diversity considerations, there are more international supervisory board members with different corporate governance backgrounds. There is the need for convenient translations to keep them informed and enable them to make truly informed decisions. If foreign companies come from the United Kingdom or United States, they are usually used to disclosures related to compensation and performance and can coach these interactions.

Application to U.S. Companies in Germany

So far, the policies appear headed in the right direction. However, there is a trend to more complex compensation policies. This increased complexity decreases transparency, whereas VorstAG sought increased transparency. What does this mean for U.S. companies in Germany?

These companies in usually are not listed in Germany. Thus, they only have to comply with a reduced set of regulations according to VorstAG. There is a need to inform the supervisory board members about the existing compensation program to perform checks on the internal and external appropriateness of pay on a regular basis. The results as well as the ratio and assumptions for peer groups, market positions and similar items should be documented.

If a U.S. company also is listed in Germany, then the additional regulations on sustainable variable pay and the GCGC have to be addressed. Usually, common U.S. LTI plans do not fulfill the legal requirements in Germany. This may lead to conflicting discussions with corporate human resources in the U.S. as some members of the German management board have international roles and also participate in corporate (U.S.) plans that do not comply with the German VorstAG.

Executive Compensation in Family-Owned Businesses

An important area that has received insufficient attention lately involves common executive compensation issues arising in family-owned businesses. Specifically, two different situations are addressed:

- Private-family companies, in which the family owns the totality of the business
- Publicly listed family businesses, in which the family is the dominant shareholder and part of the shares float on the stock market.

Of course these situations often are linked: many private-family companies decide to go public to sustain international expansion and/or acquisitions. The listing is also often seen as an opportunity to attract leadership talent from the market and to improve management quality. In fact, executive compensation and the ability to offer more competitive packages and therefore attract high calibre top managers is one of the most frequently cited reasons for a family business to publicly list its shares.

Listed family businesses are frequent in many European countries (notably in Germany, France and Italy). The considerations we discuss are mostly based on a European perspective.

Setting a Competitive Pay Package

Consider, for example, a large, privately owned family company in the fast-moving consumer-goods sector. The market for leadership talent in this business is dominated by a few large multinational players and their compensation packages are heavily based on equity compensation and long-term incentives.

What should the family business do? Offer the same elements of compensation and mirror the market? Offer higher base salary to make up for the missing equity component or provide (for the same reason) higher annual bonus opportunities?

On the other hand, listed companies might be driven to use deferred bonus arrangements for compliance with corporate governance codes or government policy requirements. Should a family privately owned business do the same? Or should it instead to consider taking advantage of the higher degree of freedom a private business enjoys compared to the more regulated listed companies and completely forget about the deferral approach?

There is no straightforward solution to this problem. However, it can be worthwhile to look at how typical private-family businesses set the main components of executive pay: base salary, annual bonus and long-term incentives.

The following considerations are not based on statistical evidence, but instead rely on our consulting experience to large, privately owned family companies.

Base Salary

Base salary typically is very competitive, often to make up for the lack or lower value of LTIs and equity compensation. Also, high base pay tends to compensate for the risk of moving from well-known public companies to companies with a less-known employer and leadership brand.

Merit increases often are strongly linked to individual performance and their amount typically is higher than market practice, even if such increases are granted to a smaller number of executives. Base pay increases are seen as an effective way to reward individual performance and they are not viewed only as a tool to keep up with inflation and market pay rates.

Annual Bonus

Annual bonus programs typically are more discretionary and less formulaic than in publicly listed multinationals. Very often the family still has a strong say on the amount of the bonuses of the top executives of the company.

The bonus structure is often based on a "bonus pool" approach, reflecting the annual level of profitability of the company. On rare occasions it is structured as an add-on cost, with no reference to company profit. A typical question the owner of the company asks is, "How much of the profit should I share with my executive team?"

One consequence is that bonus payouts are linked not only to the degree of achievement of the annual targets set in the budget, but also depend on the level of the profit the company expects to achieve. This approach is very much entrepreneurial in its nature, reflecting the owner's view of executives' bonuses as linked to a satisfactory level of profitability of the company.

Long-Term Incentives

LTIs are much less common in private-family businesses than in publicly listed companies. When present, they typically are based on cash rather than equity. They might use measures related to an increase in equity value or on economic profit. But even if related to measures of value creation for the owners, the reward typically is set in cash, not equity.

In listed companies where a family is the dominant shareholder, the LTI plans tend to be based on measures of operating/business performance, rather than stock market or TSR. The investor perspective often is not fully considered. Top executives can be rewarded, if the operational performance of the company is considered satisfactory, even if the stock price has not performed adequately.

In listed companies, the family owners typically do not like to focus management attention on stock price increases. Rather, the family shareholder often is more interested in a stable flow of dividends. This makes it difficult to balance the different perspectives of institutional investors and the dominant shareholder. In fact, the design and implementation of LTI in a family business often tends to be a long and difficult process.

A further reason is very likely related to the fact that LTIs have very detailed rules, whereas the family owner generally prefers to maintain some degree of freedom and discretion as far as the actual payouts of the plan are concerned.

Risk and Reward in the Family Business

Family-owned businesses tend to be more risk averse than public companies. This different orientation is explained by the fact that the family shareholder typically is an undiversified investor, whereas institutional investors have a diversified investment portfolio.

Risk aversion in a family business often is increased when the top executives are family members and in particular when the

CEO is a family member. This is also because their human capital is totally invested in the company with limited or nonexistent opportunities to sell their managerial services to other companies. Risk aversion also varies across different generations of family members involved in the management of the company — the executive chairman, typically the father, is often more risk averse than top managers (typically the sons). However, the family CEO and executives are much less worried by quarterly results than their counterparts in public companies. This attitude is observable also in family-owned listed companies in which the CEO is a family member.

The implications of this specific attitude toward risk on CEO and executive pay packages are relevant. Compensation contracts may in fact reinforce conservative managerial decisions. Incentive plans may reward "not making mistakes" rather than encouraging innovation or getting into a new geographical market or product area. LTIs might have limited upside so that senior executives are not encouraged to take excessive risks. On the other hand, the family member CEO and executives do not need complex clauses to deal with severance or change-in-control situations.

The CEO Role in the Family Business

There are four different situations characterizing the role of the CEO that relate to whether the CEO is a family member and whether the company is privately held or publicly listed:

- **The CEO is a family member in a privately held company.** CEO pay might be very low, with no reference to market rates. The key issues are not mainly related to pay, but to the effectiveness of the CEO and his/her performance. The critical question is often if a professional manager can be more effective in managing the company. There is evidence of companies moving from a family CEO to a professional CEO as long as the importance of research and development, innovation and velocity of market cycles increases.

- **The CEO is a family member in a publicly listed company.** The main issues to consider are the excess pay risk, performance management and succession planning. Often it is important to ensure that the CEO is 100 percent dedicated to the company and not involved in other family businesses, such as sitting on other boards with executive responsibilities. In the past few years, active investors have tried to extract value from this type of situation by acquiring a material stake in the target company and then pushing for corporate governance reform. This activism has brought significant improvements in corporate governance standards of listed family businesses.

- **The CEO is not a family member in a privately owned company.** The relationship between the CEO and the family in this context is often very critical. The more complex the business, the more difficult it is for the family to evaluate the CEO's performance. However, the family though can exercise in many cases an effective monitoring of the CEO's performance. Pay levels tend to follow market rates, but the reward system often is focused on operational/ annual performance without long-term upside opportunities for the CEO because often the family has a very important say on the strategy definition, leaving the CEO more focused on execution.

- **The CEO is not a family member in a publicly listed company.** This is the case where the CEO's pay is mostly market driven, even if the compensation package may be based more on cash rewards rather than equity. The rewards system may be still based more on operational/business results rather than total return for the investors. See Table 21-1, "Key Points/Issues Concerning CEOs in Family-Owned Businesses."

Role of the Compensation Committee

Only a minority of private-family companies have a remuneration (compensation) committee in place, whereas if the company is listed, such a committee is a given. However, more privately owned companies are considering or actually establishing a compensation committee within the board, even if the lack of independent directors is very often an issue for the correct functioning and the effectiveness of the committee. For this reason, a presence of an external expert on executive compensation is often seen as a way

TABLE 21-1

Key Points/Issues Concerning CEOs in Family-Owned Businesses

	Privately owned business (family owns 100% of the business)	Listed company (family is the dominant shareholder)
The CEO is not a family member	• Reward system very often focused on operational/annual performance • CEO's pay levels tend to follow market rates	• CEO's pay strictly market driven • Reward system based more on operational/annual results rather than total return for investors
The CEO is a family member	• CEO's pay might be low/immaterial • Performance evaluation • Succession planning	• Risk of excess pay • CEO might not be fully dedicated to the business • Performance evaluation • Succession planning

to ensure more independence and to help the committee to take more informed decisions.

In listed companies the committee might be weak, especially if the CEO is a family member and the family has significant influence on the board. Privately owned companies increasingly recognize the importance of having well-defined processes as far as executive pay, performance and succession at the top is concerned. For example, some family companies have in place very clear policies dealing with the hiring of the family members in the company. These policies may require, for instance, a minimal external working experience before hiring a family member or a formal assessment carried out by an external provider.

When the CEO is a family member, the main risk for the company is that he/she might stay in charge even if the performance of the company is poor. In this regard, some family-owned companies have in place clear procedures to remove the family member and appoint a professional executive when company performance falls below industry norms.

Choices

Large, privately owned family businesses are competing for leadership talent with public companies and are therefore very concerned about the competitiveness of their executive pay packages. We see privately owned family businesses increasingly considering the use of LTIs to motivate and retain their executives and to link rewards to company performance. Sometimes the most difficult choices for the family concern the role of the family members within the top management of the company, especially considering the CEO's role.

Executive pay has to be carefully tailored regardless of whether a company opts for a professional manager or a family member for the CEO job or another top position. Governance processes are generally improving to ensure better control on some critical areas such as executive pay, performance management and succession planning for the top positions. Investors' activism also is driving corporate governance improvements in companies where families are dominant shareholders, with significant opportunities to extract value from this type of investment.

Executive Pay Practices of A-share Listed Companies in China

Without much administrative supervision from the government, the executive pay practices of listed Chinese companies in China's A-share stock markets are highly market-oriented and diversified. Technically, a company usually can obtain approval of its executive pay program from the China Securities Regulatory Commission (CSRC) if it follows the general regulations and already has been approved by the board and at a shareholder meeting. Even with a very high pay level, there should be no problem as long as the board thinks the executive pay levels are necessary to retain and motivate the top team.

Yet companies have much more to worry about nowadays — sometimes called supervision from the media and the public, who are focusing on social fairness and harmony. Such pressure could be a reason why a listed company may revise its executive pay program immediately after releasing such information.

Pay Philosophy

A modern executive pay program with concepts of benchmarking, job evaluation, a pay-performance link and the introduction of an

LTI plan has been widely accepted and used in China. However, the most difficult task has been for the owner of a privately owned listed company to buy in to the concept of target incentives, whether through annual bonuses or LTIs. These individuals have relied too much on the "afterward reward" concept that has no pre-set performance target but rather a pay link to the past. An owner can have a philosophy of no incentive pay (not a penny) in the same way that he/she compensates sales personnel, enjoying the huge flexibility so that the owner can pay as much as he/she likes, perhaps irrationally, when in a good mood.

Pay Level

The trend of an enlarging gap of CEO pay between A-share listed companies has been mitigating in recent years, largely due to the supervision from the media and the public. In 2007, the highest total cash compensation paid to the chairman of a privately owned bank was skyscraping — more than $3 million ($10 million of total direct compensation that year), with a gap of 1,500 times to the lowest level of $2,300 of a CEO from the manufacturing sector. Facing massive attack from the media, the total cash of the same chairman of this bank shrank to zero in 2008. In 2010, the board decided to pay $1.4 million in cash to the chairman, which it thought to reflect the performance of chairman in a more reasonable way. The median of a CEO's total cash at an A-share listed company recently has been between $60,000 to $80,000, with highest paid CEOs found in the finance and real-estate sectors.

Another interesting observation is the relatively small internal pay gap between top team members. Due to the unique corporate governance structure, in many cases the vice presidents are not reporting up to the CEO; instead, they work more as peers in a team and report to the board as a whole team. Some companies consider the relationship as between peer and boss. The pay policy of those vice presidents would be described as if they have similar responsibilities as the CEO, they should have similar compensation as the CEO. Market practice for such gap ranges from 80 percent to 85 percent.

Pay Mix

Although an information release on the pay mix of executives of A-share listed companies is not required by the CSRC, in our experience the range is from 6:4 to 7:3 with the majority in base salary. The concept of performance-based salary, rare elsewhere but popular in the China market, can be tricky because some companies consider it as a part of fixed compensation while others do not. Some executives like the name because it takes the form of variable pay, although there is actually no link with performance. In other cases there may be some degree of link but the proportion could vary annually.

Until 2010, only about 15 percent of roughly 2,000 listed companies released their LTI programs in annual reports. The prevalence increased quickly in the past three years, although the current proportion is still relatively low compared with the U.S. market. Stock options are still the most popular LTI vehicle with a prevalence of 70 percent. Around 27 percent of companies with an LTI program use restricted stock and 9 companies grant stock appreciation rights.

The prevalence of stock options was even higher years ago, with the proportion of 75 percent to 80 percent. However, with a falling share index in 2009 and 2010, so many option programs went underwater. After that, more companies tended to implement full-value share plans instead of granting options.

Performance Link of Executive Incentives

The performance conditions of an annual incentive plan are a combination of company-level financial performance and individual key performance indicators (KPIs). Although in many companies vice presidents have the same level of target bonus, more compensation committees tend to differentiate their vice presidents' individual KPIs.

Most companies with an LTI program use net profit growth and/or return on equity as the performance conditions of their LTI programs. Most of them set the above two indicators as the vesting performance condition and only a small proportion have both granting and vesting performance requirements.

Executive Pay in China: The 'Red CEO'

Quite different from what most Westerners likely imagined, the topic of executive compensation has always been of great interest in China, especially cash compensation, benefits and equity incentives for "Red CEOs," who are CEOs from state-owned enterprises (SOEs). Many of these SOEs, although majority-owned by the state, have their equity listed on a Chinese or overseas stock market. The design of compensation for Red CEOs is an interesting story, with various considerations unfamiliar to Westerners.

Red CEOs are chosen and appointed by the Organization Department of the Communist Party of China (ODCPC) Central Committee, instead of being recruited from the talent market. It is very common for the former top executive of a giant SOE to be appointed as CEO of its largest competitor, the governor of a province or head of a government bureau virtually overnight by the ODCPC. Also, a CEO never gets demoted or fired for poor performance (unless there are serious safety accidents or moral issues such as corruption), so he/she seldom is concerned with job loss.

The compensation of Red CEOs is determined by the State Asset Supervisory and Administration Commission (SASAC), which provides very detailed regulation of base pay, the bonus range and the percentage of LTIs to total remuneration.

Bonuses range from zero to a maximum of three times base pay. As for the annual total cash level, the unwritten law is that the cap on CEO pay is $170,000 U.S.; all Chinese companies know that rule and follow it during pay design.

Another rule requires that the grant value of LTIs for CEOs from domestically listed SOEs be less than 30 percent of total direct compensation (including LTI); for CEOs of overseas-listed companies, the cap is 40 percent. Any extra money that a CEO actually receives from LTI in excess of 40 percent of total direct compensation would be confiscated by the government for domestic-listed companies; the limit is 50 percent for overseas companies.

It would be interesting to ask "How much of the performance of the SOE is contributed by its CEO?", because even the government admits that some state-owned mega companies (Fortune 500 companies such as Sinopec, State Grid and China Mobile) became what they are now by monopolization power. How should the individual contribution of the CEO be evaluated here?

In most cases, the career path of a Red CEO is closely related with his/her political promotion. As mentioned, a CEO would not complain about unreasonably low pay if he/she could sense even a very slight chance of political promotion. We have seen a CEO even refuse to have his/her salary increased due to a worry that it might hurt the harmony between executives and workers which, in turn, could reduce the executive's promotion chances.

A CEO is not always the "king" at a red company, even when the chairman is not considered. Sometimes the Party Secretary is the top position, if the job is not held simultaneously by the CEO. The Party Secretary is in charge of Party affairs, and in most cases he/she also plays a very important role in business operations.

Besides the unique characteristics of Red CEOs, China recently has been experiencing unprecedented change. For example, the unreasonably low pay level of CEOs at listed SOEs, especially those listed overseas, is facing challenge from investors on how CEO pay links to their performance. Also, increases in the cost of living weaken the purchasing power of CEO pay.

Importance of Compensation Design in China

Despite all of the challenges and uncertainties mentioned, compensation design for Red CEOs remains a critical move in helping Chinese organizations work. Whether Red CEOs can obtain externally competitive and internally fair pay could even play a role in determining whether China could be successfully transformed into a globally trusted and influential nation because the SOEs employing these CEOs play such a decisive role in the country's macro economy. Organizations have to compete globally regardless of the country; investors do not care whether a CEO is Red when their ROI target is not met.

Executive Compensation in Brazil

The Brazilian marketplace has undergone major transformations in recent years. Key factors driving this shift include the control over inflation, a significant effort on poverty reduction and the increasing price of commodities. Although much remains to be done on infrastructure, education, regulatory standards and the never-ending battle against corruption, the overall mid- and long-term scenarios for the economy are very positive, leading to an expectation of steady growth in gross national product for several years ahead.

A fast-growing economy has been able to attract large foreign investments. In addition, the privatization of several state-owned industries and the professionalization of an increasing number of family-owned businesses have combined to push the demand for seasoned executives with greater and more sophisticated management skills. Currently there are not enough qualified executives to fulfill all senior management positions available in the Brazilian market.

As a natural consequence of this war for talent (which is expected to continue for several years), the executive compensation model in Brazil shifted very rapidly, moving from a base salary and benefit driven approach (1980s and 1990s) to a much more leveraged model. Thus, in the early 2000s programs became bonus-driven while recently there has been a new shift as the LTI tends to drive compensation.

In considering the executive pay scenario in Brazil and its unique characteristics, it is important to understand some basic issues that directly affect the mindset of local executives and have affected pay over time.

History of High Inflation

Although inflation has been under control for several years, the memory of those times lives on and some pay practices are still linked to that heritage. Table 21-2 shows the evolution of inflation over 20 recent years in Brazil.

TABLE 21-2

Evolution of Inflation in Brazil

Year	1990	1992	1994	1996	1998	2000	2002	2004	2006	2008	2010
Annual Inflation	1,585.185%	1,149.05%	929.32%	09.12%	02.49%	05.27%	14.74%	06.13%	0.281%	06.48%	06.46%

On a timeline perspective, inflation moved from over 1,000 percent per annum in the early 1990s to much more reasonable levels after the stabilization period of the "Plano Real" after 1994. Nevertheless, there have been some spikes, such as in 2002, due mainly to the market expectations of an upcoming election of a union leader as the country's president. This history demonstrates why worries about inflation still affect pay at all levels.

The most direct effect on pay is that a decade ago more than 61% of Brazilian companies extended their union agreement salary increases to all executives instead of driving pay through market competitiveness. This practice has been reduced dramatically, as now less than 20 percent of companies follow this practice; these are mainly subsidiaries of multinational companies that have not reviewed their union agreements.

Another unique effect of this heritage is on stock option plans. It is not unusual to find local companies opting for premium price stock options, where the strike price is indexed to inflation as a "safety net," just in case inflation rises again in the long term. This approach leads to a higher dilution to fund the plans and increases the risk of the awards going underwater, as the stock prices have almost no correlation to inflation indexes.

There is a clear trend to move toward plain stock option plans as companies become more confident of a stable environment and as a risk analysis of the compensation elements becomes a key decision factor in plan design.

High Cost of Pay

In Brazil, the basic labor obligations, taxes and social charges on base salary are relatively high as shown in Table 21-3. The result is that every time there is a salary increase of R$1,000, it will cost the company approximately R$1,511. Therefore, over the years, companies have struggled to provide a fair pay structure to executives while avoiding, to some extent, direct salary increases.

The high labor cost ultimately led to government action in the form of "profit sharing" legislation in an effort to reduce overall labor costs and enable the Brazilian economy to compete in a global economy.

---

382 Understanding Executive Compensation

TABLE 21-3

Effect of Stock Option Usage on Overhang

Item	Brief Description	Effect on Salary
13th salary	One additional monthly salary paid at the end of the year	8.33%
Vacation premium	One-third of a monthly salary due when the employee leaves on vacation	2.78%
Termination fund (FGTS)	Compulsory monthly contribution to build a fund to be paid upon termination of employment	8%
Social charges (INSS)	Public social security contribution	20%
Other social charges	FGTS and INSS contributions on 13th salary and vacation premium	12%
	Total	51.11%

Profit- and Results-Sharing Legislation

In December 1994, just after implementing the economic stabilization plan (Plano Real), the central government drafted a bill stating that all companies could implement a profit- or results-sharing program (PPLR) that, if done according to some basic guidelines, would not be considered as salary so that all labor costs would not apply.

The intention was to reduce overall labor costs and enhance productivity of all industries and sectors. To fall under this special category, a PPLR program must:

• Extend to all employees of the company
• Have clear metrics and predefined goals
• Not have more than two payments per annum, with a minimum of one semester between payments
• Contain plan conditions negotiated directly with the unions or through a internal employee commission together with a delegate of the applicable union.

The PPLR bill became law in December 2000 and companies subsequently have systematically shifted their compensation emphasis and now drive their short-term incentive programs toward PPLR programs.

The effect on executive pay came very quickly. Bonus arrangements were partially or fully migrated to this model; base salary increases were reduced as bonus targets increased significantly over the years. Annual variable pay became a very significant portion of the total compensation package and plan design grew more sophisticated as companies focused on the year-end results.

Brazilian companies were able to respond faster to the new environment than their global competitors whose subsidiaries still struggled to obtain approval from their headquarters of some degree of flexibility on global bonus arrangements for the local executives. This factor enabled local companies to gain competitiveness in compensation and consequently became capable of attracting high-level executives from global organizations. The market in Brazil became "all about the short term," so multinational firms now have a hard time competing at the same level with the Brazilian companies.

In addition, leveraged bonus programs increase the focus on the short term and provide a whole new level of liquidity to an executive's compensation package. In a business environment in which the focus is shifting from annual to multi-year business plans and there are plenty of job opportunities within the marketplace, it has become imperative to move into LTI arrangements. This development brings up the lack of regulation regarding equity compensation.

Regulation of Equity Compensation

The regulation of executive pay is a recent topic in the Brazilian market. According to a Hay Group executive survey, 35 percent of the companies in 2006 granted some kind of LTI to their top local management. The vast majority were multinational companies granting equity through their global programs. These figures changed significantly as Hay's 2011 survey found that 70 percent of the companies are currently granting LTIs and, of those, approximately half of them are Brazilian-based companies with local programs.

The grant levels and the number of participants in these programs are still below what is expected in developed markets, mainly due to the absolute lack of regulation on that theme. As a consequence of the lack of regulation on equity-based pay, there are several concerns from the labor legislation perspective on how to address stock options, performance shares and restricted stock awards.

The biggest concern is the possibility that equity compensation might be considered as salary, in which case the full labor cost (51 percent) would be applicable. Several companies, even listed firms, choose to grant cash-based plans as a proxy to the actual equity programs, typically through phantom options or phantom restricted plans to avoid any taxation risks.

Those companies that award actual equity manage their tax risk through assumptions such as "the higher the risk of a plan not paying out, the lower the risk of it being considered as compensation." It is advisable to obtain legal advice before implementing any equity-based plan to obtain a thorough risk assessment of each modality.

Roughly assessing the labor risk (and not the inherent risk) involved of the major types of equity plans, it would be fair to state:

- Stock options are viewed as at a lower risk level because there is a greater chance of not performing. In addition, the fact that the executive is paying for the exercise of a stock option may support the concept of the arrangement being of a mercantile nature and not remuneration, provided the strike price is at a reasonable value at the grant date.
- Performance shares would be considered as at an intermediate risk level as the performance condition would bring a risk element into the plan.
- Restricted share awards could be considered at a higher risk level, as there is no additional condition other than the time vesting.

To summarize, it is clear that to be competitive now in the Brazilian market, having a LTI program is no longer a differentiation from the marketplace; rather LTI pay has become a regular piece of the compensation package in Brazil and it tends to increase in size and perceived value by executives. Nevertheless, the implementation process for local plans is still complex and a better understanding of the taxation environment, especially regarding the labor perspective, is needed.

Urban Violence

Unfortunately, questions on the topic of urban violence are common from people outside of Brazil. It is sadly true that in Brazil's major cities there is an intrinsic risk of urban violence and it is a market practice to provide armored cars to senior executives. As these problems are far from over, the continued use of this kind of benefit is expected.

Disclosure

As a developing market, the issues around corporate governance and disclosure are developing quickly in Brazil. Since 2010, all publicly quoted companies have to disclose annually through the "formulario de referencia 480/481" details of their compensation strategy regarding all elements of pay for the board of directors and group administrators (top executives that represent the owners of the company).

Although there is not yet full disclosure (because companies do not provide individual figures for each executive), companies now must disclose the average compensation packages for each group as well as both the highest and the lowest individual compensation packages. This is a major step in terms of transparency and we expect that, in the coming years, the level of details regarding executive compensation likely will increase, leading inevitably to a full disclosure.

Finally, managing executive compensation in Brazil is very similar to doing it in any other country, with its own issues and complexities. Local operations are not disconnected from the global businesses and should be treated accordingly. Understanding the local environment and what drives compensation in this market allows a better planning process and awareness on how to compete in attracting, retaining and motivating these scarce resources called executives.

About the Editors

Irving (Irv) S. Becker is National Practice Leader of the Executive Compensation Practice at Hay Group. Over the course of his career, Becker has worked with boards and senior management at major public and private corporations across multiple industries to design and develop rewards programs that align executive efforts and results with the success of the company. His financial background provides him with a grounded perspective on performance measurement and management. Becker's clients have included Fortune 50 financial services companies, major foreign owned banks, global industrial and consumer products companies, large professional service organizations, national chain retailers, small pre-IPO companies, and large private businesses. He also has worked with companies in distressed or turnaround situations.

Prior to joining Hay Group, Becker was the National Practice Leader for Executive Compensation Consulting at a Big 4 accounting and tax firm. During his combined 10 years at this firm, over two time periods, he worked with numerous clients to assist them with developing overall reward philosophies, as well as more specific executive compensation programs.

Becker also has 10 years of in-house corporate experience heading up the compensation and benefits functions at Goldman Sachs, First USA Bank, The Home Depot and Young & Rubicam.

He is a frequent speaker on executive compensation topics, and has been quoted in numerous notable publications, including *The Wall Street Journal, The New York Times, The Financial Times, The Economist, Agenda* and *Human Resources Executive.* Some of the organizations for which he has presented include: The Conference Board, National Association of Stock Plan Professionals (NASPP), NACD Directorship Forum, Outstanding Directors Exchange (ODX), The Directors Roundtable, RiskMetrics (ISS) Governance Exchange, Society of Corporate Securities and Governance Professionals,

National Foreign Trade Council (NFTC), Financial Executives International and WorldatWork. Becker has been named to the Directorship 100 for each year from 2008 through 2011, a list published by *Directorship* magazine, recognizing the most influential people who are shaping agendas and corporate governance issues in boardrooms across America.

Becker received his master's of business administration in finance from Columbia Business School and has a bachelor's degree of business administration in accounting from the University of Massachusetts. He is a licensed CPA in New York State.

William (Bill) M. Gerek is the U.S. Regulatory Expertise Leader of Hay Group's Executive Compensation Practice and heads the regulatory and legal team. He assists organizations on all aspects of executive compensation, with a particular focus on tax, corporate, securities, accounting and other regulatory matters that can affect executive compensation.

Gerek helps employers and executives obtain a clear understanding of the relevant issues involved in design and implementation of executive pay programs, including base pay, annual incentives, long-term incentive programs (especially those based on or settled in equity), deferred compensation, severance and change-in-control arrangements, executive benefits and perquisites. Gerek also designs executive compensation packages, works on employment agreements, incentive plans and deferral programs, and critiques both existing and proposed executive pay arrangements. In recent years, Gerek frequently has been retained to consider and address the reasonableness of compensation of executives across various litigation perspectives, including income taxes, shareholder derivative suits, disputes among shareholders, securities law disclosures, and other instances where the reasonableness of pay is a core issue. Gerek's experience spans taxable and tax-exempt organizations, corporate and noncorporate entities, and public and private companies.

Gerek is editor and publisher of *The Executive Edition*, Hay Group's quarterly newsletter on executive compensation. In addition to this book and his authorship of numerous Hay Group publications and alerts, Gerek has written over two dozen articles on executive compensation, deferred compensation and benefits topics that have been published in a wide variety of professional journals. Gerek is active in numerous professional organizations, including the National Association of Stock Plan Professionals and bar association committees that address executive pay issues. He also is a frequent speaker at executive compensation, benefits and tax forums.

Immediately prior to joining Hay Group, Gerek was a partner in the executive compensation and employee benefits practice of the 100-plus attorney Chicago-headquartered national law firm of Ungaretti & Harris. He also was a partner for many years in the executive compensation and employee benefits department of the 600-plus lawyer international law firm now known as Katten Muchin Rosenman.

Gerek earned his Juris Doctor degree from the University of Michigan Law School after graduating magna cum laude and Phi Beta Kappa from Dartmouth College with a bachelor of arts degree in psychology. In addition, his post-graduate studies earned him a master of laws in taxation degree from the DePaul University School of Law.